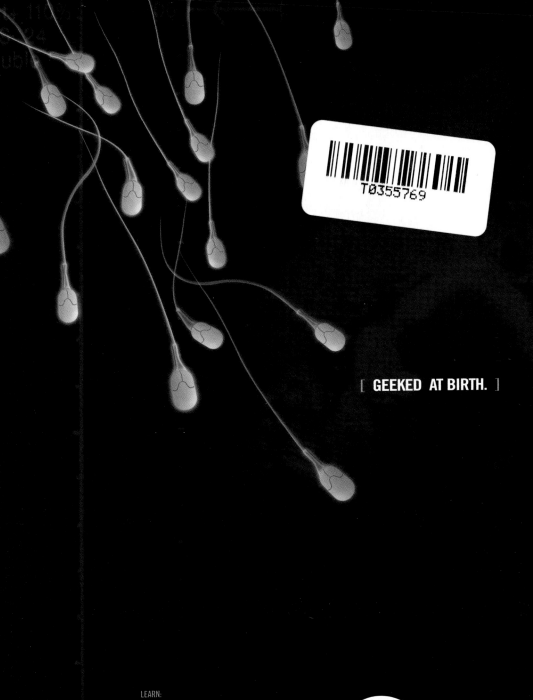

[GEEKED AT BIRTH.]

Make:

Volume 13

technology on your time™

MAGIC TRICKS

ON THE COVER: Our lovely assistant, Katharina Worthington, demonstrates the magical escaping blocks. Photographed by Garry McLeod and styled by Alex Murphy and Sam Murphy.

Columns

FISTFUL OF FIRE:
Build a simple
electronic flash gun,
a stalwart of close-
quarter magicians.

Vol. 13, Mar. 2008. MAKE (ISSN 1556-2336) is published quarterly by O'Reilly Media, Inc.in the months of March, May, August, and November. O'Reilly Media is located at 1005 Gravenstein Hwy. North, Sebastopol, CA 95472, (707) 827-7000. SUBSCRIPTIONS: Send all subscription requests to MAKE, P.O. Box 17046, North Hollywood, CA 91615-9588 or subscribe online at makezine.com/offer or via phone at (866) 289-8847 (U.S. and Canada); all other countries call (818) 487-2037. Subscriptions are available for $34.95 for 1 year (4 quarterly issues) in the United States; in Canada: $39.95 USD; all other countries: $49.95 USD. Periodicals Postage Paid at Sebastopol, CA, and at additional mailing offices. POSTMASTER: Send address changes to MAKE, P.O. Box 17046, North Hollywood, CA 91615-9588. Canada Post Publications Mail Agreement Number 41129568. CANADA POSTMASTER: Send address changes to: O'Reilly Media, PO Box 456, Niagara Falls, ON L2E 6V2

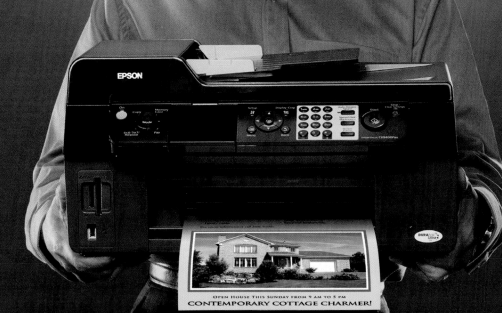

Make: Projects

Boom Stick

This PVC air cannon delivers maximum bang for the buck. By Edwin Wise

114

Toy Music Sequencer

Let babies play with shapes, sounds, and lights on this electronic music player. By Brian McNamara

124

Smart Structure

Build and demonstrate an active vibration-damping system. By Steven Griffin

134

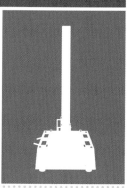

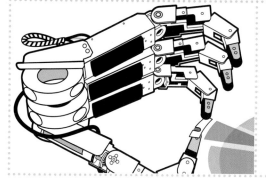

UPLOAD

Fake sun photography, home music control, tweak songs for car speakers, rip and burn movies, and more.

104

Volume 13

Make:
technology on your time™

READ ME: Always check the URL associated with a project before you get started. There may be important updates or corrections.

Maker

32

MAGIC MAKER: Illusion designer John Gaughan plays with his very real 45-year old parrot, Luther, in his workshop.

DIY

143

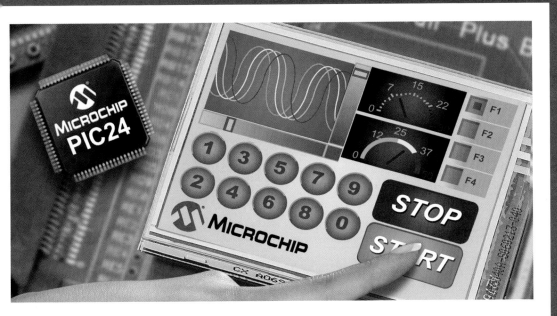

Make:
technology on your time™

EDITOR AND PUBLISHER
Dale Dougherty
dale@oreilly.com

EDITOR-IN-CHIEF
Mark Frauenfelder
markf@oreilly.com

MANAGING EDITOR
Shawn Connally
shawn@oreilly.com

ASSOCIATE MANAGING EDITOR
Goli Mohammadi

SENIOR EDITOR
Phillip Torrone
pt@makezine.com

PROJECTS EDITOR
Paul Spinrad
pspinrad@makezine.com

STAFF EDITOR
Arwen O'Reilly

COPY CHIEF
Keith Hammond

EDITOR AT LARGE
David Pescovitz

CREATIVE DIRECTOR
Daniel Carter
dcarter@oreilly.com

DESIGNERS
Katie Wilson
Alison Kendall

PRODUCTION DESIGNER
Gerry Arrington

PHOTO EDITOR
Sam Murphy
smurphy@oreilly.com

ONLINE MANAGER
Terrie Miller

ASSOCIATE PUBLISHER
Dan Woods
dan@oreilly.com

CIRCULATION DIRECTOR
Heather Harmon

ACCOUNT MANAGER
Katie Dougherty

MARKETING & EVENTS COORDINATOR
Rob Bullington

MAKE TECHNICAL ADVISORY BOARD
Evil Mad Scientist Laboratories, Limor Fried, Joe Grand, Saul Griffith, William Gurstelle, Bunnie Huang, Tom Igoe, Mister Jalopy, Steve Lodefink, Erica Sadun

PUBLISHED BY O'REILLY MEDIA, INC.
Tim O'Reilly, CEO
Laura Baldwin, COO

Visit us online at makezine.com
Comments may be sent to editor@makezine.com

For advertising inquiries, contact:
Katie Dougherty, 707-827-7272, katie@oreilly.com

For sponsorship inquiries, contact:
Scott Feen, 707-827-7105, scottf@oreilly.com

For event inquiries, contact:
Sherry Huss, 707-827-7074, sherry@oreilly.com

Contributing Editors: Gareth Branwyn, William Gurstelle, Mister Jalopy, Brian Jepson, Charles Platt

Contributing Artists: Howard Cao, Gunnar Conrad, Steve Double, Nick Dragotta, Howard Hallis, Timmy Kucynda, Tim Lillis, Garry McLeod, Pars/e design, Nik Schulz, Damien Scogin, Jen Siska, David Torrence, Noah Webb

Contributing Writers: Ian Alejandro, Mitch Altman, Tim Anderson, Nick Archer, Joost Bonsen, Gareth Branwyn, Christophe Caron, Brian Dereu, Cory Doctorow, Kes Donahue, Nick Dragotta, Tim G. Drew, Andrea Dunlap, George Dyson, Caterina Fake, Dan Fost, Steve Griffin, Saul Griffith, Johanna Hallin, Karen K. Hansen, Marlow Harris, Joel Johnson, Frank Joy, Richard Kadrey, Andrew Lewis, Mike Lin, Steve Lodefink, J.J. Loy, Carl Malamud, Brian McNamara, Dug North, Tom Parker, Bob Pennington, Harry Porter, Michael H. Pryor, Donald Simanek, Rick Polito, Douglas Repetto, Randy Sarafan, Gene Scogin, Andy Seubert, David Simpson, Bruce Sterling, Bruce Stewart, Cy Tymony, Daniel Weiss, Megan Mansell Williams, Edwin Wise, Lee Zlotoff

Interns: Eric Michael Beug (video), Matthew Dalton (engr.), Adrienne Foreman (web), Arseny Lebedev (web), Brian Lewis-Jones (edit.), Kris Magri (engr.)

Customer Service cs@readerservices.makezine.com
Manage your account online, including change of address at:
makezine.com/account
866-289-8847 toll-free in U.S. and Canada
818-487-2037, 5 a.m.–5 p.m., PST

NOW GREENER THAN EVER!
MAKE is now printed on recycled paper with 30% post-consumer waste and is acid-free. Subscriber copies of MAKE, Volume 13, were shipped in recyclable plastic bags.

Contributors

Daniel Weiss (*Uncle Bill's Magic Tricks*) is a computer geek at heart but likes to work with materials he can touch in the real world as well. "That," he says, "leads to my strong interest in being a maker." He lives in "steamy Saint Louis" with his wife, Jan, and two kids who are makers themselves and love to perform the tricks he's built. He's currently working on yet more magic-related projects, including a set of magician's tables "designed for easy setup, teardown, and carrying around." A consultant for IBM by day, he loves "to create things people can appreciate for the final result, but also (hopefully) for the effort or technique that went into the project."

Tall, dark, and geeky, rogue technologist **Edwin Wise** (*Boom Stick*) admits to working in "anything except wood, 'cause a guy has got to have limits. And I hate sanding." He loves Halloween, and volunteers as an actor, designer, and special effects maker for a charity haunted house. A bit of a maverick, he says, "Some people collect money; I collect skills. I'm not the best at any of them, but I have a nice collection and it's growing every year." Among them are writing, ballroom dancing with his wife, jewelry making, robotics, and working with metal and digital hardware.

Dr. Steven Griffin (*Smart Structure*) is an aerospace engineer who enjoys finding simple solutions to multidisciplinary problems. He has explored the use of smart structures in applications from musical instruments to space launch vehicles and is always on the lookout for new opportunities. He's currently working on "a musical shoe, and an active bridge for a guitar or violin." He lives in Albuquerque, N.M., with his wife and two children, and loves hiking with them in the mountains for fun (as well as training for local trail runs and triathlons).

Kris Magri (engineering intern) became enamored with R2-D2 at an early age and built her first robot from plans in a book when she was in high school. Before returning to school to study mechanical engineering, she earned a degree in electrical engineering and worked at Parallax, where "my crowning achievement was to get eight robots to do the Hokey Pokey." She's also worked in the oil field, detonated dynamite, and taken down many a machine, from the smallest micro to big Unix servers, with her stellar programming skills. She teaches robotics to eighth-graders, and hopes to someday make a clean, neat, reliable robot with no visible black tape.

Brian McNamara (*Toy Music Sequencer*) has been pulling things apart since he was 2 or 3; many years later, he has figured out how to put some things back together. Some of them even seem to be useful. After working in a wide range of electronics workshops, from avionic to scientific, Brian finally decided to set up his own workshop at home and started inventing fun stuff. Apart from electronics, Brian loves music, gardening, and taking his two kids on hiking adventures.

As the youngest child of three, **Noah Webb** (*Proto* photography) always had to sit in the back of the "sparkly brown" family station wagon, so he gained a sharp eye at an early age. That back seat, he says, "forced me to become a photographer. Looking through that window was like looking through a big view camera watching the world go by." He lives in Los Angeles in a 1910 Craftsman home, and loves cookies, swimming, snowboarding, and "pushing my body's limits as I grow older." His latest project is a handmade book about a trip to Ecuador.

SLOW MADE: TAKE IT EASY

By Dale Dougherty

THIS MAGAZINE EXPLORES NOT JUST how to make things but also why. Why make things when you can buy them? Why spend hours on a project when you could be doing something else? Why?

I often reference cooking when explaining why people make things. I love to cook and grow my own food. Food is such a basic need that all of us have to figure it out on a daily basis. We become food makers.

Cooking is not something everyone likes to do, I realize. Two people can view this same activity very differently, one as the worst kind of drudgery and the other as the practice of something like an art form. The former wants as little hands-on involvement as possible, while the latter sees multiple ways to enhance his or her own pleasure and enjoyment.

One's level of engagement makes all the difference. If you want to cook well, you'll be willing to learn about cooking from books, from friends, and from eating out. You'll become better with practice and challenge yourself by trying out new recipes. You'll also fail now and then, but you'll enjoy the process as you discover new ways of creating meals that you really enjoy. Moreover, you don't have to aim to become a professional chef. Being a good everyday cook is rewarding if you can satisfy family and friends.

Simon Hopkinson writes in his cookbook *Roast Chicken and Other Stories* that good cooking "depends on common sense and good taste." He says cooking is "a craft, after all, like anything that is produced with the hands and senses to put together an attractive and complete picture."

MAKE is about creating that kind of picture using the technology at hand (and in this issue, sleight of hand). There are plenty of DIY magazines for cooks, woodworkers, and gardeners. But until MAKE, it had been decades since there was a true DIY magazine for technology enthusiasts. Our mission is to help anyone become a better everyday maker.

We recently signed with Twin Cities Public Television (TPT) to create a *Make: TV* program for PBS. I envision it fitting in with cooking programs such as Julia Child's or woodworking shows like *The New Yankee Workshop*. The goal of *Make: TV* is to show how to make things yourself and share them with others.

Lately I've been learning about the Slow Food movement, which developed in Italy as a response to fast food. In short, they advocate wholesome, local food over processed food with dubious ingredients and obscure origins. They want to develop alternatives to the industrial system of food production and distribution, which is optimized for speed and efficiency. The Slow Food movement encourages us to slow down, enjoy the simple pleasures of life, and make connections to real people creating real food. It's good for you, good for your community, and good for the Earth.

At the heart of the Slow Food movement are local farmers' markets. These markets have become the hub for locally produced food. However, the Slow Food movement wants us not just to become better consumers of food, but also to see ourselves as co-producers. It's a higher level of engagement. If we become more involved in the process of bringing food to our table, then we can have a positive impact on the local environment as well as the local economy.

I see makers, too, exploring alternatives to what the consumer culture has to offer. DIY is essentially the slow way. To do it your own way allows you to optimize for values that are important to you. You can choose to put fun, coolness, or pride of craftsmanship ahead of efficiency. It's the sum of these very personal choices that makes the work of an artist or craftsperson unique.

I'd like to propose using *slow made* to identify the work of makers. A slow-made object is created when a maker guides the process by making personal choices. *Slow made* is like *handmade* but allows for using machines to make things. *Slow made* values the creative effort — a combination of manual and mental processes — that generates something new. Whether it's building things from scratch or from a kit, or taking an idea all the way from design through build, we shift from consumer to producer. I can imagine makers' markets that feature slow-made goods from local makers. We could all become more connected to the things in our lives and to the real people who make them. Why not?

Dale Dougherty is editor and publisher of MAKE and CRAFT.

Maker Faire ™

Meet the Makers

Build.
Craft.
Hack.
Play.
Make.

SF BAY AREA May 3 & 4, 2008
SAN MATEO FAIRGROUNDS

AUSTIN October 18 & 19, 2008
TRAVIS COUNTY EXPO CENTER

MakerFaire.com

FEATURING: EepyBird.com
Diet Coke & Mentos Fountain Show,
Life-Sized Mousetrap Game,
MAKE and CRAFT Labs, MAKE
Play Day, Swap-O-Rama-Rama,
Bazaar Bizarre Craft Fair, Rockets,
Robots, Food Makers, Fire Arts,
Art Cars, and more!

MAKER'S CALENDAR

Compiled by William Gurstelle

Our favorite events from around the world.

Jan	Feb	Mar
Apr	May	Jun
July	Aug	Sept
Oct	Nov	Dec

» MARCH

»Pragyan Science and Technology Festival
Feb. 28–March 2
Tiruchirappalli, India
This festival of maker technology is carried out in true Indian metaphysical fashion. Say the organizers: "The Pragyan wheel shall resume its endless journey on the path of creative innovation." pragyan.org

»Cambridge Science Festival
March 10–20
Cambridge, England
One of the best science fairs in a country rich with science festivals, this one will offer over 100 free events on subjects ranging from astronomy to zoology.
cambridgescience.org

»Smithsonian Kite Festival
March 29, National Mall, Washington, D.C.
If the wind cooperates, kite enthusiasts display their artistry and technical skills as they fly amazingly unusual and interesting kites.
kitefestival.org

2008 FIRST Championship
April 17–19, Atlanta, Ga.
Each year tens of thousands of students compete to build robots that can best solve problems and handle complicated tasks. The FIRST Championship is open to the public and free of charge. usfirst.org
»

» APRIL

»Rube Goldberg Contest Finals
April 5, West Lafayette, Ind.
Inspired by the cartoons of Rube Goldberg, college students across the nation compete to design machines that use an overabundance of imagination to accomplish a simple task.
makezine.com/go/rube

»Weak Signals R/C Expo
April 4–6, Toledo, Ohio
This is one of the nation's premier events for radio-controlled vehicle enthusiasts.

Modelers and suppliers from across the nation come to this show to see the latest and greatest in R/C kits, electronics, gadgets, and parts.
toledoshow.com

»Yuri's Night
April 12, various locations
Yuri's Night is the outer space lover's equivalent to St. Patrick's Day. In 2007, more than 90 space-related events in 30 countries were held. Parties ranged from a huge event at NASA's Ames Research Center to a small meetup in Lower Hutt, New Zealand.
yurisnight.net

» MAY

« 40th Annual RTMC Astronomy Expo
May 23–26
Big Bear City, Calif.
This is one of the three largest gatherings of astronomy enthusiasts in the country. From naked-eye observation to advanced telescope-making techniques, all things astronomical are shared and discussed.
rtmcastronomyexpo.org

IMPORTANT: All times, dates, locations, and events are subject to change. Verify all information before making plans to attend.

Know an event that should be included? Send it to events@ makezine.com. Sorry, it is not possible to list all submitted events in the magazine, but they will be listed online.

If you attend one of these events, please tell us about it at forums.makezine.com.

Make Free

PREDICTING THE PRESENT

By Cory Doctorow

SCIENCE FICTION WRITERS MAY NOT accurately predict the future, but they're often excellent predictors of the *present* — people who notice just how futuristic the world's become while we weren't looking.

In my last column, I introduced you to Tom Jennings, the virtuoso queerpunk anarcho-engineer who invented FidoNet, one of the earliest networks for exchanging conversation. For nearly a decade, bulletin boards around the world used FidoNet, until the internet came to the average info-civilian.

Here's an amazing story from the paleo-internet that Jennings told me, which illustrates what this "predicting the present" business is really about.

William Gibson coined the term "cyberspace" in 1982, describing a virtual "place where telephone calls happened," depicted in his fiction as "bright lattices of logic unfolding across that colorless void." Gibson's cyberspace lived in the 21st century, but it had more to do with 1982 than 2012.

I suspect the future is probably weirder than the Singularity — it's usually weirder than we think.

Just as Gibson's seminal novel *Neuromancer* was going to press in 1984, Jennings launched FidoNet. Jennings is full of great Fido war stories. So many of the standard fights seem to have survived the transition to Usenet, message boards, and then blogs and LiveJournal. Nothing new under the sun, right?

Wrong. There's one standard FidoNet flame war that didn't make the transition: in 1984, FidoNet users would upbraid one another for being rude while "a guest" in each other's homes. When one FidoNetter called another FidoNetter a sack of spuds, the putative spud would get up in arms about being insulted "in his own home." While you're a guest, they'd say, you'll behave yourself.

"What?" I said. "They thought that BBS discussions happened in the room where their computer was?"

Jennings nodded emphatically. "But that's crazy!"

Then I thought about it for a moment. Where *do* flame wars happen? "They didn't know the term *cyberspace*!" We both nodded vigorously. That was it! The spread of the term *cyberspace* killed the "guest in my home" flame war, because once we knew that term (which, after all, described 1984, not 2054) we knew that flame wars didn't happen in our houses! They happened *out there*, in the notional network of pure ideas. It didn't have bright lattices of logic, but it had plenty of cyber and plenty of space.

Today, there's a hell of a lot of science fiction being written about "the Singularity." This is the moment at which it becomes possible to make a computer as smart as a human, which will shortly be followed by the moment at which a computer becomes twice as smart as a human, then four times as smart, and shortly, 40 heptillion times as smart. This is like a spatial singularity — a black hole — in that it's a break with history as we know it, a precipice that we can't see over. Once we hit the Singularity, human destiny becomes unknowable and unpredictable. We cease to be humans as we understand "human" and become something ... else.

I suspect the future is probably weirder than the Singularity (it's usually weirder than we think — Bell thought the telephone would be used to uplift the masses by bringing opera into their living rooms, not to beam atrocity photos out of Burma). But the popularity of the Singularity tells us something about our present day. We're apparently living at a moment with a boundless appetite for stories of humans using technology to transcend our destiny and even our species.

Are we disappointed that our tools haven't transformed our lives enough? Anxious that we can't keep up anymore? Or just so overjoyed by the new mind candy all around us that it seems like we're headed for a kind of techno-spiritual uplifting?

Cory Doctorow (craphound.com) is a science fiction novelist, blogger, and technology activist. He is co-editor of the popular weblog Boing Boing (boingboing.net), and a contributor to *Wired*, *Popular Science*, and *The New York Times*.

You can't learn everything from a book.

In the web-based O'Reilly School of Technology, you learn by doing. In our courses and accredited certificate programs, instructors provide feedback and encouragement, while students experiment with emerging technologies and build real-world projects. Courses are self-paced and can be taken from anywhere in the world.

Get the skills and experience you need to succeed. Find out about the OST today at **http://oreillyschool.com**. Use code **make-school** for a **20% discount**.

Certification available through

Office of Continuing Education

Tips and news for MAKE readers.

■ Looking for a Few Good Kit Makers

Ever had a cool idea for a kit, but weren't sure how to bring it to market? Or maybe you're already selling kits but you'd like to expand your market reach. If so, we have some exciting news for you. We're significantly expanding our line of kits and we're interested in meeting new kit makers.

The Maker Store (store.makezine.com) exists to unite, inspire, inform, and entertain imaginative and resourceful people who want to pursue science, craft, and tech projects in their backyards, basements, garages, and even kitchen tables — tech enthusiasts, teachers, amateur scientists, hobbyists, renegade crafters, hackers, students, and inventors of all ages.

We offer life-enriching challenges and exploration through carefully curated projects for a range of interests and experience levels. Our motto: "Permission to Play!" And talk about playing. We shipped more than 25,000 items in 2007! Not bad for our first full year in operation.

So what do we look for in a kit? We look for unusual and hard-to-find projects designed and produced by backyard scientists, basement engineers, artists, teachers, and individual makers and small suppliers who typically lack channel distribution but not creativity and ingenuity.

Areas we're particularly interested in include robots, circuit bending, games, electronics, optics, chemistry, lasers, magic, rockets and airplanes, boats and submersibles, and a broad cross-section of crafts. Pretty much any project you might find in MAKE or CRAFT magazines.

We're building a kit lineup that offers DIY entry points for virtually all skill levels and budgets, with an emphasis on middle-schoolers and beyond. Our most successful kits tend to fall in the $15 to $39 range, but we have a number of kits over $100 as well.

Three kit characteristics we find ourselves particularly drawn to are openness to hacking and modding, family appeal, and appropriateness for group builds and meetups. It probably goes without saying that we encourage kit builders to take kits in new directions: hack it to no end, do something we never thought of, and then come back and show us what you did. If a kit lends itself to that, it gets extra points.

We're also looking for kits that parents and mentors can do with kids on rainy weekends. Who knows, if you keep your mind open you might learn something from a kid. And we're getting a lot of interest from Dorkbot groups and MAKE groups who like to tackle projects at their monthly meetups. So project kits for less than $25 that can be tackled in a couple of hours work well there.

Two questions I get asked often by prospective kit makers: What about packaging? And documentation? We do look for the kit vendor (that's you) to deliver the kits in their own package. Basic, planet-friendly and/or reusable packaging is the goal here.

As for documentation, we prefer a combination of basic printed instructions and a PDF, which we host online with the product information in the Maker Store.

Interested in getting your kit in front of millions of makers and DIY enthusiasts? If so, drop me an email at dan@oreilly.com and tell me about yourself and the kind of kit you have in mind. We keep the process friendly, down to earth, and straightforward.

Dan Woods is associate publisher of MAKE and CRAFT magazines. When he's not working on circulation and marketing or finding cool new stuff for the Maker Store, he likes to hack and build barbecues, smokers, and outdoor grills.

Photograph by Howard Cao

NO POSTAGE
NECESSARY
IF MAILED
IN THE
UNITED STATES

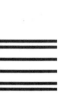

BUSINESS REPLY MAIL
FIRST-CLASS MAIL   PERMIT NO. 273   CONGERS NY

POSTAGE WILL BE PAID BY ADDRESSEE

ROBOT

PO Box 310
Congers NY 10920-9822

The latest in
hobby,
school contest,
science,
consumer
robotics

**BECOME A
SUBSCRIBER
AND ENJOY:**

■ Robot kits and
accessories

■ Homebuilt robot
projects

■ Techno hacks for all skill
levels

■ Consumer robot
reviews

■ School contest
coverage, from FIRST
to Botball, BBIQ, BEST,
and more

■ Worldwide robot news
from academia, the
military, and industry

■ Tech updates

■ Space robots

■ and more!

**BONUS WEB
FEATURES:**

■ Expanded coverage

■ Online forum

■ Source code, videos

Use the attached card to **CHECK OUT A FREE TRIAL ISSUE
OF ROBOT** and to **SUBSCRIBE FOR ONLY $19.95**

OR GO ONLINE AT:

www.botmag.com/make

3¼-Cent Lure

By Tom Parker

Sometimes it costs more to buy it than to make it from the money itself.

$7.99
Store-bought fishing lure.

⬆ ## $1.04
Hook, hardware, solder, and 4 pennies.

Photograph by Tom Parker

5 Hot New DIY Books

From the makers behind CRAFT, MAKE, and Maker Faire

Eccentric Cubicle

Who says cubicles need to be dreary? Eccentric Genius creator Kaden Harris introduces a highly entertaining parallel universe of surreal office-based projects — from desktop guillotines and crossbows to mood-enhancing effects and music makers — that are sure to pique the curiosity of even your most jaded office comrades.

"Educational and entertaining, whether or not you want a mail-flinging ballista on your desk."
–Wired.com

Making Things Talk

Programming microcontrollers used to require a development environment that broke the bank. Not anymore. New open source platforms with simple I/O boards and development environments translate to affordable options for makers on a budget. This book is packed with projects that show what you need to know and do to get your creations talking to each other,

"Projects that are accessible for all levels of expertise and budgets."
–Myworkinprog.blogspot.com

connecting to the web, and forming networks of smart devices.

Illustrated Guide to Astronomical Wonders

Authors Robert Bruce Thompson and Barbara Fritchman Thompson show how serious astronomy is now within the grasp of anyone. An indispensable guide to the equipment you need and how and where to find hundreds of spectacular objects in the deep sky — double and multiple stars as well as spectacular star clusters, nebulae, and galaxies.

"The best single-volume guide to the hobby of observational astronomy."
–Max Loudenback, Amazon review

Building the Perfect PC

Learn everything you want to know about building your own system, from planning and picking out the right components, to step-by-step instructions for assembling your perfect PC, to why you'd want to do it in the first place. Regardless of your level of technical experience, Building the Perfect PC will guide you through the entire process.

"A superb, well-done book that will end up being the basis of at least one father-son project in this household."
–Thomas Duff, Duffbert.com

The Best of MAKE

Featuring the editors' picks for the best projects from MAKE's first ten volumes, this book is a surefire collection of fun and challenging activities.

"A wish book for geeks and handymen alike." – North Adams Transcript (Mass.)

Ponoko

A LONG-TAIL, PRO-AM, DIGITAL MAKER THING.

By Bruce Sterling

PONOKO, WHICH IS PRONOUNCED *po-NO-ko* with a New Zealand accent, is a Web 2.0 startup that makes physical objects. Ponoko's plans are deep and limpid and philosophical, but they break so many 20th-century paradigms that they're hard to parse. For instance, so far, Ponoko makes mostly plastic jewelry and furniture. But Ponoko's not an industrial factory or an artist's atelier.

It's a "platform," which means that Ponoko's a "place" (the ponoko.com website), a "tool" (a bunch of laser cutters), a "marketplace" (to buy and sell objects, or to buy and sell files for the objects), and an "online community" (to get all chummy with customers and/or attempt to befriend designers). It's also an informal trade school, because it attempts to recruit people who are just floating by and turn them into helpful Ponoko producers. Yeah, kind of a long-tail, pro-am, digital maker thing!

But wait, there's so much more! It's also a promotional service, and it's a blog. Ponoko is also a mashup, because you can't create with Ponoko unless you already use design software.

Still, I don't want to describe Ponoko in this tech-centric geek way. Let me approach this subject from the point of view of the material differences potentially made in the real world. So let's imagine a hands-on encounter with Ponoko products, in a future scenario where web-based "personal manufacturing platforms" are as big a deal as, say, Facebook, Wikipedia, or Amazon are today.

Scene: A hipster's living room somewhere in Iowa, during the late 20-teens. There's a Goodwill couch, some hand-crocheted clothes, a third-hand plywood Eames chair held together with shoe glue, and a wi-fi repeater sitting on a checkerboard table. JANE WEBGEEK is idly playing with a shiny toy when her country cousin, JEFF NEWBIE, comes in,

banging the screen door behind him.

JEFF: What's that thing?

JANE: (Mesmerized) It's a spinning top.

JEFF: (Sitting on the busted couch) Does it spin good?

JANE: It's OK. Yeah. Try it yourself.

JEFF: (Bug-eyed) Hey, wait a minute. When it spins, this little top has got *your face* engraved on it.

JANE: Yeah, I was gonna give it to my niece, but see this? (She deftly pops the plastic top into separate gleaming tab-and-slot components). You think little Vicky might swallow this pointy part? She's 3, you know.

JEFF: Is it from China?

JANE: It's from New Zealand.

JEFF: Well, then at least it's not poisonous. (With some small effort, he reassembles the toy.) It doesn't spin as good now.

JANE: You gotta push hard till that little bump clicks and locks right in there. Yeah, that's it. You gotta really work those slot affordances.

JEFF: Yeah, it's real pretty, but it's, uh, pretty slotty.

JANE: Well, when you've got pieces lasered from laminar sheets, they're plenty stout on the x and y axes, but the z — where you kinda stress it orthogonally to the grain of the material — you gotta watch that.

JEFF: (Putting his feet up) Say again?

JANE: It's like my coffee table here. See how it's waxed sustainable plywood all mitered along the edges? My boyfriend fell over this while we were drunk last night, and it kinda tooth-chipped right here on the vertex. Knocked that strut clean loose.

JEFF: Your table's from New Zealand, too?

JANE: The *plans* for my table are *stored* in New Zealand, but they cut this one with a water-saw down at the local Kinko's. I gotta get a new strut.

JEFF: You can get all the pieces separately?

JANE: Oh sure. Zillions. Many as I want.

JEFF: And they're cheap?

JANE: (Scoffing) What's cheaper than plywood? And I got a laser cutter right next to my laser printer.

JEFF: (Gazing at ceiling) That's a new lamp up there, isn't it?

JANE: (Preening) You like it?

JEFF: It's a giant fanfold thing made out of your face.

JANE: Yeah, that's called "profile cutting." The barriers to entry are so low! I just downloaded the starter kit, put my face against my scanner sideways, then kinda rotated myself. So now the lamplight shines out of my eyes, but in a tasteful rose-colored shade of Perspex.

JEFF: You sell any of those?

JANE: My mom bought one.

JEFF: My mom's my best customer, too. How is Aunt Susan? I haven't seen your mom around much lately.

JANE: That's because Mom's gotten so deep into the post-consumer alteration of all her IKEA goods. It's not just about the community sharing of furniture plans — she is much more into the remixing, the mashup scene, you know, surface glossing, alternate parts. I keep telling her, "Mom, that's close to piracy! You need to really master the tolerances and the material behaviors!" But, you know, my mom's old-fashioned.

JEFF: She's still way into Second Life, huh?

JANE: They call it "Second Retirement."

Ponoko is super-friendly to makers, and one naturally wishes them well. But my greater concern is Ponoko's cousin: that visibly heaving groundswell of entities that are all trying to make real-world, nonvirtual objects. It's like there's a kind of gnawing hunger upon the land because all the heavy industry has fled to China.

So we're seeing a whole panoply of innovative efforts, arising in a haze of neologisms. They might once have been websites or think tanks, but now they are "think-and-do labs," "patching zones," "creative industries," a "laboratelier" (I really love that one, though it's almost impossible to pronounce), "unconferences", "skunkwork foo-camps," "practice-based research," "transdisciplinary collaboratories," "commons-based peer production," and (as Ponoko might slot it all together) a "place-tool-market platform." None of those seem to me to hit the mark yet. But boy, they sure are suggestive.

They are a set of shaded Venn diagrams: overlapping conceptual circles. And at the core of that overlap, there is a lot of white light. In 2008, it's still a hobbyist thing, a fringe activity, a prototype and/or experiment. That's where it's gestating now and sucking up its energies. When it emerges from those verbal mists, it's going to be strong, fast, world-scale, and deadly serious.

Bruce Sterling is a science fiction writer and was the guest curator of the SHARE Festival 2007 in Torino, Italy.

Photography by Andreas Nilsson

Erik and the Submarine

Erik Westerberg was 5 years old when he first saw a large oil tank standing next to a neighbor's barn in his rural hometown in northern Sweden. "I started dreaming of a submarine," he remembers. "I wanted so badly to see what was down there."

The underwater world still calls to him, but the construction itself is now the biggest driving force. "When I first started building, I looked around for information, but there wasn't a lot out there, since submarines are mostly classified as military. So I gave up. I decided to build it completely from my own imagination and common sense."

For the past two years Westerberg, 26, has spent more than 2,400 hours, apart from his day job as a freelance mechanic, building his submarine. He had to invent a special device to bend the 30-millimeter, matte-finish sheet metal for his 6-meter-long hull. He used 200 kilos of filler metals in welding, and thought out all the tiniest details — from the Volvo seat and racer steering wheel down to the smallest, well-oiled mechanical bearing.

Now finished, the submarine weighs 8.7 metric tons and can dive to a depth of 100 meters. Down in the dark waters of the Gulf of Bothnia, the submarine is powered by an electric motor from a lathe, giving a modest top speed of 2.5 knots.

Westerberg's submarine is only the second civil submarine in Sweden. The first was built in the 1960s by Håkan Lans, who can also claim the invention of a Neanderthal computer mouse on his list of merits.

But there are other submarines in Swedish history. In October 1981 the Soviet submarine U137, armed with nuclear torpedoes, ran aground in the Swedish archipelago, and for many years holidaymaking Swedes, wearing Speedos and sunscreen, kept a wary eye on the horizon.

"It would be funny to put the hammer and sickle on the sub," Westerberg says laughing. "Then there could be a little action when I'm out and about."

—Johanna Hallin

Westerberg's Submarine: makezine.com/go/eriksub

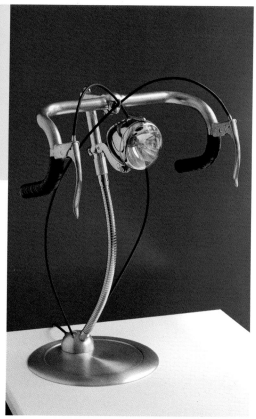

Hello Moto

If the headlamp on a classic Vespa or Lambretta scooter can illuminate a twisting Italian roadway at night, why couldn't it light up a desk?

In the hands of Milanese artisan **Maurizio Lamponi Leopardi**, the polished chrome, handlebars, and headlights of the iconic 1960s motorbikes now find new uses in gorgeous halogen lamps.

Leopardi was trained as an engineer and surveyor, but decided to pursue the artist's life in the 1970s. He made high-end artworks, including lamps, but followed another passion as an art world photographer and graphic artist until the bottom fell out in 2001.

At that point, according to the broken English on his website, he decided to devote "new ideas and energies to what, since child, always has been the most important and amusing job of all his life: 'TO BUILT.'"

And what wonders he has built. The object does not exist that Leopardi cannot turn into a fantastic lamp, perhaps because his middle name sounds so much like *lampioni*, the Italian word for large lamps. Seltzer bottles, coffee pots, hand irons, and hair dryers are all balanced ethereally on slender wire stems. Even giant razor blades and German helmets with the wings of Mercury find themselves central players in Leopardi's whimsical creations.

"I found some old parts in a junkyard and decided to bring them back to a new life with a different function, to make light in houses," Leopardi says in an email, translated from his Italian.

All of his work is informed by another of his passions: airplanes. His lamps not only seem to float on air, but many of them also feature handles that jut from the sides like the wings on a plane. He even makes a series of lamps out of model planes, in shiny aluminum and in wood, evoking everything from the dawn of flight to the Space Age.

In the motorcycle lamps, it's the handlebars that give flight to the light. In bright primary colors, the lamps have such a realistic look that you want to grip them and feel the wind blowing back your hair as you soar above the farms of Leopardi's native Lombardy countryside. —Dan Fost

≫ **Leopardi's Lamps:** lamponislamps.com

Photography by Maurizio Lamponi Leopardi

Right on Track

Photograph by Jonathan Jamieson

Jonathan Jamieson of Dumfries, Scotland, did more than whittle away his vacation in the summer of 2006. While on a break from school, he turned common bamboo barbecue skewers into a delicate sculpture that gracefully delivers a rolling metal ball bearing down a series of chutes and turns.

Jamieson built the 2-foot-tall wooden sculpture, and a smaller, dual-track one, in the glass garden room of his parents' house. The structures are rather delicate, so their 17-year-old architect probably won't be taking them to university when he goes to study mechanical engineering this fall.

But his parents have other messes to worry about. There's an entire room in their house devoted to their son's projects — microcontrollers, an R/C car made from K'nex, a Van de Graaff generator that stands hair on end. There are also juggling and unicycling gear, guitars, and an amp cluttering up the room.

"I like the look of them," Jamieson says, explaining why he constructed the tracks. "It's fun watching these, because the ball keeps changing direction and, because you can't see a direct track, it looks like the ball is moving around randomly."

Working from the bottom up, Jamieson stacked 10-inch bamboo skewers into a scaffolding and connected them with 3-inch strips of garden wire. He didn't begin with a preconceived plan, so he had to adjust as he went. The ramp lengths and angles, for example, needed tweaking the higher he went, lest the ball get moving too fast and derail.

"You decide where you want to take it. That's the freedom of it," Jamieson says. "You have to test it constantly 'cause you often put something in and it goes wrong and you take the piece out and try again."

To show his far-flung friends his creation, Jamieson posted video of his sculptures in action on YouTube. The video-inspired comments include, "You are my idol!" and "Better than LSD." Guess they liked it. —*Megan Mansell Williams*

Rolling Ball Sculpture: ohthebanter.com/rbs

Topsy-Turvy Expression

Riding a red double-decker bus in London is all about the view. The yellow *Topsy-Turvy School Bus*, currently touring the United States, is all about point of view.

Usually, when **Tom Kennedy** builds and drives art cars, he's taking his own artistic vision for a spin. This time, the driving forces were graphic artist Stefan Sagmeister and Ben Cohen, who makes Chunky Monkey ice cream and roving political statements. Their point of view is straightforward: federal budget priorities are topsy-turvy. Their school bus motif suggests one alternative to reserving half of discretionary spending for the Pentagon.

Cohen and Sagmeister chose Burning Man denizen Kennedy to transform a political viewpoint into mobile artistic expression — anything but straightforward.

Kennedy and visual artist **Haideen Anderson** were the initial team that cut up two buses, revealing structural challenges that would send most people looking for an exit ramp. Destined to be driven by volunteers during the long 2008 presidential campaign, Topsy-Turvy had to be strong, but not top-heavy.

This artwork was not for the faint-fingered. Kennedy describes the organically formed crew of joiners as "multi-skilled freaks." Making it up as they went along, they operated a ceiling crane, welded, ground, cast, fabricated, lighted, wired, and painted in a West Oakland, Calif., warehouse. Engineer **Michael Prados** assessed structural progress weekly.

To convey point of view artistically and practically, the makers transformed the passenger compartment into a theater. They painted budget charts on the ceiling and the stop sign, and constructed a speechmaker's platform atop the wheels-up roof. A second gas tank uses biodiesel fuel.

During Kennedy and Anderson's delivery drive to Vermont, Topsy-Turvy proved roadworthy, and rain revealed the exact location of holes in time to fix them. Now its makers and shakers hope the yellow double-decker bus reveals the exact location of national priorities, in time to redirect them.

—*Karen K. Hansen*

≫ **Tom Kennedy's Art Cars:** tomkennedyart.com

Photograph by Tom Kennedy

Photography by Kay Canavino

Wind-Up Whimsy

Gina Kamentsky's *Mechanical Confections* are one-of-a-kind kinetic sculptures ranging from wind-up toys to comical automata, lamps, and motorized pieces. "Humor is really important," she says. "I love old comics and animation from the 30s."

Kamentsky started making art with found objects more than 20 years ago. Walking around her neighborhood in industrial South Boston, she'd pick up pieces from abandoned vehicles and take them home to make small, toy-like objects.

Growing up, Kamentsky's scientist-inventor father was a big influence. "A typical weekend project would be commandeering a toy, taking it apart, and supercharging it in some way. Our model train set was voice controlled; we had a model plane which flew around the room dropping bombs."

After studying industrial design and film animation at Philadelphia College of Art (now the College of Art and Design), she went to work for Fisher-Price. She couldn't believe she got paid to design toys — it was like a wonderful sort of grad school, as she learned how to work in plastic and develop mechanical proto-types. "When I started in the 80s, we were still using Ozen units to put sound in a toy," she explains. "You would pull a string, which powered a spring-wound motor driving a miniature record inside the box!"

After branching out on her own as a freelance toy designer, she got into sculpture. She starts with an idea about motion and progress, then finds objects and forms that fit. She scours flea markets, yard sales, thrift stores, and eBay for raw materials, and scavenges old toys, computers, and video games. Her life's work will be on display until November at the Fuller Craft Museum in Brockton, Mass

Today, Kamentsky splits her artistic time between sculpture and animation, and teaches interactive information design at Northeastern University. Lately she's interested in combining these favorite pastimes by exploring kinetic interfaces for operating the menus on cheap DVD players, and tinkering with Arduino open source electronics. Along with a smattering of humor, of course.   —*Bruce Stewart*

≫ **Gina Kamentsky:** ginakamentsky.com, pixeltoon.com

PlayStation Wizard

Learning to use an oxyacetylene torch was just the spark **Max Maruszewski** needed to set his interest in building things afire. Now, when he's not working on a school play or racing around a parking lot in the "wheelchair" he and a buddy made out of a shopping cart, this 16-year-old's almost certainly "coming up with crazy stuff to build."

Boredom can play a large part in a teenager's life, but for Maruszewski, it's often his muse. Take, for instance, his Lego PlayStation conversion. "The PlayStation box came from pure boredom, late at night when my friend Doug West came over," he remembers. "Mainly I just get bored and decide to go make something weird."

Maruszewski's interest in making things started when he was a youngster, hanging out in his father's bicycle shop in San Francisco. From there, he was lucky enough to find a venue for learning often-neglected maker skills. "It really started to pick up when I started a machine shop class at Petaluma High School," he says. "I learned how to use an oxy torch and how to use lathes and such. These skills

motivated me to acquire some more 'hardcore' tools."

He's now working on a remote-control "shopping bot" that he and a pal hope to send down to the local 7-11 for chips and salsa. "It will hand the cashier a credit card and get the receipt and bring it back. It's going to be quite a challenge," he predicts.

Maruszewski continues to take machine shop classes, and after school he's earning his second-level credential with the National Institute for Metalworking Skills (NIMS). The NIMS credentials will allow him to apply for a degree in CNC machining later on, something he's very keen on doing.

For now, he's content to continue his schooling and have a little teenage fun. "Doug and I like to go to the local [grocery store] and get a train of carts attached to the back of the wheelchair. We zoom around the store grabbing coupons, then leave really fast."

Ah, the vagaries of the youthful mind. Maybe next he'll build coupon-dispensing robots.

—Shawn Connally

≫ **Maruszewski's Projects:** makezine.com/go/maxm

Photograph by Max Maruszewski

Bottled Up Visionary

The idea of building with bottles isn't new, but most existing bottle buildings have fallen into disrepair. It's rare to find such a perfect and intact edifice as the bottle chapel built by restaurant owner and folk artist **Martin Sanchez**.

Sanchez has created an urban oasis, a Garden of Eden, hidden behind shrubs, trees, and a wrought-iron fence at his Tio's Tacos restaurant in Riverside, Calif. Sanchez' complex is located on a city block near the historic Mission Inn, and has several outdoor elements that he's continually creating, appending to the complexity of his design.

There's the sculptural chapel made out of ferro-cement, beer and soda bottles, bits of tile and glass, and fabulous statuary from his home country of Mexico. There are several gardens created out of found objects — trash and ephemera otherwise thrown away — that he's rescued and put to his own visionary use.

Down garden paths made of stone and bottle caps, remnants and rummage, you're led to a unique urban environment where broken Barbie dolls and other children's toys grow like flowers amidst the tree branches and handmade wrought-iron arches.

Sanchez has been working on his creation for almost ten years. Patrons of the restaurant can walk beneath cooling streams of water flowing from a fountain garden made of broken pieces of clay and old pipes, discarded bicycles, and other items. There's an incredible path through an archway lined in tubing that's pumping jets of water, creating an obstacle course where one can walk without getting wet.

Inside the restaurant, tile mosaics of sea creatures such as lobsters and marlins cover the tables and floors. Sanchez welcomes everyone to view his beautiful creation, and he hopes it will bring the viewer as much joy as it has brought him to build it.

—*Marlow Harris*

≫ **Tio's Tacos:** makezine.com/go/sanchez

Photograph by Marlow Harris and Jo David

ART WORK
Simple Rules

By Douglas Repetto

ONCE IN AN ART CLASS AT CAL ARTS our teachers, Sara Roberts and Hillary Kapan, told us we were going to play a game to get to know each other better. There were about 15 students, and they divided us up into two groups and gave us some simple rules:

• Sit in a circle.
• Look at the person to the right of the person (or space) directly across from you.
• Do exactly what that person does; otherwise do nothing.

That might not sound like a very interesting game, and it's not clear what's supposed to happen. Many of us were skeptical; how were we supposed to get to know each other by sitting around doing nothing? We weren't even making eye contact, since following the second rule ensures that no two people are looking at each other.

In fact, in one group, nothing did happen. They stared at the sides of each other's faces, bored, dutifully doing the nothing they'd been instructed to do, wondering what all of this had to do with the "integrated media" seminar they'd signed up for.

The group I was in, however, seemed to be playing an entirely different game. After a minute or two of sitting quietly, someone shifted in a chair, or scratched a nose, or maybe just blinked. I wasn't looking at that person, so I didn't see exactly what happened. All I remember is that suddenly a gesture went zipping around the circle. The woman across from me scrunched up her face, so I scrunched up mine. A moment later she grunted, so I grunted too. In a few seconds the scrunch came back, but now it was a full body scrunch/grimace/hunching action. Followed, of course, by an elaborate grunt/heehaw/raspberry. Each action was amplified and modulated as it made its way along the zigzag path around the circle, each person

reacting a bit differently, some hamming it up, others playing it cool, some reacting right away, others taking a while to process what they'd seen and heard.

The simple rules set up a feedback loop, and like many feedback loops, the signals in ours were folding back on themselves and starting to squeal. Before long people were jumping up and down, standing on chairs, shouting, contorting their faces and bodies, doing little dances, in general having a grand time. Meanwhile the other group sat idly, wondering what in the world had gotten into us. After a while they gave up on their own circle, and started watching ours; the simple "get to know you" game had turned into a full-blown performance.

Roberts and Kapan, having played this trick before, knew that something interesting would happen. They didn't know what, exactly, but they knew it would be fun and it would get us thinking about simple systems as generators of complex, often surprising behaviors. Lots of artists have used games, rule sets, algorithms, processes, and procedures as ways to generate new materials or explore novel situations. You don't know what you'll get, and sometimes you'll get nothing much, but giving up a little control can be a powerful creative technique.

Many artists have used text-based instructions or scores to explore algorithmic art-making ideas. Some of the most compelling are concise. La Monte Young's *Composition 1960 No. 10* consists of a single instruction: "Draw a straight line and follow it." Sol LeWitt's many *Wall Drawing* pieces are a bit more involved, but not much; #65 is: "Lines not short, not straight, crossing and touching, drawn at random, using four colors, uniformly dispersed with maximum density, covering the entire surface of the wall." Composers and musicians get in on the action as well; Yoko Ono's "Voice Piece for Soprano" suggests various ways of screaming, while Christian Wolff's "Stones" encourages players to "draw sounds out of stones" and ends with the request: "Do not break anything."

Text-based instructions for making drawings or music are cool, but what about instructions for making instructions? Larry Polansky's *Four Voice Canon #13 ("DIY Canon")* is just that, a kind of second-order music-making system. From Polansky's description:

> The four-voice canons are a set of pieces I have been working on since around 1976. *#13 ("DIY Canon")* is intended as a general template for making new four-voice canons: a kind of meta-canon. This "score" *(#13)* describes the ideas behind the previous canons (permutation lists, mensuration canons, heterophony), and suggests ideas for future ones. It is a how-to manual, a technical description, and an invitational "cookbook" for performers and composers to make their own pieces.

Sometimes, rather than defining a new algorithm and using it to generate materials, artists work with data or artifacts that are the result of some pre-existing process. Rachel Beth Egenhoefer recorded the moves in a game of Chutes and Ladders and then used bubble gum, lollipops, and string to turn the game play into sculpture. I once saw a very beautiful, and seemingly abstract, geometric sculpture/painting by Candy Jernigan: a board covered with small, colorful plastic caps arranged in clumps with a grid in the center. On closer inspection I discovered the caps were from crack vials that Jernigan had found during walks in her neighborhood. The grid was a map of the surrounding blocks, and the caps were placed on the board according to where they were found.

Often the goal isn't to make a thing at all, but to have an experience or create an interesting situation. At "psychogeography" events like the recent Conflux Festival in Brooklyn, N.Y., participants often use games or systems to explore unfamiliar parts of a city or find new ways of appreciating familiar ones. Mary Flanagan introduced Mapscotch, a combination of hopscotch and mapmaking used to explore social issues in public spaces. And Christian Croft and Kate Hartman introduced the Energy Harvesting Dérive, a pair of Heelys roller sneakers with a wheel-driven generator and two light-up arrows that generate random turning instructions. Sneakers for getting lost!

You don't know what you'll get, and sometimes you'll get nothing much, but giving up a little control can be a powerful creative technique.

Being creative is hard work, and it's easy to fall into a routine or rely too much on ideas and techniques that you're comfortable with. If you feel yourself coasting, why not dream up a game or system of some sort and give yourself over to it? You might end up someplace unexpected and marvelous. Or horrible, but in that case it's not my fault. Why can't you just draw pretty pictures like a normal person?

Assistant executing Sol LeWitt's *Wall Drawing #65* (top), on a wall in the National Gallery of Art's concourse galleries. In Energy Harvesting Dérive (bottom), all electronic components are housed in the tongue of the sneaker. The arrows on the toe light up to direct you where to go.

Douglas Irving Repetto is an artist and teacher involved in a number of art/community groups including Dorkbot, ArtBots, Organizm, and Music-dsp.

Making Magic

Illusion designer John Gaughan is the man behind the curtain.

By David Pescovitz
Photography by Noah Webb

ARTHUR C. CLARKE FAMOUSLY SAID, "ANY sufficiently advanced technology is indistinguishable from magic." In response, modern conjurers like to say, "Any sufficiently advanced magic is indistinguishable from technology." At the intersection of both maxims sits John Gaughan.

For five decades, he's designed and built illusions for everyone from Doug Henning to Siegfried and Roy. Ever seen David Copperfield fly? Gaughan gave him those invisible wings. Scratched your head as David Blaine makes a person's watch disappear and rematerialize behind a shop window across the street? Gaughan's handiwork in action.

Gaughan makes the magic behind the magician.

"I'm fascinated with how primitive the human mind still is," he says. "It can be misdirected so easily."

Gaughan's Los Angeles workshop more closely resembles a theatrical scene shop than a master craftsman's studio. Large props lean against the walls, hand tools are scattered on tables, one assistant cuts lumber outside the shop's garage door while another paints a classic Oriental motif on a large wooden box.

Look closely, though, and you begin to get a feel for the real magic of the place. Two elderly parrots roost overhead. A clarinet-playing robot stands frozen inside a glass display case. Off to one side, an android in a turban awaits the next move in a game of chess.

Their stories Gaughan is happy to tell. However, the various other illusions under construction aren't part of the tour. The maker behind the magic does not intend to reveal his secrets, or those of his clients.

Like many kids, Gaughan was first enchanted with magic as a young boy hanging around a magic shop in his hometown of Dallas. When he was 14, a local magician, Mark Wilson, hired the enthusiastic teen as his gofer and handyman. At 21, Gaughan followed Wilson to Los Angeles in 1960 to work on

his national television series *The Magic Land of Allakazam*. Later he studied industrial and furniture design at California State University, Los Angeles, and went on to teach at CSU Northridge with famed designers Gerald McCabe and Sam Maloof. The fine craftsmanship he learned designing furniture translates directly into his work for the stage. His magic wand is a screwdriver.

"I like working with my hands," Gaughan says. "And I always liked magic. If you have an interest in something, you can usually find a way to learn to do it yourself."

A legend in magic circles, Gaughan has become the go-to maker for magicians in search of a new spectacle. He has an arsenal of ingenious mechanisms to vanish people, levitate them, and subject them to multiple swords thrust through the body.

"There are some common illusions we build that may be ho-hum to the audience, but I've enjoyed working on every mechanism," Gaughan says.

Many of Gaughan's best-known gimmicks are modeled on classic illusions from a century ago, or before. For example, in the late Doug Henning's 1980s Broadway show, the hippie magician hugs a young woman who then vanishes right before the audience's eyes. That was based on a 19th-century illusion that Gaughan had to reverse-engineer just by reading old articles about it. Other illusions, like Blaine's mind-blowing street magic routines, are fresh off the drawing board, or rather the workbench.

"We don't do any design work on a computer," Gaughan explains. "We start full-scale so you can walk around the object and see it like the audience would. That's hard to do with CAD, so we prototype with duct tape and cardboard. Then we start cutting wood."

Not only are magicians always looking for bigger and better illusions, Gaughan's ingenuity is also

LEGEND OF LEGERDEMAIN: John Gaughan plays with Luther, one of his two parrots. Luther, 45, is a former circus performer from Argentina. Luther's companion, Max, is 85 years old. Gaughan says that when he's in the next room, he often overhears Luther and Max talking to each other.

sought out by Broadway directors and rock stars. He's old pals with Alice Cooper, created stage effects for Ozzy Osbourne and The Doors, and most recently delivered levitations and vanishings for the forth-coming musical *Merry-Go-Round*, composed by the Sherman Brothers, who previously wrote the songs for Walt Disney's *Mary Poppins*.

"We turn away much more work than we take in," Gaughan says. Hours to spare are essential, he says, so that he has ample time to make magic for himself. That means restoring and re-creating the wonder of magic history. In the dusty storage space and office behind Gaughan's shop lies his own in-credible museum of illusions past. A glass showcase filled with exquisitely crafted "ball and vase" tricks from a century ago sits near stacks of magic boxes, collapsible metal urns, tables with secret storage compartments, and piles of unidentifiable mecha-nisms from long-lost illusions.

"I like looking at these mechanisms and asking what the maker could possibly have been thinking," Gaughan says. "I can usually figure out what some-thing does, but why it does it — what the illusion was that required the mechanism — is often a mystery."

Not far away from a display of original Houdini handcuffs is Houdini himself, or rather a life-size animatronic model of the famed magician sitting in a re-creation of his study from 1922. Press the button and the Houdini robot signs an autograph. "It's very close to his real handwriting too," Gaughan proudly points out.

Every surface, every shelf, in these cramped quarters is packed with apparatuses and ephemera that once delighted audiences. It's a cabinet of curi-osities that even P.T. Barnum would line up to see.

In fact, if Barnum were alive, he'd be thrilled to encounter the Android Clarinetist in Gaughan's shop. Built in Holland in 1838, it was bought by Barnum for his own museum, which eventually burned to the ground. The Clarinetist made its way to a University of Michigan warehouse where it sat in disrepair for 100 years until Gaughan got wind of it.

"It was a wonderful mechanism but it was so rusty and broken that it looked like it came off the *Titanic*," Gaughan says.

Several years of maker surgery brought the Clarinetist back to life. Its new owner is quick to point out that this is no music box stuffed inside a mannequin. The fingers are articulated, enabling it to actually play Beethoven and Weber compositions on its custom instrument.

OPPOSITE: One of Gaughan's many display cases packed with 18th- and 19th-century magic apparatuses. Inset shows 19th-century French boxwood ball-and-vase tricks. THIS PAGE, CLOCKWISE: The Harry Houdini automaton in a re-creation of his 1922 office; dowels of every size; Psycho, an 1875 automaton formerly owned by Harry Kellar and Houdini; one of 12 clocks built by Gaughan entirely from Brazilian rosewood.

"I'm fascinated with how primitive the human mind still is. It can be misdirected so easily."

The Android Clarinetist was the poster child for a massive 2001 exhibition at the Getty Center titled Devices of Wonder. Gaughan appreciated the opportunity to introduce the public to several of his own wonderful devices, including a re-creation of a famous robot named The Turk, who played chess against the likes of Napoleon Bonaparte and Ben Franklin and was written up by Edgar Allan Poe.

The Turk was built in 1770 by Hungarian inventor Wolfgang von Kempelen. Then the world's most advanced automaton, The Turk drew huge crowds as it toured Europe and America. To satisfy doubting Thomases, von Kempelen would open the machine to reveal a system of gears and levers resembling a wristwatch's grand complication. Of course, The Turk turned out to be a hoax anyway: a human chess master hid inside the cabinet. In 1854, The Turk was destroyed in a fire and instantly became the stuff of legend. A century later, engravings of the machine reprinted in magic magazines caught Gaughan's attention.

"I kept asking myself how they hid a full-size person in there with all the gears and levers?" Gaughan recalls. "So I decided to rebuild it."

Twenty years, three prototypes, and more than a few dollars later, Gaughan's Turk is a near-perfect re-creation of von Kempelen's. He even replicated the original Turk's chessboard that wasn't caught in the blaze. The reborn Turk is a marvel to behold, but even a close examination begs the question that captured Gaughan's imagination: how does a person fit inside the box with all the mechanics? When asked, Gaughan doesn't miss a beat.

"You've got to keep some of the magic alive," he says with a wry smile.

MAKE Editor-at-large David Pescovitz is co-editor of boing boing.net and a research director at Institute for the Future.

OPPOSITE: Gaughan shows his replica of an 1830s French illusion where water was transformed into wine. A fortune-telling bell from the same period was secretly triggered with electricity, itself a "magical" phenomenon at the time. THIS PAGE, CLOCKWISE: Android clarinetist plays a 32-note scale; Gaughan restored this massive clock mechanism from a French cathedral; The Turk awaits its next chess opponent; at a magician's command, this little devil would produce cards, rings, and keys vanished from the audience.

Making Trouble

THE FAIRYLAND OF SCIENCE

MAGIC IS IN THE MIND OF A FIFTH-GRADER NEAR YOU.

By Saul Griffith

"**I HAVE PROMISED TO INTRODUCE YOU TO** the fairy-land of science — a somewhat bold promise, seeing that most of you probably look upon science as a bundle of dry facts, while fairy-land is all that is beautiful and full of poetry and imagination. But I thoroughly believe myself, and hope to prove to you, that science is full of beautiful pictures, of real poetry, and of wonder-working fairies … and though they themselves will always remain invisible, yet you will see their wonderful power at work everywhere around you."

These are the words of Arabella B. Buckley from *The Fairy-Land of Science*, penned in 1891. If I thought about a modern-day equivalent to this little book, I suspect it would be about the wondrous land of invention, and how it promises more reward and delight than the magical land of special effects. I'd like to see kids inspired by the fantastic feats of their big-screen heroes to produce real-world equivalents, to invent their own magic, through a deep understanding of the fairyland of science, with a good application of engineering.

I love magic as much as the next person: I love the illusions, I love the sleight of hand, I love the spectacle. To me, however, the real magic is in trying to explain the phenomenology of the trick. You know you're watching a great magician when you're struggling to explain the physics or even the optics of what's going on.

Why not use magic as an entrée into the world of science, engineering, and invention? The phenomenon is the science, the props the invention, the execution the engineering. This way of imagining the world allows kids to envision their own magic, and then to make it.

I recently returned from a tour promoting our first *Howtoons* book (*see page 178 for our regularly appearing MAKE Howtoons*). My co-author Nick Dragotta and I visited seven or eight cities in the United States and talked to groups of 50 to 400 kids at a dozen or so schools. The kids were third- through seventh-graders, and the experience was delightful and inspiring for a host of reasons.

I'd like to see kids inspired by the feats of their big-screen heroes to produce real-world equivalents.

Nick and I would do a presentation with the kids where we would describe what we do in our professional careers. It turns out kids are amazed to find out that someone can make a living drawing superheroes, and are inspired to find out that one can also grow up to be an inventor and build kites as large as their school auditoriums. (They were, however, horrified when I said I was in school for 26 years. I don't think they thought that was possible, and when faced with more years of school than their current age, it must have seemed like a nightmare.)

After showing kids how to make projects from our book, they became extremely excited when we finished our time with a Q&A. It was actually less a Q&A than an invitation to imagine: if they could invent or draw anything, what would they most like to invent or draw? While I would then discuss how

A 10-year-old girl dreamed of inventing a robotic cow: "It would live in my bedroom, and walk around and eat up my dirty clothes that I left on the floor." In response, Nick Dragotta drew a robotic cow pooping out clean clothes.

Illustration by Nick Dragotta

one would go about inventing those things, Nick would draw what the kids were describing. It was pretty apparent that in the normal curriculum, kids weren't often encouraged to take inventive flights of fancy outside of story time. They were excited not only to be listened to, but also to have me describe how their ideas were possible and what would have to be done to realize them. They were even more excited as Nick would whip up a drawing of their invention coming to life.

The inventions were often fantastic, occasionally impossible, frequently altruistic, and generally wonderful. Of course some were predictable — flying skateboards and homework-completing machines — but many were lovely flights of fantasy. I was delighted at the proportion of suggested inventions that dealt with clean energy, more efficient cars, and healthier people.

But my favorite came from a 10-year-old girl. To paraphrase: "I'd like to have a robotic cow. It would live in my bedroom, and walk around and eat up my dirty clothes that I left on the floor." And this is where it got interesting. Her tone changed to educational, as she was now teaching me. "As you should know, cows have four stomachs, so my robotic cow can clean my dirty clothes after eating them. The first stomach will be the wash cycle. The

second stomach, of course, will be the rinse cycle. The third stomach will be the dryer, and the fourth stomach will neatly fold my clean clothes."

You can imagine what comes next: in a now very excited tone she said, "And then the robotic cow will walk into my closet and poop out my clean folded clothes." I was inspired by this vision, and by the depth to which it had been thought out. If only iRobot would produce this as the follow-up to the Roomba (the Moomba?). Nick, of course, drew a surreal-looking robotic cow pooping out clean clothes, to roars of laughter from the audience.

I'd like to ask every kid what they'd like to invent. I want to live in the world of magic that these kids dream up — cars that run on water, a vending machine for any combination of soda flavors, an automatically loading marshmallow-making cannon, a single book that feels like paper and contains all the library books in the world, a backpack helicopter, clothes that never need washing, a series of trampolines so you can jump all the way to school, 200-foot leaps at a time.

Magic is in the minds of our fifth-graders. We should talk to them.

Saul Griffith is a co-author of *Howtoons* and was recently named a MacArthur Fellow.

THE BARRAGE GARAGE

Meet the Tool-Zine

Outfitting the all-purpose maker's workshop.
Part 2 in a series. By William Gurstelle

IN THE PREVIOUS VOLUME OF MAKE, I detailed the construction of my all-purpose maker-style workshop, which I've nicknamed the Barrage Garage. It's turned out beautifully, and as anticipated, it's the envy of my maker friends.

Small? Sure, it's a mere 20 feet by 14 feet, but it has all the space required to do serious creating. It's loaded with features, including a way-cool vinyl tile floor, a high-tech wall storage system, fluorescent lighting, 240-volt power, and lots of electrical outlets.

After the infrastructure was completed, it was time to outfit the Barrage Garage. Choosing tools and supplies is a subjective question to be sure, and one that a dozen people would answer a dozen different ways. My goal was to make the Barrage Garage into the Platte River of workshops: a mile wide and three feet deep. Like the Platte, my workshop covers a lot of different areas but is not particularly deep in any single genre. Flexible as a yoga instructor, it provides an environment in which I can attempt projects in wood, metal, chemistry, home repair,

Photography by William Gurstelle

electricity, even the odd bit of pyrotechnics (*see "Making Black Powder," page 54*).

If you're a maker with dreams of metalworking, woodworking, building electronics projects, customizing your rod, or simply keeping your house up and running, read on. In this installment, we'll examine the must-have tools and equipment that make the Barrage Garage such a maker-enabling space.

The Workbench

Building a workbench was my first consideration, for it's literally the foundation on which all subsequent work will be built. I considered the design carefully, evaluating possibilities ranging from a complex Scandinavian design with a beechwood frame mounted on self-leveling hydraulic cylinders, to an interior door nailed to two sawhorses. I chose something in the middle — a solid, heavy, counter-braced construction made from 2×6 fir lumber.

The work surface is two-thirds wood and one-third granite. From a local countertop maker I was able to inexpensively obtain a beautiful 2'×2' piece of polished granite left over from a bigger job. The ultraflat, smooth granite is perfect for doing fine work or electrical projects. The plywood-covered

2×6s are great for everything else.

I finished the workbench by outfitting it with a wood vise with bench dogs (wooden inserts mounted opposite the vise to hold oversized work pieces), a portable machinist's vise, and a pullout shelf.

The typical advice from experts to novices is to buy the best quality tools you can afford. And I believe it's good advice. Cheap screwdrivers, for example, can be a big mistake; the soft metal edges of inferior blades can bend or even break under stress, and the plastic handles chip when dropped. For any tool you use frequently, it makes sense to go with quality.

On the other hand, when you've got a one-off job, and you're not sure if you'll ever have another application for piston-ring pliers or a gantry crane, then buying an inexpensive tool may make sense.

Besides raw materials and tools, I stocked up on general supplies: duct tape, electrical tape, transparent tape, powdered graphite, rope or cord, twine, light oil, white glue, super glue, quick-set epoxy, extended-set epoxy, sandpaper, heat-shrink tubing, zip ties, pencils, ink markers, rags, wipes, and towels. Now, on to the tools.

William Gurstelle is a MAKE contributing editor.

Maker

BASIC TOOLS

A. Electric drill, cordless or corded A drill with a variety of screwdriver tips and drill bits may well be your most frequently used power tool. In the Barrage Garage, where I have power outlets everywhere, I appreciate the lightness and torque of a corded drill. But many people appreciate the flexibility of a cordless model. The higher the top voltage (e.g., 14.4 or 18 volts) of a cordless drill, the greater its torque and the more it weighs.

B. Files and brushes Flat and round bastard files and a wire brush. (A bastard file refers to one with an intermediate tooth size.)

C. Cutters You'll want diagonal cutters, a utility knife, tinsnips, a wire cutter/crimper/stripper, and a good pair of scissors. You'll find a self-healing cutting mat to be a great help; buy one at any fabric store.

D. Mixing and volume-measuring equipment Sturdy plastic bowls in different sizes, disposable spoons, measuring cups, and measuring spoons.

E. Hacksaw For those occasions that require cutting through something harder than wood.

F. Handsaw Most often, you'll likely be cutting dimensional lumber (2×4s, 2×6s, etc.) to size, so choose a saw with crosscut instead of ripping teeth.

G. Linear measuring gear Tape measure, protractor, and combination square.

H. Socket and wrench set If you work on things mechanical, you'll appreciate the quality of a good socket set. Spend the money and get English and metric sockets, as well as Allen wrenches (hex keys).

I. Pliers come in a variety of shapes. At a minimum, you should have standard, needlenose, and vise-grips.

J. Hammers Start with a claw hammer for nailing and a rubber mallet for knocking things apart.

K. Digital multimeter If you do any electronics work, a volt-ohm meter with several types of probes and clips will be indispensable.

L. Screwdrivers Choose an assortment of high-quality Phillips and flat-headed (and possibly Torx) screwdrivers in a variety of sizes.

M. Scale A triple beam balance or electronic scale is a necessity for chemistry projects and mixing stuff.

POWER TOOLS
N. Belt sander

O. Drill press I simply can't live without my drill press, because it provides far more accuracy than a hand drill ever could.

P. Cut-off saw

Q. Grinder

Beyond these basics, there are hundreds, if not thousands, of tools available, all of which may be useful depending on the project. In regard to stationary power tools, it's a tough call. Because they're expensive and require a lot of shop real estate, it really depends on what you're going to do *most*. I use my table saw all the time. But I know people who consider a band saw an absolute necessity and others who say a scroll saw is their number one power saw priority.

SPECIAL TOOLS
Soldering iron Choose a variable-temperature model with changeable tips.

Magnifying lens You'll find a swing-arm magnifier with a light a very helpful addition to your shop. It mounts directly to your workbench and swings out of the way when not in use. It's great for everything from threading needles to examining surface finishes.

Safety equipment Safety glasses, hearing protection, a fire extinguisher, goggles, a dust mask, and gloves are very important.

All safety glasses, even inexpensive ones, must conform to government regulations, so they all provide adequate protection. However, more expensive ones are more comfortable and look better, making you more inclined to always use them. (*See MAKE, Volume 12, page 44, "The Safe Workshop."*)

» If you've got opinions on what is an absolutely necessity for the well-equipped maker's shop, let us know. Post your recommendations at makezine.com/13/garage.

Basic Tools

Power Tools

Safety Equipment

General Supplies

The Tool-Zine

OK, once you've got all this stuff, where are you going to store it? I use a combination of bins hung on Store-Wall panels, and my own contrivance that I call the Tool-Zine. It's easy to build and provides an incredible amount of storage in a small area.

The Tool-Zine is like a magazine for tools; you store your tools on "pages" and simply turn to the correct page when you need a particular tool. You'll be amazed at the convenience and organization it brings to your shop. A 4-page Tool-Zine provides the equivalent of 64ft^2 of wall space in a space slightly larger than 8ft^2. That's a highly leveraged storage solution!

Conceptually, the Tool-Zine is straightforward. It consists of four 1" PVC pipes slotted lengthwise. A 2'×4' piece of ⅜" pegboard is inserted into each slot and fastened with machine screws. Next, wood lath is bolted to both sides of the pegboard to make it rigid. This entire assembly makes a single page of the Tool-Zine.

Four pages are assembled and then mounted vertically on wooden brackets that are firmly affixed to wall studs, reminiscent of the way the pages in this magazine are bound to the spine.

MATERIALS

» **1" Schedule 40 PVC pipes (4)** 5' long
» **1" PVC pipe end caps (4)**
» **1" wood laths, 4' long (4)**
» **⅜" pegboard in 2'×4' sections (4)**
  Other pegboard thicknesses might work, but you'll have to adjust the slot width.
» **2×6 lumber** about 8' long
» **¼" machine screws, 1½" long (20)** with nuts and washers
» **#8 machine screws, 1½" long (20)** with nuts and washers
» **Wall anchors** or wood screws

MAKE YOUR TOOL-ZINE

The diagram shown here has all the information you need to build the Tool-Zine. Here are a few pointers to make the task easier.

1. The most difficult part is making the long slot in the PVC pipe. To fit the pegboard, it must be straight, with a constant width. You will likely need a table saw to do this successfully. I bolted the PVC to a 2×2 piece of dimensional lumber so I could use the saw's rip fence to keep the cut as straight as possible.

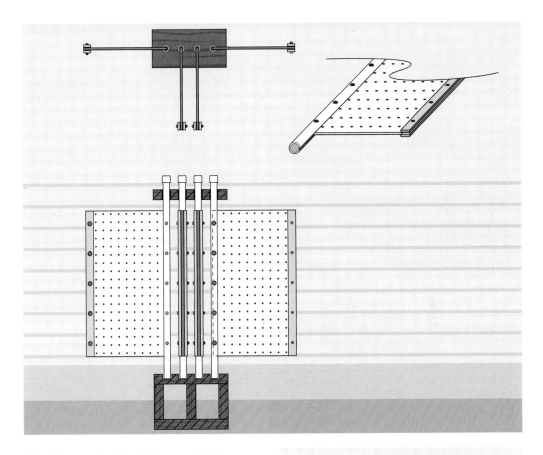

2. Set the saw blade height on your table saw so that it's just high enough to cut through the bottom of the PVC, but doesn't cut into the bolts used to attach the PVC to the 2×2 guide piece.

3. Depending on the kerf width of your saw's blade, it may be difficult to slide the pegboard into the slot. If so, use a rubber mallet to pound it in.

4. Be sure to anchor the top bracket firmly into the wall studs.

5. I chose to build a platform to support the lower bracket. The platform rests on the concrete floor and is attached with a concrete anchor. As an alternative, the bottom bracket could be wall-mounted like the top bracket. It you do this, make sure the brackets are securely mounted to structural members that can handle the weight of your tools.

6. The Tool-Zine is customizable. You can easily add additional pages or increase the distance between pages by extending the size of the brackets. However, if you do, be sure the brackets are adequately anchored to the wall studs.

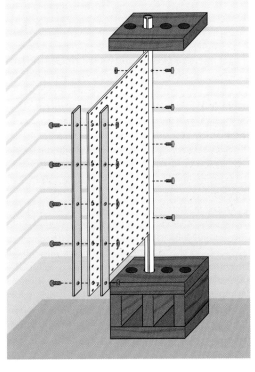

Illustrations by Tim Lillis

Post-Industrial Idyll

The 2007 Robodock festival in Amsterdam. By Dale Dougherty

EACH GENERATION LAYS CLAIM TO THE past with much the same force as it imagines the future. Sometimes we look to a period in the past and call it the Golden Age, whether it's the Golden Age of TV or the Golden Age of DIY.

I was reminded of this while sitting on a plane to Amsterdam. I read about a Dutch painting from 1605, *The Golden Age* by Joachim Wtewael, that had gone on display at the Met in New York City. The painting depicts an idyllic forest, bathed in blue light, and full of resting sheep and goats, colorful birds, and cats and dogs. People inhabit this forest, without need of clothes or shelter, and live off the fruit from the boughs of trees. This is not a dark forest filled with wild creatures. It is a dreamlike state. *The Golden Age* is a picture of how we wish it might have been, even if it never was.

I recalled this painting after spending several days at Robodock (robodock.org), an art and technology festival held in September on the abandoned grounds of an enormous shipyard north of the city. Robodock reinhabited this industrial landscape that working men and large machines once dominated. Artists transformed the factory into a playful fantasia, something beautiful and carefree, yet pulsating, with extreme machines bathed in purple light. Here, we were invited to take control of the machinery in this giant factory and make our lives more wondrous and vibrant. I wandered around in a trance, not wholly conscious that I was living for a few nights in a made-up world.

ROBODOCK KICKOFF

Drumming signals the opening of Robodock. Acrobatic drummers are suspended down the outside wall of the main shipyard building, and come to life

Photography by Steve Double

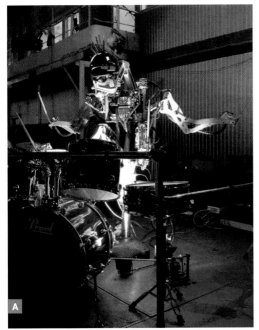

A

B

once a spotlight hits them. Next, the door to the warehouse opens to groaning sounds, harsh lights, and a blanket of fog. Soon, a train car emerges. Imagine this: the boxcar moves 20 feet on a section of track, pulled forward on chains by one man; when the train stops at the end of the track, two sets of hydraulic legs descend and lift the train up off the track; now, the man pulls the section of track forward before the train is lowered upon the track and then tugged forward another 20 feet. It is a Sisyphean task to move this train, and it's repeated to move the boxcar back inside.

As I follow it inside, the rest of the warehouse comes to life: a large fan puffs up the parachute of a dress worn by a woman in mid-air; an ice sculpture holds a flame burning inside; a mobile coffee shop built out of an old motorcycle serves java; a chef's knives have piezoelectric pickups so that he makes music while he slices onions; and a man made of sawdust has his head buried in the side of a building topped with surreal clocks. I stop at Robocross for a drum solo by a brilliantly lit, spike-haired robotic drummer created by Frank Barnes of Berlin (robocross.de).

Delinus (delinus.com) of the Netherlands is zooming around in a delightful red-and-white plane that looks like a childhood toy. His other creation, *Chez Jopie*, is a small engine pulling a train of barstools. Soon, the Ferris wheel from Time Circus (laika.be) of Belgium begins to spin, next to a carousel designed as the underside of a hoop skirt.

Then La Machine (lamachine.fr) starts to play. This French musical troupe, directed by François Delarozière, created a workshop with 35 different machines — they're playing mechanized instruments of their own making. Ever heard someone composing on a lathe?

ORIGINS OF ROBODOCK

Robodock celebrated its tenth anniversary in 2007. Maik ter Veer is the founder and organizer of the festival, which runs for four nights in September. The event grew out of an artists' collective that squatted in abandoned buildings in Amsterdam, and they have struggled to stay in the areas they've brought back to life. Ter Veer dreams of building a permanent home for Robodock so it becomes a year-round activity.

He has managed to get increasing funding from the city and the national government. This has given him a budget to bring in artists from around the world, and this year he has quite a few groups from the Bay Area. Ter Veer is especially happy to have Mark Pauline and Survival Research Labs, calling Pauline the "father of the machine art movement." SRL produced a show for the finale of Robodock on Saturday night.

SERPENT MOTHER: The Flaming Lotus Girls from San Francisco warmed the night with a fiery dragon. Fig. A: **Berlin's Frank Barnes created a robotic drummer that likes to solo.** Fig. B: **Delinus of the Netherlands toyed with his plane on wheels.**

All the facilities at Robodock are designed by members of this artistic community — the ticket booths, the bar, the coffee and food stands (the latter serving quite good vegetarian food). Most things are old and repurposed. Nothing is new. Nothing is commercial.

ROBODOCK BY DAY

Coming in early the next day, I visit Pauline and his team of about 25 people from San Francisco. Their orange, 40-foot shipping container, filled with machine tools as well as machines of destruction, was late in arriving and they're feeling rushed to complete their work in time. Pauline speeds by on an orange bike with a black basket.

The artists are late sleepers for the most part. Jarico Reesce of San Francisco's Cyclecide looks haggard and complains about the rain and the tent he's been sleeping in.

There's much work to be done by day to create this wonderful illusion at night. The warehouse looks plain, almost uninviting.

A very loud noise catches my attention. Ben Blakebrough of Australia is testing his twin-engine hovercraft he calls Triclops. It's a "re-appropriation" of an original idea from the 1950s. It has two wooden propellers that create a column of air and allow him to glide across the concrete floor of the warehouse.

FIRE AND RAIN

There's plenty going on outside on the piers at night. The Flaming Lotus Girls have set up *Serpent Mother*, a spectacular fire sculpture: a large head sits atop a long body that coils around an egg. Along the serpent's spine are 41 "poofers," which Jessica Hobbs, one of the Girls, describes as a "participant-activated flame effect." In the cool mist, people huddle in the middle to be heated and surprised by the bursts of flame. Across from the *Serpent Mother* is the giant mechanical hand built on-site by Christian Ristow's Robochrist Industries (see *"Talk to the Hand,"* page 50).

I run into Jon Sarriugarte of SRL and we walk to the end of the pier where a Russian freighter named *Stubnitz* has been converted into a night-club. Sarriugarte says he thinks that subsequent generations will look back on our time as the "golden age of gasoline." Pauline has restored a V-2 rocket engine to working order and it's part of an incredibly loud performance that consumes lots of fuel. SRL will use 70 gallons of propane, 110 gallons of gasoline, and 10 gallons of diesel in rehearsal and in their Saturday midnight performance. Sarriugarte adds, "The next generation won't be able to burn fuel the way we're doing here."

Rusty Oliver of Hazard Factory organized Power

Fig. C: Survival Research Labs prepared a V-2 rocket for its show. Fig. D: Musicians from La Machine tune their instruments for a performance. Fig. E: The human-powered Ferris wheel, from Belgium's Time Circus troupe and Laika theater company, creates a carnival spirit. Fig. F: Paka the Uncredible from London rides his robotic war-horse. Fig. G: A handmade ride from Time Circus and Laika. Fig. H: Charlie Gadeken, one of the Flaming Lotus Girls, shows a youngster how to raise *Serpent Mother*'s head.

Maker

Tool Racing. He and about ten others came from Seattle and they're staying in a yurt on the other side of the shipyard. One custom-built racer is Apocapony, a blue belt sander with a My Little Pony doll glued on top. Holding a bullhorn, Oliver is having a great time coaxing people to step forward and race. After one pair of racers screech to the finish line, he bellows: "Ladies and gentlemen, something has gone horribly right!"

On the end of the pier is the *Pendulum of Fire*. The pendulum has openings on both sides, and alternating bursts of fire shoot out to cause the pendulum to swing. To a bystander, the giant flamethrower seems to be doing fine. However, once I walk behind it to meet one of its creators, Joe Bard of Pyrokinetics, I hear him grumbling. The pendulum isn't swinging far enough.

He stops the pendulum and apologizes to the crowd: "It's just not working. I'll get it working. Please come back." He explains to me what is wrong. "I'm having serious problems with the European propane tanks. The internal valves are different. I can't get a constant flow of vapor."

Someone says that Bard needs an accumulator tank. "That's what we're trying to get," he responds. After a few minutes, a member of the team spots the tank coming and cries out in joy. Kimric Smythe of SRL is operating the forklift that delivers the white tank. Bard presses his hands together and exclaims, "Oh! Great!" Everything will be perfect now for the final performance.

My route home from Amsterdam took me through New York, and I made time to visit the Met and see this Dutch painting that was part of the Age of Rembrandt exhibition.

I had trouble finding it at first, mostly because I was looking for a large painting. Wtewael's *The Golden Age* turned out to be surprisingly small, slightly larger than an ordinary sheet of paper: such an idyllic fantasy captured in the smallest frame.

📷 See more photos of Robodock:
makezine.com/go/robodock

Dale Dougherty is the editor and publisher of MAKE.

TALK TO THE HAND
By Christian Ristow

FROM THE TIME I FIRST HEARD ABOUT ROBODOCK, I knew I wanted to participate. Having executed large-scale robotic performances for several years under the moniker Robochrist Industries, I was going to bring my stable of machines to the industrial docks of Amsterdam and stage a performance.

But ... for years, I'd had the nagging thought that the person having the most fun at one of Robochrist's performances was always me. I wanted to figure out a way to let anyone have those amazing feelings of power and control that really only come from totally destroying things from a distance!

In September 2006 I attended Robodock for one evening as a tourist, just to get a feel for the event and see how I could fit in. As I walked around, I felt two things were missing: audience interactivity and violence. I came up with an idea: build a really huge hydraulically actuated hand, large enough to pick up and crush cars, and make a controller that anyone could fit their hand into. Any audience member would have the opportunity to show a tremendous increase in their physical strength, if only artificially and temporarily.

Robodock has a bit of a tradition of people coming from all over the world and building things on-site specifically for the event, usually out of nothing but reclaimed scrap metal. This is exactly what we decided to do.

Four Americans, Doyle Shuge, Justin Gray, Conrad Carlson, and I, arrived in Amsterdam in early September with nothing but a few hand tools and the controller, which I built at home before traveling. We met up with two local artists, Jens Schendel from Germany and Tom van der Stelt from the Netherlands, who supplied most of the tools we'd need to build it over two weeks.

About 90% of the materials we used in building the hand were salvaged from local wrecking yards, and the other 10% were purchased from surplus dealers. Strangely, the stuff we purchased was the only stuff we had problems with! We unknowingly bought some really leaky hydraulic cylinders. I had no idea that the word *lek*, which was written on them, means "leak" in Dutch! And the fellow who sold them to us didn't say a word!

We actually used parts of the building where we worked. We pulled wire down from the walls to use in the controller, and used steel tubing from the oxyacetylene plumbing system to complete the hydraulics on the fingers.

We really pushed *Digitalis Ex Machina* to the limit and let a lot of people crush cars! I really hope they had as much fun as I think they did.

Christian Ristow is a robotic artist based in Taos, N.M.

Fig. I: The giant hand built by Christian Ristow of Robochrist Industries and friends, bathed in blue and red light. Fig. J: Kids lined up for the security camera that contained a water spray. In the background is the *Large Hot Pipe Organ*. Fig. K: The *Pendulum of Fire* from Pyrokinetics starts to swing in the shadow of a shipyard crane.

One Man's Junk, The Same Man's Treasure

Meet the Junk Brothers: they filch people's curbside castoffs, transform them, and give them back. By Rick Polito

IF STEVE AND JIM KELLEY HAD A TREASURE map, it would probably be scrawled on the back of the garbage pickup schedule. The power tool-toting stars of *The Junk Brothers* aren't looking for diamonds in the rough, they're digging through castoffs at the curb.

Their HGTV show has the Kelleys prowling nocturnal neighborhoods in their pickup, scooping furniture and flotsam off the curb and carting it back to their workshop where they turn trash into treasure, or at least into unexpected reinterpretations and reprieves for landfill-bound refuse.

Who knew a sink would make an interesting grandfather clock? Or a pair of broken-down bikes could become a karaoke stage! But the Kelleys don't put their creations in a shop window with a price tag. They take them "home," back to the curb from whence they came. Then they ring the doorbell. And run.

It's an odd intersection of prank and project, but the brothers seem perfect for it. Growing up in the sawdust of their father's Ottawa furniture restoration shop, the Kelleys learned an appreciation of the craft and what it took to rescue a neglected treasure. And they each gained an eye for any object's potential — even before the production company found them.

"We're not necessarily dumpster divers," says Steve. "But if we see something on the side of the road it's usually in the back of the truck in a minute."

It's this attitude that turns a rusty lawnmower into a rolling drink caddy and an ill-used rowing machine into a chair fit for George Jetson's den. We pulled the brothers away from the workbench to find out how they find the odd in the odds and ends, like turning an old traffic light into a tasteful bedside table.

"You got to have vision," says Jim.

"And a big garage," Steve adds.

AT LEFT: Jim Kelley (left) and Steve Kelley (right), sharpen up the logo they attach to all their finished projects. THIS PAGE: An Americana cabinet (right) was originally a bed set (top), and a modern bench folds up into a writing desk made out of an old fridge door (bottom).

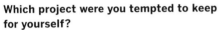

Which project were you tempted to keep for yourself?

Jim Kelley: The one I was most tempted to keep was the first one we did. It was an old console TV. We cut it out and turned it into a fish tank. When it lit up for the first time, we got really excited about it.

Steve Kelley: There was an antique chair that was from about 1880. They obviously didn't know what they had. We completely restored it. It was such a nice, quality piece of furniture. If I could have kept one, that would be it.

What's the one tool you can't live without?

SK: Probably the cordless drill. It just makes life so much easier. It works as a screwdriver, a drill, and it's convenient. You can take it wherever and you don't have to have a power source.

JK: I wish there was just one. I would say the reciprocating saw. It's just a tool that I can use for a bunch of different projects. It's great for demo[lition]. It pretty much revolutionized the saw. You can use it for any kind of material: wood, metal. You can cut holes out.

What does your show teach us about modern society?

SK: It teaches us we live in a throwaway society but we don't have to. We sometimes have to peel the onion back to see that there is some value. We can maybe make this into something or fix it, or make it

better. It doesn't have to be, "Hey, it's paid for. I don't like it. I'm going to throw it out."

JK: If you pick something off the curb, you think you're a garbage picker. But that's not necessarily the way it is; you're basically saving it. We just have to get past this stigma. My next-door neighbor was throwing out the coolest ice cooler I've ever seen. It was metal, from the 50s. I'm using it right now. It's right at the end of my bar.

What do you need to get rid of?

SK: I really have a hard time throwing anything out. That's probably a good question for my wife. If I can't use it on this project, I can use it on the next project. I like to hang on to everything.

JK: I've stopped accumulating and I've started to reduce what I have by reusing things, but I guess the one thing that I need to get rid of is the rest of my carport. I tore it out so I could get a truck through. I took all the 2×10s. I took all the nails out. I'm down to the sheets of plywood I had on the roof. I can't find a use for it. I guess I need to get rid of it.

⊞ For the complete interview and more images, go to makezine.com/13/junkbros.

Rick Polito is a newsprint refugee and freelance writer posing as a slacker in Boulder, Colo.

The Fire Drug

A maker's history of black powder. By William Gurstelle

IT TRANSFORMED THE FATE OF NATIONS;
it changed the way wars were fought, made
weak countries strong and strong kingdoms
weak. It ended the Middle Ages and ushered in
the Renaissance with a bang. Its gush of hot,
expanding gas blew away feudalism, for no longer
could chain-mailed knights on horseback, invulner-
able to hand-held weapons and arrows, maintain
domination over their fiefdoms. In my estimation,
black powder, or gunpowder, is the most important
chemical discovery in the history of mankind.

For a thousand years, black powder was the only
propellant and explosive in existence, making it the
most powerful, deadly, entertaining, and politically
potent chemical on Earth.

Because gunpowder was cheap and relatively
simple to make compared to fashioning armor, it
was the great equalizer among those who fought.

It led to the supremacy of technology over arm
strength, making engineers and scientists more
important than knights and ninjas.

Francis Bacon, the English statesman, essayist,
and philosopher, wrote that gunpowder (along with
printing and the magnetic compass) had "changed
the whole face and state of things throughout the
world ... insomuch that no empire, no sect, no star
seems to have exerted greater power and influence
in human affairs."

Despite its essential simplicity, compounding
black powder is not for everybody. While relatively
tame compared to its high-energy cousins, flash
powder and smokeless powder, black powder has
more than enough brisance to blow off valuable
body parts if handled carelessly. But after reading
several books dealing with the subject, I decided
that I couldn't intimately understand the stuff until

MAGIC INGREDIENTS:
Combining saltpeter, charcoal, and sulfur in the right proportions is the first step to making high-quality black powder.

SALTPETER 75% SALTPETER

CHARCOAL 15%

SULFUR 10%

I made it myself. Making black powder is intellectually stimulating and historically revealing, and it gave me a degree of insight into this important discovery that simply reading about it never could. The first time I smelled the smoke and saw the fire issuing from the magic powder I'd compounded, I knew immediately that this was something special. I'll remember that bang for the rest of my life.

THE FIRE DRUG

The Chinese invented gunpowder, which they called "the fire drug" or "magic black powder." The exact dates are uncertain, but by the 10th century, gunpowder was in use for ceremonial and entertainment purposes, if not in warfare.

Gunpowder is composed of three ingredients: potassium nitrate (often called saltpeter), sulfur, and charcoal. In parts of China, gunpowder makers could merely scoop up saltpeter lying on the ground, the result of the fermentation of soil and animal waste in the humid subtropical climate.

Europeans living in a dryer, colder environment had to work harder to get their saltpeter. The early European method of obtaining potassium nitrate involved aggregating great heaps of rotting organic matter, especially that which contained high percentages

of rotted meat and animal dung. "Petermen" would search out promising places to collect their smelly treasure (abandoned outhouses and animal pens being especially prized). The petermen would taste the earth, and when they found a place that tasted right, they'd cart out the soil, boil it in vats, then evaporate and strain the residue. The result was high-purity saltpeter.

But once you have the ingredients, you can't just shake them up in a jar. The ratio and the manner in which they must be combined are precise and unforgiving. Mixed in the right way, the chemicals become the magic black powder. Combined incorrectly, they're a mound of unimpressive black dust.

HOW IT WORKS

Each ingredient has a specific job to do in producing the desired chemical reaction. The charcoal is the fuel. Made correctly, it is virtually pure carbon. Unlike other forms of pure carbon such as coal or diamond, charcoal's lattice-like structure is filled with microscopic pits and voids that are critical for rapid burning.

The saltpeter is what chemists call an oxidizer. It willingly gives up the oxygen locked within its chemical structure to a nearby fuel, allowing for

Maker

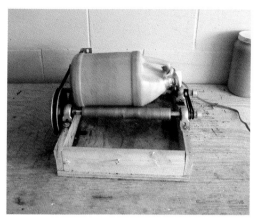

LEFT: Making black powder requires a ball mill for proper mixing. RIGHT: Willow branches make for good charcoal.

burning. Of course, charcoal burns with ordinary oxygen available in the surrounding air. But if the oxygen for burning is supplied chemically, by an intimate mixing with an oxidizer such as saltpeter, the reaction happens far faster and with great gusto.

The sulfur, called brimstone by alchemists in the Middle Ages, plays a dual role: it facilitates detonation by lowering the temperature at which saltpeter ignites, and then it increases the speed and intensity of the ensuing chemical reaction.

Obtaining these three ingredients in sufficient purity and quantity wasn't a trivial effort in today's times, but it wasn't overly difficult either. I would guess that any maker of legal age and average capability would have little trouble doing so. A short time on the internet visiting the websites of chemical supply companies yielded many likely sources.

Once I procured the saltpeter and sulfur, the final and most difficult step was obtaining the charcoal. This may run counter to intuition since bags of charcoal briquettes are piled up by the front door of any grocery. But bagged briquettes won't work, adulterated as they are by chemical binders and additives. No, I had to make my own charcoal to obtain the purity required.

Roasting wood in the absence of air creates charcoal. I found I could obtain all the charcoal I needed by wrapping small hunks of willow wood in airtight aluminum foil, and leaving them overnight in the remains of the still-hot charcoal briquettes from an earlier cookout.

So now I had everything I needed. It was time to combine the three chemicals into the final stage of the project: real, live black powder.

IS THIS A SMART THING TO DO?

I can't begin to tell you how many people laughed, turned pale, and/or ran away when I explained my intention to make gunpowder.

"That's illegal!" they shouted.

"That's what terrorists do!" they cried.

"That's too dangerous!" they warned.

I beg to differ. In much of the United States and many other countries, possessing small amounts of black powder is assuredly not illegal. In most places, if you're old enough, you can buy much larger quantities of higher-power, higher-quality black powder at any sporting goods store than you can make at home.

As for the terroristic potential of homemade black powder, it's nearly nonexistent. Even underage delinquents have easier opportunities for finding materials with which to cause trouble than to go through the rather long and demanding processes required to make a primitive explosive like this.

And as for danger, well, of course it's dangerous if you're not careful. But so are driving a car and mowing your lawn. By working carefully and limiting quantities, I found I could reduce my risk to a level with which I was comfortable.

Now, I would love to explain in detail the recipe for black powder. And, I believe, so would MAKE magazine's editors and publisher. Heck, so would the art director, the advertising staff, and the interns. Everybody at MAKE is onboard, with one exception: the company lawyer.

We live in a litigious society. Anybody can sue anybody for any reason. So, to allay the fears of our attorney, I'll delve only into the procedure for the manufacturing of high-quality charcoal. Making your own charcoal is fun, easy, and worthwhile for reasons beyond making gunpowder. You can cook with it and you can draw with it. It's worth doing at least once.

Black powder led to the supremacy of technology over arm strength, making engineers and scientists more important than knights and ninjas.

MAKING CHARCOAL

As noted earlier, charcoal briquettes are not usable for black powder because they have additives that are convenient for barbecuing steaks but lousy for making powder. Pure lump charcoal, or wood char, is simply wood roasted in the absence of air. Without air, the wood doesn't oxidize or burn. Instead, it more or less bakes, the process removing water, oils, tar, and other volatiles, and turning what's left into a dark, carbony residue.

After all the goo and moisture have been heated away, the wood char weighs about 20% as much as the original hunk of wood. This is pure charcoal, which burns hotter and more slowly than the original wood ever could.

1. Wrap small hunks of wood (willow wood is the traditional choice for gunpowder charcoal) in heavy-duty aluminum foil. Fold the edges tightly to make it airtight.

2. Poke a small hole approximately ⅛" in diameter in one end of each hunk of foil-wrapped wood.

3. Line the bottom of a grill with regular charcoal briquettes and light them. When they're covered with white ash, the coals are ready. (Incidentally, the white color comes from the addition of lime, which acts as a signal that the coals are ready. The lime is another reason you can't use briquettes for black powder.) The number of briquettes you need depends on the amount of lump charcoal you wish to make. Keep in mind that a 5oz piece of wood becomes a 1oz piece of charcoal.

4. Place the wood bundles in the grill and cover them with hot briquettes.

5. Allow the briquettes to burn to ash. This will take several hours. When the briquettes have burned away, remove the wood bundles.

6. When cool, unwrap the charcoal and set aside. Your charcoal is ready to be used to grill steaks, draw fine art on canvas, or, if you're the daring type, make black powder.

THIS STUFF WORKED

The final steps involved in making black powder include measuring, mixing, and grinding. When I was finally finished, I scooped up my first-ever batch of powder and placed a little on a piece of paper to test it. With a match I lit the corner of the paper. The closer the flame came to the small mound of powder, the farther back I stood, unsure of what would happen when the fire reached the powder. There was a flash of orange light, an audible fizzle, and then a great plume of black smoke. This stuff worked.

I now had a small vial of homemade explosive. Strong, primal urges to use it hovered over me like smoke over a battlefield. Now I wanted to make something to blow up. And that meant making a firecracker.

I'm not stupid; I've seen enough pictures of mangled hands and empty eye sockets to not attempt an M-80. The federal legal limit for explosives in commercial firecrackers is 50mg, which equates to a pile of powder a bit smaller than half an aspirin. The good thing about this is that at that size, your powder goes a long way.

I made a triangular paper case to hold the powder, and added a fuse. It took a while to figure out how to contain the expanding gas long enough to rupture the paper case so that a reasonable bang ensued. Once I mastered this skill, other gunpowder projects soon followed: blackmatch, quickmatch, rocket motors, and a few I don't care to talk about in print.

A sense of pride and accomplishment washed over me, and I thought of myself as a bit like the Professor on *Gilligan's Island*. I now know how to do something scientific as well as useful and practical. And I understand the most important chemical discovery in the world with a degree of intimacy the average non-maker can never attain.

William Gurstelle is a contributing editor for MAKE magazine. Visit williamgurstelle.com for more information on this and other maker-friendly projects.

Tin Can Copper Tan
By Andrew Lewis

Copper-coat a tin can, turning it into an aesthetically pleasing, reusable container.

You will need: A tin can (tin-plated steel, not aluminum), muriatic acid (sold in hardware stores as a brick cleaner), hydrogen peroxide (from a drugstore), scraps of copper, splash-proof goggles, rubber gloves, waterproof apron, plastic container, soap, hot water

1. Wearing protective clothing in a ventilated area, mix 9 parts of muriatic acid to 1 part hydrogen peroxide in a plastic container. Slowly add scraps of copper, which will react with the acid solution and turn it a blue-green color. When the reaction slows and the copper stops dissolving, remove the remaining pieces of copper. The blue-green component is cupric chloride, which reacts with tin and leaves a shiny new layer of copper in its place.

2. Thoroughly wash a tin can, removing all traces of glue and grease from the inside and outside. An abrasive plastic dishcloth might be useful for this. Dry the can and gently place it into the acid solution. The can need not be completely submerged, but keep it turning to expose all parts to an equal amount of the solution. After a few seconds, the can will start to change color, and you should see a pale copper tan appearing within minutes.

3. Remove the can from the acid bath and rinse with water. Leave the can to dry naturally. Then you can finish it with clear acrylic spray, coat it with wax, or just let it oxidize to create a dark, neglected, antique look.

Andrew Lewis is a keen artificer and computer scientist with special interests in 3D scanning, algorithmics, and open source software.

Photography by Andrew Lewis

Make: MAGIC TRICKS

More than a dozen fiendishly ingenious illusions you can build to prove your powers of prestidigitation!

FOR YOUR EYES ONLY: Keep these secrets to yourself or you'll spoil the magic for others.

Photograph by Garry McLeod

Uncle Bill's Magic Tricks

Revive five captivating classics.
BY DAN WEISS

My father was a professional magician and a maker, among many other things. His stage name was Uncle Bill and his business card was Uncle Bill play money (get it?). He's been dead for nearly 20 years now (don't worry — he was born in 1909) and I fondly remember the tricks he built. Here are five of his "gadget tricks," which rely primarily on equipment rather than sleight of hand. They're all easy to perform after a little practice, but the audience should be at least a few feet away. I've included my dad's usual script and patter, but these are just starting points. As with any jokes, you should fit these to your audience and the current moment.

By the time my dad stopped performing, he was in his 70s and walked with a cane. Yet he still had no trouble captivating young and old with these tricks. They're classics, and I haven't seen them since.

Dan Weiss is a second-generation maker who as a kid served as his father's magic assistant. He remains a big fan of the brotherhood of magicians who perform simple tricks like these for the delight of their audiences.

Photography by Dan Weiss (left) and David Torrence (right)

CAN I GET A WITNESS: Many of my dad's favorite tricks were "gospel magic," with patters ranging from moral to flat-out religious. Here I am demonstrating his explicitly religious Burning Bible trick.

The Burning Bible
Dramatic flames leap out of an open Bible,
and return every time you close and open it again.

PREPARATION

1. Dilute some white glue with an equal amount of water, and paint it on the edges of all the pages and the entire inside back cover of the book. Use lots of glue and riffle the pages to help it soak in. You want the book to be a solid block except for the front cover.

2. Place wax paper or plastic wrap under the front cover to keep it from gluing shut. Clamp the book or press under very heavy weights to prevent the pages from warping. If you can open any pages after it's dry, use more glue.

3. Cut a piece of cardboard to the book's page size, then measure in 1½" from all sides, and cut out a frame shape. Use this template and a utility knife to cut the center out of the first page or two. Don't try to cut through more than that yet. If the page comes loose, go back and apply more glue. Repeat and continue cutting down into the book. After a dozen pages or so, you shouldn't need the template anymore, but be sure to cut straight down; a long blade helps. Also keep the corners square. Cut until you reach the back (Figure A), and don't worry if the last few pages won't come out.

4. Paint the inside of the hole with more diluted glue, then insert the wax paper and press dry as before.

5. Now we'll line the cavity with metal. Trace your template's inner rectangle onto the bottom of a foil baking pan. Cut off the outside corners of the pan to meet the corners of the rectangle, then score and fold in the sides so the pan fits into the cavity. Press the tabs snug against the sides of the hole and fold them out flat at the top (Figure B). Trim them so they don't stick out, and staple the metal in place. I found that a desk stapler works better than a staple gun. Staples in the bottom will come out the back of the book; fold these over by hand.

6. Out of the second pan, cut a piece of metal to line the inside cover, and staple it in place.

7. Paint the entire inside of the book with black heat-resistant spray paint. You don't want to get the rest of the book black, so be careful or mask the other areas.

8. Paint the page edges with gold paint. You'll be amazed at how much this "sells" the book as a Bible.

9. Cover the book with the black textured paper, glued on with spray-on glue or diluted white glue. You can tuck a bit in around the edges, but don't go in too far or it could burn!

PERFORMANCE

Ready the prop by pouring a little lighter fluid on a handful of ceramic wool (not the whole bag) and putting it in the cavity along with your lighter (Figure C). At the start of the performance, light the lighter and tilt the book to bring the wool close to the flame. Doing this without being obvious takes practice. The lighter fluid will immediately start burning dramatically. I suggest you first try this outside, and be careful.

Do not place your face over the book. Practice holding it out in front of you, which is safer and more theatrical anyway. Hold the book open flat and tilted toward you slightly, to hide the inner workings from the audience. The black paint helps obscure the details.

Practice opening and closing the book, keeping your thumb at the lower right corner so it doesn't shut completely. If flames shoot out the sides, you used too much lighter fluid or didn't close the cover enough. If the fire goes out, you used too little or closed it too tight. After a few openings and closings, shut the book completely and place it under your arm for a while to extinguish the fire.

The type of lighter used won't catch on fire or explode, but it will get very hot, so you need to watch for that. The ceramic wool cools quickly. One possible upgrade is a clip to hold the lighter, to make it easier to flick.

PATTER

You need some patter, but understand that no one is listening; they are looking at the fire. From the moment you light it until you extinguish it under your arm (and everyone is worried that you will catch on fire) the fire is the star of the show.

Regardless of this, your patter should somehow explain why the book is burning in the first place, and why the fire continues even after you close the

A

B

C

MATERIALS

Large hardcover book at least 1"–2" thick that you don't mind destroying

White glue

Cardboard I got mine from the back of a used writing pad.

Disposable foil baking pans (2) at least as large as your book; I used lasagna pans.

Metal, non-butane lighter and lighter fluid I use a Ronson WindLite.

Ceramic wool sold as "glowing embers" for gas fireplaces

Black textured paper 24"×36" for book cover

Black heat-resistant spray paint

Gold spray paint

Paintbrush

Utility knife

Stapler

Wax paper or plastic wrap

Clamps or very heavy weights

book. Something like, "The fire represents the power of God that is always available in the Bible, even when you're not reading it. And when you open it again, it roars forth as powerful as before." After 2 or 3 times, the audience will be amazed when you close the book for good, since they now believe the fire is nonextinguishable.

Hippity Hop Rabbits

Black and white rabbits invisibly trade places, and the audience thinks it knows how — until they magically appear pink and green.

PREPARATION

1. Cut 6 pieces of hardboard: 5"x11½" (4) and 4½"×11" (2). These are the main pieces for the rabbit houses and the 2 rabbits.

2. Cut 10 strips of ¼" plywood: 11½"×1½" (4), 4½"×½" (4), and 5½"×2" (2).

3. Primer-paint all the pieces. Then paint one side of each 5"×11½" piece matte black and the other side gloss white (Figure A). Paint all the plywood strips gloss black (Figure B).

4. Cut a paper stencil following the rabbit pattern at makezine.com/13/unclebill. It should be a bit taller than the printable area of letter-size paper, so print it full-page on legal size.

5. You can either cut your rabbits to shape, or keep them rectangular. If you keep them rectangular, paint all sides of the two 4½"×11" rabbit pieces matte black. Otherwise, cut them out along the outside edge of the pattern, making the shapes as identical as possible.

6. Stencil the rabbit pattern on both sides of the hardboard pieces. On the rougher sides, paint one rabbit neon green and the other neon pink (this may take several coats), then finish with the outline and details in gloss black. On the smooth sides, paint one gloss black with a gloss white outline and details, and the other gloss white with gloss black details.

7. Glue each rabbit onto a 5½"×2" base, centered and sandwiched on either side by two 4½"×½" strips. Glue all pieces together and clamp until dry.

8. Build the houses out of the remaining pieces, facing the matte black inward. Glue and clamp together until dry. You can optionally reinforce the boxes with nails (Figure C). The rabbits should now stand up straight, and the houses should fit neatly over them.

9. Now for the trick part. Cut the sheet magnet, with the less-magnetic side facing you, into 2 rabbit shapes — following the template, but not including the base. If the less-magnetic side has adhesive, peel off the backing and replace it with heavy stock paper. Paint these sides as a black-on-white and a white-on-black rabbit, just like the hardboard. Then fit them over the colored rabbit sides and trim the edges so they don't stick over (Figure D).

10. Using leftover scraps of sheet magnet, create a magnetic edge for the colored rabbits, within the black outline, and paint it gloss black. With adhesive-backed magnet material, you can just stick it directly; otherwise use glue.

PERFORMANCE

Place the magnetic cover of the white rabbit on the back of the black rabbit, and vice versa. Place them in their houses so that one has the black rabbit facing front and the other has the white rabbit facing front, with the magnet cover sides both facing back. At the end of the trick, pinch the magnet cover against the inside of the house as you grab it to lift it off, lay the house down with the magnet inside, and rotate the rabbits around to reveal the colored sides.

PATTER

Explain that all magicians have rabbits, and yours live in these 2 houses. Reveal each rabbit and cover it back up. Show that the houses are empty by looking through them at the audience.

"White rabbit called black rabbit to invite him over. So white rabbit left his house (turn the house around) and started going to black rabbit's. But black rabbit got impatient, and went over to white rabbit's (turn the other house around) to see what was taking so long (reveal that the white rabbit is now at the black rabbit's house, and vice-versa)."

"Then both rabbits went back home." Turn both houses, and show the rabbits in their original places.

Repeat this story at least 2 or 3 more times. You will hear calls from the audience like, "Turn the rabbit around!" Pretend to not understand, then take off both houses, along with the magnetic covers.

Hold one rabbit closely in front of you. When asked to "turn it around," you turn around yourself, hiding the color. Then turn the rabbit clockwise or counterclockwise. Finally, feign a flash of understanding and turn the rabbit to reveal the colored side. In the stunned silence, turn the other rabbit around to show its colored back as well.

Photography by Dan Weiss (A, B, C, D) and David Torrence (far right)

A

D

B

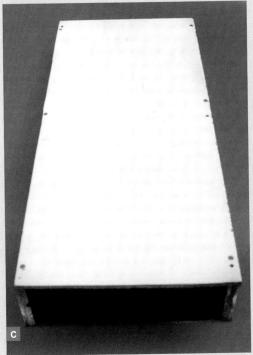

C

MATERIALS

Sheet magnet 10"×12"

Heavy stock paper **several sheets**

Hardboard 2'×4' **aka masonite**

Spray paint **Get primer (1–2 cans), plus matte black, black gloss, white gloss, neon green, and neon pink.**

¼" plywood 2'×2'

Table saw and scroll saw **A small hand saw or jigsaw will also work.**

Clamps

Glue

Masking tape, hobby knife, paper

Hammer and nails (optional)

Six Bill Repeat

You count out six dollar bills (or play money), keep giving bills away, and always still have six. Since my dad's business cards were his Uncle Bill play money, this let him give them away at every event.

PREPARATION

1. Make a pocket by loosely taping 2 bills together so they're aligned to look like a single bill. The best way to do this is to tape them from the inside of the pocket, starting at the bottom and leaving a slight gag between bills. This hides the tape and ensures that no sticky stuff faces toward the bills, so they slide out easier.

2. Cut a V-shaped notch on the back side of the pocket, along the long edge. Make it just big enough for your finger to rest in (Figure A).

3. Load some bills in the pocket, all aligned in the same direction as the pocket.

PERFORMANCE

Put 4 bills under the loaded bill with its notch facing down. Then slide the free bills from the bottom, and make a production out of each one.

This will cover any trouble you have working with the loaded bill.

For the fifth bill, slide one bill out of the pouch, and then count the loaded bill as the sixth. Making this believable takes practice. It helps to keep the stack of bills tilted toward the audience, and they should not be too close.

PATTER

There are many patters for this trick, ranging from the religious (the wages of sin) to the silly (I can magically make money).

The core of the patter is to give a reason for the money to keep appearing, even when you give the excess away. Be sure to give the bills out to the audience so they know you aren't just picking up the same money you set down.

A

MATERIALS

Full-sized play money or real money uncreased and all of one denomination. I've never found play money that's full-sized sold anywhere, so you may need to make your own.

Transparent tape

Scissors or utility knife

Mouth Coil

A torn scrap of paper put into your mouth turns into an impressively long, colorful streamer.

PREPARATION

1. Cut tissue paper the long way into 3"-wide strips, the more precise the better.

2. Glue strips end-to-end, overlapping them by about ⅜" and mixing colors, until you have a streamer 20'–30' long.

3. Tape or glue 1 end of the streamer to itself around the paint-stirring paddle, then continue wrapping the entire streamer around the paddle in a tight coil. You'll slide the coil off later, so I rub bar soap on the paddle beforehand to lubricate it.

4. Slice the coil along its middle across one flat side of the paddle and both edges. You can go around the other flat side a bit, but don't cut it all the way around. Be sure to cut all the way to the stick.

5. Slide the coil off the stick and fold it back at the cut to expose the center, then tape the coil around the outside in this position (Figure A).

6. This is the hardest part: reach into the centers of the 2 coil halves and pull out just the innermost 1" of each streamer. These tails are what you'll pull on (Figure B).

PERFORMANCE

After you've secretly popped the coil into your mouth (see Patter), tail facing out, push it against your teeth with your tongue. This will provide the pressure to hold it in place while it unravels.

Practice pulling the streamer out in front of a mirror. If you lean back and pull the streamer up, it looks like it's coming from deep in your throat.

PATTER

Show a drawing on a piece of paper, and tell the audience that you can destroy it and put it back together before their eyes. Rip it up, say some magic words, and then act as if you believe the object repaired, only to find it is not. People love it when magicians mess up!

Pretend to repair it a few more times, offering a different excuse each time: not the right magic words, the audience wasn't loud enough, the audience was too loud, everyone needs to sing, and so on. The lamer the excuse and the funnier the audience participation, the better. Get more frustrated each time, and cap the final attempt by vowing that if you do not get it this time, you will eat the drawing!

Finally, palm the mouth coil, then pick up the torn pieces with both hands, and make a big noisy show of shoving the pieces in your mouth as you get the mouth coil positioned. Palm the pieces and get rid of them; you can even just drop them. Make a loud coughing/retching sound, and start to pull out the streamer. The sudden change from failure to colorful streamer will surprise and delight the audience, and you can toss it into the audience afterward.

A

B

MATERIALS

Package of colored tissue paper

Glue, glue stick, or double-sided tape

Single-sided tape

Utility knife

Disposable paint-stirring paddle

Ruler

The Fiery Furnace

You tie three identical silk handkerchiefs together and place them into a "fiery furnace" container. When you remove them, a fourth, different-colored silk is tied between them.

PREPARATION

1. Make a pouch by sewing 2 dark silks together on all 4 sides, except for about 1" on each side of 1 corner.

2. Tie the contrasting silk to one of the open corners, then stuff it inside and position its opposite corner just inside the opening.

If the contrasting silk (the "load silk") is obvious peeking out of the pouch, then dye or magic-marker its corner to match the outer silk (Figure A). My dad used blue silks and a white load silk with a blue corner.

PERFORMANCE

Tie a corner of an undoctored silk to the corner of the pouch silk opposite the opening (Figure B), then pretend to tie the corner of the pouch silk to the other undoctored one, but actually tie it to the contrasting silk loaded inside (Figure C).

Stuff the silks in the jar. For the "fiery furnace" effect, turn the lid upside down on top, and then pour in and ignite a bit of lighter fluid.

Afterward, take the silks out and keep them bunched up in one hand. Then pull vigorously, which will extend the load silk and make it seem like it was always there.

PATTER

The 3 blue silks represent Shadrach, Meshach, and Abednego from the Old Testament story of the Fiery Furnace (Daniel 3:1–30). Each time you say the names, you should hold up the corresponding silk to emphasize the fact that there are 3 and only 3 silks.

"A long time ago there was a king named Nebuchadnezzar who had three favorite advisors, Shadrach, Meshach, and Abednego. King Nebuchadnezzar liked these advisors so much, it made his other advisors jealous. They wanted to get rid of Shadrach, Meshach, and Abednego, and started working on a plan.

"They realized that Shadrach, Meshach, and Abednego only worshipped God, so the evil advisors convinced the king that he was as important as a god, and that people should worship a statue of him. What's more, they said, anyone who didn't worship this idol should be burned in the Fiery Furnace.

"The king liked this idea, so he passed it as law. The advisors watched Shadrach, Meshach, and Abednego to see if they would worship the idol, and when they did not, they told the king. This angered King Nebuchadnezzar, and he called for Shadrach, Meshach, and Abednego to appear before him.

"'Why won't you worship the idol?' he demanded. 'We can only worship the true God,' they said. The king said he would throw them in the fire if they did not comply, but still they refused. Even though he liked Shadrach, Meshach, and Abednego, he could not change his law, so he told the guards to tie them up and throw them in the fire."

Stuff the silks into the jar and light the fire, continuing the story as it burns.

"The king was upset, but he had to watch. He couldn't believe what he saw. Shadrach, Meshach, and Abednego were not burning up — in fact, they seemed to be walking around as if nothing was happening. But what was even more amazing was that they were not alone. Right there, inside the fire, was another person, all in white! How was this possible?"

By now the fire should have gone out. If not, use less lighter fluid next time. Knock the lid off (it will be hot) and remove the wad of silks.

"The king told the guards to pull Shadrach, Meshach, and Abednego out of the fire (don't count the silks this time, keep them in a ball). He rushed to see them and find out how they had survived. 'What happened?' asked the king. 'How did you survive? And who was that in the fire with you?'"

"Calmly, the three answered that their God protected them, because he was always with them."

Pull the silks apart, revealing the white silk.

➕ For the Hippity Hop Rabbit stencil design, see makezine.com/13/unclebill.

Photography by Dan Weiss (A) and David Torrence (B, C, and far right)

A

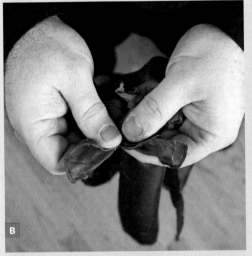

B

C

MATERIALS

18" silks (5) You need 4 in a matching dark color or loud pattern, and 1 in a light or contrasting color. Available at magic shops, or make your own out of lightweight material; true silk is best.

Needle and thread

Small glass jar with metal lid **like a peanut butter jar**

Lighter fluid

Dye or marker (optional) **that matches dark silks**

THE Escaping Blocks

Remake this classic magic trick with high-quality materials.
BY CHARLES PLATT

Imagine a handsome lacquered oak box with a lid mounted on brass hinges. The magician opens the box to reveal a row of 6 brightly painted, rainbow-colored wooden blocks nestled snugly inside. A long, rigid spike passes through a hole at one end of the box, through holes in the centers of the blocks, and out through another hole at the opposite end of the box. When the magician turns the box upside down, the spike holds the blocks securely in place.

The magician pulls the spike out, and all the blocks fall onto the table. He invites a member of the audience to inspect everything, then asks the volunteer to name his favorite 2 colors of any of the blocks.

The magician stacks the blocks back in the box, closes the lid, and replaces the spike, pushing it from end to end. Holes in the lid reveal that the blocks still appear to be lined up in a row, as they were before. Yet when the magician raps twice on the lid with his knuckles and turns the box upside down, the 2 blocks that the volunteer selected fall out, while the other 4 remain inside, still impaled on the spike. How did the chosen blocks escape?

Photography by Garry McLeod

How It's Done

The Escaping Blocks trick is many decades old but still can be a source of fascination and amazement to anyone who hasn't seen it before.

The secret is simple. When the magician puts the blocks back into the box, he secretly turns 2 of them so that they lie to either side of the spike instead of being pierced by it. The lid conceals this act from the audience, but because we all saw the blocks stacked in an orderly row initially, our minds encourage us to imagine that we saw them go back into the box in exactly the same way that they came out. Thus, we are fooled by our expectations, and the cunningly arranged holes in the lid help to confirm what we believe to be true.

Remaking the Trick

This trick is still available in magic kits, but has suffered a terrible degradation in quality over the years. Instead of lacquered oak, the box is made from thin plastic, and has been downsized to less than 2" long. The blocks are the size of Chiclets, and they aren't very solid. The spike is barely more than a plastic toothpick.

I decided to re-create the original version using classic materials, and to construct the box on a scale that would enable a performance in front of an audience of 20 or more. In return for about $25 in consumables and a pleasant day in your workshop, you too can have your own Escaping Blocks, and they will be sufficiently durable to last for many decades, creating a renewed sense of wonder in each new generation that encounters them for the first time.

Materials

To build the box, I found some strips of oak, 6" wide and ¼" thick, in the hardwood section of my local home improvement store. For the blocks, I wanted softer wood that would be easy to shape, so I bought a plain old 2×4 pine stud and cut some square sections from one end.

For the rod, I found a "driveway marker" — a solid plastic, orange stake, ¼" in diameter and pointed at one end. I could have used a wooden dowel, but the driveway marker was stronger, with a shiny finish that lets it slide easily through holes in the blocks.

Size

The geometry of this trick is crucial. When the magician secretly turns 2 of the blocks sideways, they must still fit in the box while allowing a gap just wide enough for the stake to slide between them. I found that the thickness-to-width ratio of each block should be about 3:7. Since a 2×4 stud is actually 1½"×3½", it's ideal for the job.

If you want to make a smaller version of the trick, you can scale it proportionally, but remember to add a thin space between the blocks and the box so that they don't fit too tightly. Otherwise, they won't fall out when they're supposed to. In my version I allowed a total wiggle room of ¼" vertically and another ¼" horizontally.

Fabrication

I used epoxy to glue the mitered joints at the corners of the box, with thin nails for extra strength, since the box may have to withstand some abuse if kids play with it. I didn't use brads or finishing nails, because the slight extra width of their heads could have split the wood near its edges.

Instead I chose wire nails 1½" long, which were a nice tight fit in guide holes that I made with a ¹⁄₁₆" drill. I chopped the heads off with side cutters before pushing them in with pliers (a hammer might have destroyed the mitered joints before I had a chance to strengthen them). I used a belt sander to make the nubs of the nails flush with the wood.

I sprayed the oak box with several coats of semi-gloss lacquer, then coated the blocks with a sealer before I colored them with spray paint. The part of the job requiring greatest precision was mounting the hinges so that the lid would open and close nicely. The tiny screws that came with the hinges were a little too long, and protruded through the lid. They, too, were made flush with the wood by applying a belt sander.

Performance

After you finish your construction work, you'll want to perform the trick — but naturally you should restrain that impulse until you've had a chance to practice it. The most important moment occurs when you put the blocks back into the box. You have to rotate the center pair without anyone noticing, and any hesitation or awkwardness will draw attention to what you are doing. Practice the action in front of a mirror until you can throw the blocks into the box without even looking at them.

This trick is so simple, you may feel tempted to tell people how it works. Just remember the great paradox of magic: everyone wants to know the secret, but if you reveal it, they may wish you hadn't.

MATERIALS

6"×¼" oak board, 30" long
Board sold as 6" wide is actually 5½" wide, but it should be genuinely ¼" thick. Take a measure with you to the store, to check.

2×4 pine lumber, at least 24" long Actual size will be 1½"x3½".

Wire nails, 17 gauge, 1½" (1 packet)

Brass hinges ¾" long (3)
Small hinges are sometimes hard to find. They should be no less than ⁹⁄₁₆" and no more than ¹¹⁄₁₆" wide when open, and should be packaged with their own screws.

Small can of wood sealer
Polyurethane is acceptable if it has a matte finish.

Can of spray lacquer, semi-gloss finish

Spray paints (6) in the colors of your choice

Foam paint brushes (2)

Driveway marker stake, ¼" diameter, at least 18" long

Quick-set epoxy glue, clear

Sandpaper, medium grit

TOOLS

Electric drill

Pliers

Side cutters capable of chopping the nails

Chisel with ½" or ¾" blade

Saw You can use a handsaw, but a radial arm saw will make clean and precise miter joints.

Power sander (optional) A belt sander or a handheld orbital sander will greatly reduce your sanding time.

Frame clamps (optional)
These will make it much easier to glue the mitered corners of the box.

Router bit (optional) Using a router bit with your drill is the easiest way to round the edges of the holes in the blocks, but a large countersink will do.

1. MAKE THE BLOCKS.

Cut 6 square pieces from the pine 2×4. Each piece should measure 3½"×3½"×1½". Drill a ½" hole in the center of each (Figures A and D). Round all the edges, preferably using a router bit on the center hole.

2. MAKE THE BOX PARTS.

Cut the 2 end pieces from ¼" oak, 4¼" wide by 4" high. The 2 shorter edges should be beveled at 45° (Figures B and C). Make a ⅜" hole in each piece as shown in the diagram and round its edges (Figure E). Now cut the 2 side pieces of the box from the same oak, each measuring 10¼" wide by 4" high (Figure F). Bevel the shorter edges to fit the bevels on the end pieces. Finally, cut the bottom of the box from oak, 3¾"×9¾", and the lid of the box, 4¼"×10¼". Drill ½"

Photography by Garry McLeod (far left), and Charles Platt

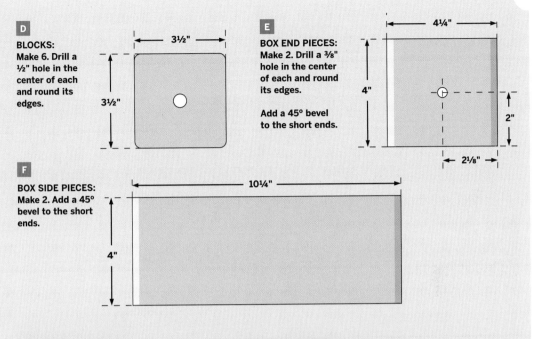

D BLOCKS:
Make 6. Drill a
½" hole in the
center of each
and round its
edges.

3½"

3½"

E BOX END PIECES:
Make 2. Drill a ⅜"
hole in the center
of each and round
its edges.

Add a 45° bevel
to the short ends.

4¼"

4"

2"

2⅛"

F BOX SIDE PIECES:
Make 2. Add a 45°
bevel to the short
ends.

10¼"

4"

G

H

holes in the bottom and in the lid (Figure G), spaced precisely as shown in the diagrams (Figures I and J).

3. MAKE SURE EVERYTHING FITS!

Stack your blocks in a row, and position the pieces of oak around them. Turn the center 2 blocks and make sure that the box will still fit. Also make sure that the driveway marker will slide easily through the holes in the blocks and through the end pieces of the box.

4. PAINT THE PARTS.

Paint the blocks with sealer, let it dry, then spray each block with paint. You'll probably want to continue assembling the box, and pause to come back to the blocks and give them another coat of paint every hour or so, till you have sufficient coverage.

5. BUILD THE BOX.

Glue an end piece of the box to a side piece and hold them together with a pair of frame clamps for at least 10 minutes (Figure H). Make ¹⁄₁₆" guide holes through the miter joint, snip the heads off your 1½" wire nails, and push the headless nails into the guide holes with pliers, to strengthen the joint. Add the remaining sides to the box, and then add the bottom of the box. You'll probably have to sand it slightly to fit.

6. SAND AND LACQUER.

Sand your joints to remove any excess glue and make the nubs of the nails flush with the wood. Remove sawdust with a damp cloth, wait 10 minutes for residual moisture to evaporate, then spray the box with lacquer. You'll probably need several coats.

I

**BOX LID: Make 1. Drill ½"
holes as shown, and round
their edges.**

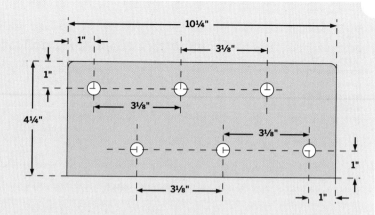

J

**BOX BOTTOM: Make 1.
Drill ½" holes as shown,
and round their edges.**

Holes are spaced the same
as the holes in the lid.

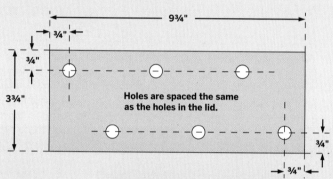

K

L

7. MOUNT THE LID.

Cut recesses for the hinges using a handsaw and
a chisel. Since a chisel can be an extremely dangerous tool, take care never to direct it toward your
hands, even when wearing work gloves.

Glue 1 hinge into place so that you can make
sure the lid closes accurately before the glue sets.
Then drill ⅟₁₆" guide holes and screw all the hinges

into position (Figure K). Most likely the screws will
protrude, and you'll have to sand them down.

After that, spray the lid with lacquer, and your job
is done (Figure L). Allow everything to dry for at least
24 hours so there's no risk of the blocks sticking
inside the box.

Charles Platt is a contributing editor to MAKE.

THE
Conjurer's Dilemma

Do you protect a magic trick, or keep it a secret? You can't have both. BY J.J. LOY

The mystique of magic depends on hiding the secrets behind the tricks. Since the beginning of modern stage magic, organizations such as the Society of American Magicians and the International Brotherhood of Magicians have enforced codes of ethics and oaths of secrecy, to prevent the willful exposure of secrets to the public and, maybe even more importantly, to recognize and respect the ownership rights of magic effects inventors.

Unfortunately, some knaves will break these codes in order to steal a particularly astonishing effect. This means magicians must resort to copyrights and patents to protect their inventions.

Copyrighting a magic trick can protect the holder, but only so far. For instance, say an illusionist had a big dance number that involves a new bullet-catching technique. The entire routine could be copyrighted and no other magician could legally reproduce the act. But copyrighting doesn't protect the technique of the original trick, and no legal steps can be taken to keep it secret.

On the other hand, if the aforementioned bullet-catching routine relied on a special mechanism to perform the trick, a patent could be issued. Inventions such as levitation harnesses, magic hats, or anything that constitutes a "conjuring device" are eligible for patents, and can be successfully protected. But then, of course, the patented invention is no longer a secret, and a clever person will be able to create an effect just different enough to fall outside the claims of the patent.

The tradeoff between protecting an effect and revealing the secret behind it wasn't too bad until the web began linking to patent databases. But today, the gimmicks behind countless tricks are available at your fingertips. For some examples of secrets behind well-known tricks, go to google.com/patents and search for the patent numbers provided here.

Saw a Person in Half

This 1923 patent by Horace Goldin was the first for sawing a woman in half, and although it was not the last, it did a lot for boosting this trick's exposure. (NO. 1458575)

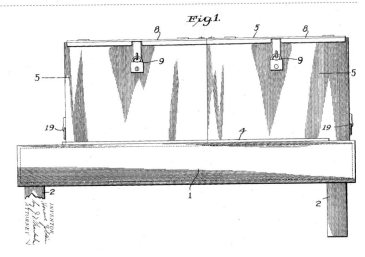

Fig.1.

Quick Change (As Seen on Oprah!)

This trick was amazing the first time I saw it. A handsome couple dances around and the lady changes evening gowns eight or nine times. Inventor David Maas even mentioned the 2001 patent itself during Oprah's show. (NO. 6308334)

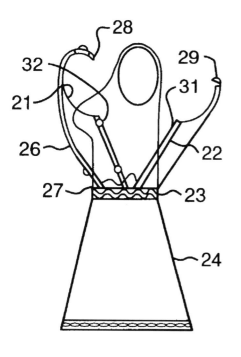

Pull a Rabbit Out of Your Hat

This patent, issued in 1956, describes a method for conjuring lots of bulky things from one's hat or any seemingly empty container. (NO. 2732207)

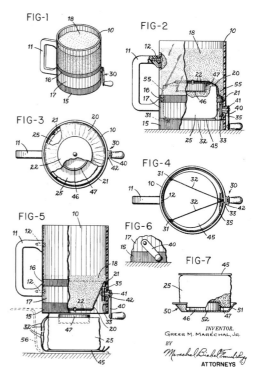

Fly Like David Copperfield!

John Gaughan (see Proto, page 32), the guy who invented Copperfield's impressive flying trick, had the whole trick exposed when this 1994 patent hit the web. (NO. 5354238)

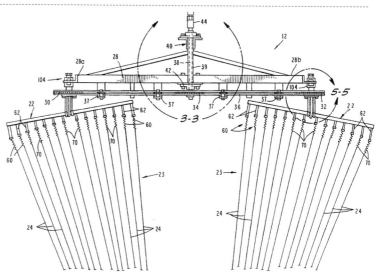

Pepper's Ghost

Here are two takes on an old stage illusion that uses angled glass to project images onstage — you know, for conjuring — one from 1877, and one from 1939 that appears to be an improvement. (NO. 187884, NO. 2155767)

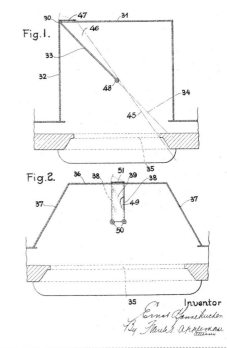

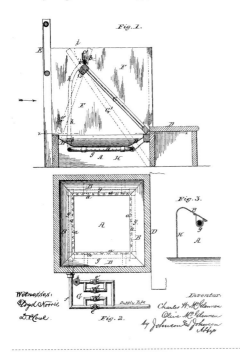

Conjuring Apparatus

A generic name, but basically, it's a patent for a chair that will make its occupant disappear, issued in 1896. (NO. 554682)

I found all this from about three minutes of searching. If you want to see more, try keywords like conjuring device, conjuring apparatus, illusion, and magic. Also, try searching magician's stage names and birth names.

It would seem that almost any attempt by magicians to keep their secrets secret will, in time, fail. My advice to magicians: don't trust anyone. Don't trust your lovely assistant, your fellow magicians, or your audience. And if you do devise the most amazing new illusion — focus on improving rather than patenting it. Because someone will be right behind you.

J.J. Loy is the creator of skablahblah.com, a podcast focusing on the traditionalist and revivalist aspects of an often-dismissed form of music. He enjoys magic, sci-fi, ska, comics, and other things that have rendered him unpopular.

THE Levitating Head

Only you can stop the head from sliding down the string.
BY CHARLES PLATT

The magician brings out a mysterious object on a tray, hidden under a velvet cloth. "Tonight," he says, "I will introduce you to ..." — he whisks away the cloth with a flourish — "my Uncle Clarence." He reveals a life-size, grinning papier-mâché head.

After a few bad jokes ("My uncle always wanted to help me get a-head in this business"), the magician selects a volunteer from the audience and helps him to thread a plastic-covered wire into one ear of the head. "Hmm," says the magician. "Seems to be a fleshy obstruction in there. Possibly the brain — although, in Clarence's case, that would be unlikely." The wire finally emerges from the other ear and the magician encourages the volunteer to make the head levitate. "Just hold the wire vertically, and exert your mental powers ..." But it doesn't work; the head falls to the floor with a thud.

"Hardly surprising," the magician says, picking up the head. He shows a clean, straight hole that runs from ear to ear, and slides a knitting needle through it to eliminate any suspicion that the hole is some kind of illusion. Then he threads the wire again, holds it vertically — and this time the head remains fixed in midair. Amazingly, as the magician speaks encouragingly to Uncle Clarence, the head descends, stops, and resumes its descent on command.

Charles Platt is a contributing editor to MAKE.

Photograph by Garry McLeod

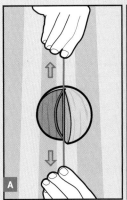 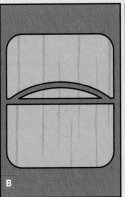 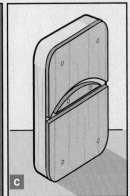 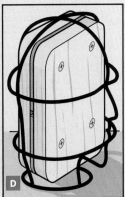

PULL A FLOATER: The traditional version of this trick used a wooden ball (Fig. A), but the principle is the same: the magician pulls tight a string or wire threaded through a secret curved hole, instead of the straight hole that the audience sees. To avoid the challenge of drilling a curved hole, cut pieces of ⅜" plywood (Fig. B) and nail them to a 2×8 board (Fig. C). Screw on a second board to make a sandwich, then attach an armature (Fig. D) to support the papier-mâché head.

How It's Done

This is an old trick that originally used a wooden ball with 2 holes drilled through it, one straight, which the audience saw, and another curved, which was concealed (see Figure A).

For the volunteer, the wire was threaded through the straight hole. Then the magician re-threaded the wire through the curved hole, and by stepping on the lower end and pulling it tight, he created enough tension in the wire to hold the weight of the ball by friction. Changing the tension made the ball fall and stop on command.

To make things more interesting, I decided to remake the trick with a papier-mâché head, although the principle is just the same.

How to Build It

1. From a 2×8 pine board, cut 2 sections, each 9" long, and round the corners.

2. Because drilling a curved hole through a solid block of wood would be too difficult, we're going to make a wooden sandwich using a center section that has channels in it. Cut a piece of ⅜" plywood to the same size as the pine pieces (9" by about 7½"). Mark channels ⅜" wide on the plywood as shown in Figure B, and cut along the lines using a jigsaw, band saw, or keyhole saw.

3. Smooth the inside edges of the channels very carefully, because you'll want your wire to thread through them easily.

4. Nail the plywood pieces to one of the pine pieces as shown in Figure C.

5. Add the second piece of pine and use 3½" screws to hold the sandwich together firmly. Add an armature of stiff wire to create the profile and outline of the head, as shown in Figure D. Tack or screw the wire to the pieces of pine.

6. Using papier-mâché technique (which you can learn from many online tutorials), build the head around the armature. Finally, paint the head. Add some black paint inside each ear to conceal the existence of the second, curved channel.

7. Use a piece of plastic-insulated electric wire when performing your trick, because wire is stiff enough to thread through the curved hole, whereas a string or rope may get stuck.

Astound Your Audience

Uncle Clarence has amused a lot of young audiences over the years, and some not-so-young ones, too. No one has ever guessed the secret behind this classic trick.

If you treat him with suitable respect, Clarence should be as helpful to you as he has been to me.

Illustrations by Tim Lillis

The Power of Negative Thinking

While they're watching the money, you'll know the trick is in the bag. BY CHARLES PLATT

Magic tricks with audience participation often entail borrowing something and then transforming it, or making it disappear and reappear. Any magician should have a variety of devices to assist in these basic operations. The double-compartment bag described here can serve that purpose, and although it's based on a design that's hundreds of years old, I haven't seen it widely sold, probably because it wouldn't be easy to mass-produce cheaply. Thus, modern audiences are unlikely to have seen it.

To give you an idea of how the bag can be used, here's a routine centered around it that I call "The Power of Negative Thinking."

Photograph by Garry McLeod

How It Looks

The magician begins by mentioning the widespread belief that a positive mental attitude can lead to wealth and success. The magician himself doesn't seem to be a stellar example, since he is still performing magic tricks and has not yet retired to the Bahamas as a billionaire, but maybe someone in the audience has a more impressive track record. If there is any such individual, would she or he be willing to step forward and contribute a 20-dollar bill for a quick field test of positive mental powers?

After a volunteer has been chosen, the magician shows him the bag and turns it inside out to emphasize that it's empty. The magician then turns the bag right side out again and asks the volunteer to fold a 20-dollar bill in half before placing it in the bag. It's important to emphasize that only the volunteer will touch the money.

The goal, now, is to transform the 20-dollar bill into a 50. The volunteer is asked to stare into the bag and think positively. "Did it work?" the magician asks after a short interval. He takes a peek himself. "Yes, I think it may have worked. Pull it out!"

The volunteer withdraws the bill, but instead of turning into a 50, it has turned into a 5. The magician becomes agitated. He accuses the volunteer of deliberately sabotaging the trick by applying negative energy. "You'd better give that to me," says the magician. He takes the 5, puts it back into the bag, and this time, he applies his own powers of positivism, such as they are.

The situation now gets worse. The magician gropes inside the bag. He frowns. There's nothing there! When he turns the bag inside out, he finds that the money has vanished completely.

What to do? Maybe a group effort will save this situation. The magician holds up the bag and asks the entire audience to exert positive energy, to save him from the humiliation of having to repay the volunteer with a check that is liable to be returned for insufficient funds. After another short wait, this time the magician claims to detect success. "Did you hear it?" he asks. "I distinctly heard the rustle of paper money." Of course no one did hear it, but the magician is now confident. He asks the volunteer to put his hand in the bag, and sure enough, there's some money in there. The volunteer pulls it out, and his original 20-dollar bill has been restored.

How It Works

The bag has 2 compartments, selected individually by shifting a divider that is attached to a semi-circular loop of stiff wire concealed under the circular wooden frame that supports the mouth of the bag. The wire extends through a hole in the center of the handle and forms a loop at the end of the handle. The magician secretly turns the loop to rotate the semicircle of wire and expose one compartment or the other inside the bag. Since this procedure requires 2 hands, some misdirection is necessary while it's taking place. The process of staring into the bag (supposedly to deliver positive vibrations) serves this purpose.

Initially, compartment A of the bag is secretly loaded with a 5-dollar bill, while compartment B is empty. This empty compartment is the one that's exposed when the magician turns the bag inside out. The volunteer can then insert the 20-dollar bill into compartment B, provided the bag is not inspected too closely.

After allowing the volunteer to beam positive vibes into the mouth of the bag, the magician stares into it himself, simultaneously flipping the ring at the end of the handle to expose compartment A. The volunteer now removes the 5-dollar bill. The magician becomes concerned, repossesses the money, pushes it into the bag — but actually palms it and withdraws it. This is quite easy to do, since all attention is now on the bag, not on the magician.

The magician turns the bag inside out to show that the money has disappeared, then looks around as if hoping to see the money somewhere. This allows some misdirection during which the magician can slip the 5-dollar bill into his pocket, since it won't be required again. He can also flip the bag back to compartment B. After the audience contributes positive vibes, the volunteer can get his money back. From this point onward, the bag is genuinely empty, allowing it to be turned inside out again for a quick inspection.

The bag must be made from thick fabric, so that when the volunteer places his money into it, he won't feel the bill that's hidden in the second compartment. At the same time the fabric must be sufficiently flexible so that it can be sewn around the semicircle of wire, allowing it to flip easily to and fro without making a sound. Felt is probably the best choice, and black the best color so that the mechanism inside the bag will be hidden in shadow.

NOTE: If you perform this trick, be careful that when you take the money out of the bag and palm it, you take your own, from compartment A, and not the volunteer's money from compartment B. It would be a major embarrassment if you had to confess that you put his money in your pocket by mistake.

Magic Bag Construction

1. Cut 3 pieces of fabric, in the shape shown here. Use heavy black cloth, such as felt, which won't reflect light.

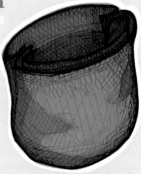

2. Stitch the 3 pieces together around their U-shaped edges, stopping 1" from the straight top edges, which you leave open. Turn inside out as shown.

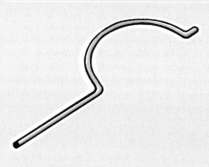

3. Bend a semicircle into a piece of stiff wire as shown, so that its curved section is the same length as the open top edge of the fabric.

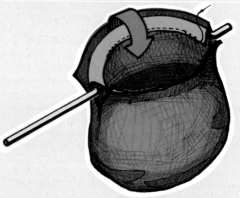

4. Fold the extra 1" of the middle piece of fabric around the curved section of wire, and hand-stitch it loosely to the wire, allowing the wire to rotate freely inside the fabric.

5. For the frame, cut a circle of wood with an inner radius smaller than your wire semicircle, and an outer radius bigger than your wire semicircle. Mine has a 3" outer radius, 6" total diameter. For the handle, cut a 4" length of 1⅛" dowel. Finish these with shellac or polyurethane, then attach the dowel to the outer edge of the circle using small metal brackets. Using a long ¼" bit, drill a hole through the center of the handle and on through the frame, and another hole through the opposite edge of the frame.

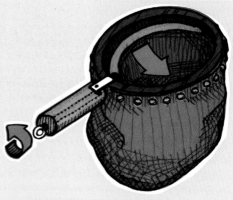

6. Thread the long end of the wire out through the handle, then make a loop in the end, to hold it in place. Fit the short end of the wire into the hole on the other side of the frame. Pull the fabric up over the edges of the frame and secure with upholstery nails.

Ghost Catcher

How to catch a spirit with a scarf.
BY STEVE LODEFINK

Photograph by Sam Murphy

You say you don't believe in ghosts? Well, my little brother didn't either — that is, until I showed him how I could catch one in a handkerchief, and he watched with his own eyes as it struggled to escape.

The secret to the illusion is amazingly simple: sewn into the hem of the scarf is an L-shaped wire with a little kink in one end. After strategically folding the scarf, pressing down on one end of the wire makes the other end lift, causing the scarf to rise, and eyes to pop.

There are variations on the haunted handkerchief setup, but the effect is always the same — some small borrowed object (or an alleged ghost) is folded into a scarf on a tabletop, and if the audience "concentrates" hard enough, the scarf will mysteriously rise!

I bought the gag at a little magic shop in Hollywood in the late 1970s, and it never failed to astound visiting relatives. With my kids showing an interest in parlor magic, I set about to reproduce the levitating scarf. Here's how to make one.

Figs. A–C: Begin by folding the corner with the inserted wire into the center of the scarf (C1). Next, fold the bottom corner, leaving the kinked end of the wire at the edge, where you can easily press it (C2). Fold in the remaining 2 corners, keeping track of the position of your secret wire (C3–C4).

1. FIND, OR MAKE, A SUITABLE DONOR SCARF

The ideal scarf will be made of as lightweight a fabric as possible. Silks are ideal, since they can be lifted easily without causing undue strain on the thin secret wire. Choose a dark color, to keep the hidden wire hidden.

If you can't find the right scarf, don't fret, making your own is about the simplest sewing project that you could hope for. I found a dark silk fabric with a funky mod pattern on sale at the fabric store, and cut myself a 24" square. Sew a narrow hem all the way around the border of the square, leaving about 1½" unsewn at one corner (Figure A). You'll sew this corner up after you've inserted the magic wire. If you're using a readymade scarf, open the seam up at one corner to insert the wire.

2. MAKE THE "LEVITATING" WIRE

Finding the right wire material was the most difficult part of this project for me. The wire needs to be pretty thin — around ¹⁄₃₂" or less — or it will be noticeable in the scarf and too heavy to be easily controlled. But it also needs to have high tensile strength, or it will bend under the stress of lifting the scarf. Good stuff to use is a springy steel wire called "music wire." This is like the stuff that steel guitar strings are made of, only thicker. I got some at a shop that makes stringed instruments. You might also get some from a piano tuner.

Cut a 6" length of wire and give it a 1½"-long, 90° bend at one end. Put a kink in the short end about ½" from the bend (Figure B). Now lay the wire flat, and press down on the "bump" in the short end of the wire. The longer end should lift up as you press on the short end. If it doesn't, adjust the bend until you have a nice little lever action.

Insert the wire into the hem of the scarf, and sew up the opening, concealing the wire within the hem (Figure C1).

3. FOOL YOUR FRIENDS

To prepare for levitation, fold the scarf so that the plain end of the wire ends up in the center, and the crimped end falls at the edge (Figures C1–C4), where you can press on it, causing the center to rise, confounding everyone in the room.

Photography by Steve Lodefink

Telekinetic Pen

An ordinary-looking Sharpie dances at your command.
BY BRIAN DEREU

Using a small battery, a magnetic reed switch, and a miniature pager motor, this device will fit concealed inside a fine-point Sharpie pen. When a magnet is drawn near, the contacts on the reed switch close, making the Sharpie dance and vibrate on a table. I call this device the Telekinetic Pen.

The entire device can be built in an hour or two, with only a couple of soldered connections and a little work with hand tools. You can even "prove" it's a real pen by writing with it.

The Telekinetic Pen is a real attention-getter, and as far as the requisite magician's patter and routines, your imagination is the limit.

MATERIALS

Sharpie fine point permanent marker

AAAA cell A Duracell 9V alkaline battery is an inexpensive source for AAAA cells, which are stacked up side-by-side in the battery can. Using pliers, peel the can away to reveal the cells, then remove them and snip away their connecting leads.

Brass tube 11/32" OD × 0.014" wall thickness, 3.3" long **MSC Industrial Direct part #79800025 for a package of six 12" pieces** mscdirect.com

Pager vibrator motor **Electronic Goldmine part #G13566** goldmine-elec-products.com

Reed switch **Electronic Goldmine part #G13078**

5/16" OD flat washer

5/16" OD light duty compression spring, 3/8" long

1/16"-diameter pin, 11/32" long **can be made from a brad**

Soldering iron with 60/40 rosin-core solder

Electric drill or drill press

Drill bits 11/32" and 1/16"

Electrical tape

Single-edge razor blade

24-gauge bare copper wire, 2"–3" **Telephone wire works well.**

Hacksaw with 32TPI blade or jeweler's saw

Fine metal file and emery paper

Crayon

Plastic coffee straw and plastic soda straw

Helping hands jig (optional) **extremely helpful**

Super glue

1. PREPARE THE BRASS TUBE

With a 1/16" drill bit, drill a cross-hole as close to the end of the brass tube as possible (Figure A). To prevent the tube from crushing, insert a regular Crayola crayon into the end before you drill.

2. SOLDER THE PAGER MOTOR, REED SWITCH, AND BATTERY

Take the motor, bend 1 lead downward, and solder to an end of the reed switch. Solder a short length of the 24-gauge wire to the other motor lead so that it extends upward and beyond the motor by 1" or so (Figures B–D).

Put a section of coffee straw around the reed switch (Figure E). Slip a plastic soda straw around the motor plus the switch, and add a little extra length (Figure F). Bend the unsoldered lead of the reed switch 90° from its original position. Solder the button end of the battery directly to the lead on the switch (Figure G). The motor/reed switch/battery assembly is complete.

3. INSERT THE ASSEMBLY INTO THE TUBE

Slide the assembly into the tube, battery first, until the top of the motor weight is just flush with the tube end (Figure H). Push on the straw to get the assembly into the tube. If the fit is loose, secure with a drop of super glue.

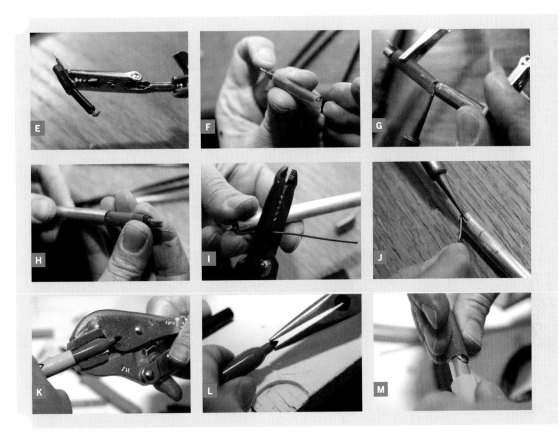

4. SOLDER THE WIRE TO THE TUBE

Bend the top wire around the tube and downward. Solder the wire onto the outside of the tube and let it cool (Figure J).

After cooling, manually check the rotation of the motor to make sure that the wire does not interfere with the counterweight. If it does, push the wire away with a pencil.

5. COMPLETE THE MODULE ASSEMBLY

Insert the spring, then the washer, and finally the cross-pin, which holds everything in place. The cross-pin can be made from a properly sized brad or any type of sturdy metal, and cut and filed to length.

6. PREPARE THE SHARPIE PEN

Pull the Sharpie apart (Figure K). Discard the large ink reservoir. With pliers, remove the writing point from the nose (Figure L), and set the point aside. With an 11/32" drill bit, drill out the nose of the Sharpie to a depth of around 1". Snip the writing point to about ¼" long, and reinsert it into the Sharpie nose. Now insert the vibrating module into the Sharpie

and snap the 2 ends together. Put the cap back on (Figure M). When a magnet is drawn near the pen, or vice versa, it will vibrate.

Neodymium magnets have the best power-to-size ratios of all magnets, and can be concealed easily. A drop of super glue can hold one under your hand, and when you sweep it over the Telekinetic Pen, it'll set it off. The magnet can be peeled off afterward, and any glue remnants will wear away.

NOTE: The Telekinetic Pen will be heavier than a standard Sharpie, so plan accordingly.

➕ **Telekinetic Pen Kit:** The Maker Store (store.makezine.com) is offering a parts kit for this project, including a cut-to-length brass tube, the micro pager motor, reed switch, spring, washer, and pin material.

Brian Dereu is a self-employed manufacturer who enjoys gadgets, fishing, and family.

Diminutive Balls of Fire

Construct a fireball shooter.
BY JOEL JOHNSON

Photograph by Sam Murphy

stalwart of close-quarter magicians for years, the electronic flash gun is a simple device: a battery-powered, hand-held ignitor that uses a "glo-plug" to light a bit of flash paper and cotton, shooting a fireball a few feet into the air.

You can buy one from most magic shops for around $50, but if you build one on your own, you'll not only save a few bucks, you'll also learn how easy it is to add fire effects to almost any electronics project. (And what gadget couldn't stand a little more spurting flame?)

I call my variant "Orpheus Shooters," after the booming voice I use before blasting a fireball into the air, cribbed without shame from *The Venture Bros.*' Doctor Byron Orpheus, my current favorite cartoon necromancer.

I'm absolutely horrible at DIY — I'd solder my fingers to my face if it were possible — so if I can cook up something like this, you should be able to take this simple design and improve it immeasurably.

My model uses a minimum of parts and is nearly concealable in my fairly large hands, but don't be afraid to tinker with the battery layout for maximum concealability. My grasp of the principles of electricity ends around "don't lick a light socket," so there may be smarter ways to rig this unit than the one I have chosen.

And of course, remember your fire safety fundamentals: it may be hilarious to shoot fireballs at your sleeping cat, but she'll have the last caterwaul when you set your bed aflame.

1. BECOME A LICENSED PYROMANCER

A glo-plug, with its platinum heating element, is a disposable part in your Orpheus Shooter, or in any commercial flash gun. Glo-plugs are usually rated for about 50 ignitions, although mine have lasted at least twice that long. While ordering glo-plugs through the mail doesn't require any special registration, ordering ignitables like flash paper does.

It's worth buying online instead of at your local magic store. My local store charged over $10 a plug, while an online shop (starlight.com) charged just $3. The savings were worth the hassle of faxing in a copy of my driver's license.

Glo-plugs (similar to those used in model rocketry, I'm told) come in two flavors: 1.5V and 3V. One isn't better than another for our purposes, but you'll want to match your plug to your power source, so just be sure to remember which one you bought.

2. BUILD THE SHOOTER BODY

2a. Cut a length of pipe with a tubing cutter, about 3" long, depending on the size of your hand. The length, width, and composition of your pipe isn't so important — so long as you're not using, say, magnesium — but anything wider than ½" will probably be less a "shooter" and more a "whoomfer."

2b. Hot-glue your nut to the bottom of the pipe (Figure A). This is one of two things holding the nut to the pipe, and as long as the glue isn't obstructing the threads on the inside, it's fine.

2c. Cut a length of heat-shrink tubing, about ¾" long. Place the heat-shrink tubing around the end of the nut, leaving about ⅛" over the end, so that it curls back around the nut when heated.

2d. Hit the tubing with a hair dryer or other heat source until it holds tightly around the end, creating a small lip that's pushed in when you screw in a glo-plug (Figure B). This doesn't really do anything, but it looks nice.

2e. Clamp the binder clip around the pipe, leaving the arms extended together (Figure C).

2f. Unscrew the nut from your pushbutton switch so that the lip of the switch and the nut sandwich both binder clips' arms. Push the switch toward the outside loop on the binder clips' arms until it's firmly in place (Figure D). You can later secure this with glue, should you choose.

2g. Get a feel for your shooter (Figure E). The only large piece missing will be your battery pack. Decide if you'd rather leave your battery pack off the main body of the unit — perhaps on a separate armband — or if you'd like to keep it all together. I chose to glue my battery pack to the shooter body, even though it's a pretty tight fit in my paw.

3. WIRE HER UP

3a. Strip a small bit of sheath from the 2 wire leads coming from your battery pack. (Red is positive; black is negative.)

3b. Solder the positive lead from the battery pack to one of the prongs on the switch (Figure F). This should take you about 10 seconds; it took me about half an hour. I'm pretty sure desire repels solder.

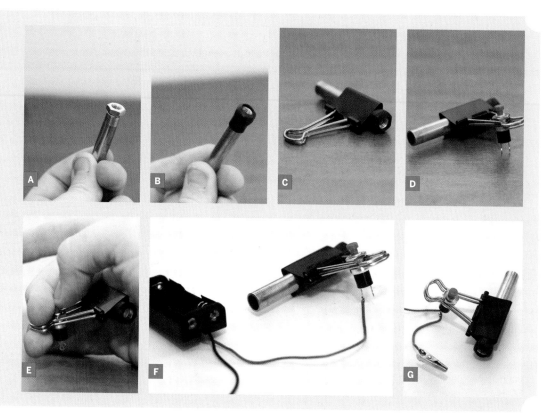

MATERIALS

Metal tubing, 2½"–3" long I used ⅜"-diameter copper, but anything under ½" should work fine.

Glo-plug, 1.5V or 3V available from starlight.com

Nut threaded to match the glo-plug I used ¼-28 jam nuts.

AAA battery holder single for 1.5V glo-plug or double for 3V glo-plug

Large binder clip big enough to snugly hold pipe in place

Heat-shrink tubing ½" diameter

Momentary pushbutton switch, open

Sheathed wire

Alligator clip

Hot glue gun

Soldering iron and solder

Tubing cutter (optional) or have them cut it at the store

Flash cotton and flash paper made of nitrocellulose, from any magic store

3c. Cut a length of wire about 2" long, stripping the sheathing at both ends.

3d. Solder one end to your alligator clip, and solder the other end to the remaining prong on your switch (Figure G).

3e. Cut a small square out of the heat-shrink tubing over the nut at the end of the firing pipe, exposing the metal below, to which you'll attach the negative (black) lead from the battery pack (Figure H). A more clever maker would solder this wire to the nut. After crying many tears, I slipped my lead under the edge of the heat-shrink hole and hot-glued it in place. It's surprisingly durable, but hardly optimal.

3f. Screw in your glo-plug. Insert the batteries. Attach the alligator clip to the rear prong on the glo-plug (Figure I).

3g. Test your shooter (Figures J and K). The glo-plug should light up in less than 1 second. If it doesn't, check your connections. You should be able to see the glow out of the pipe, without looking directly down it.

Photography by Joel Johnson

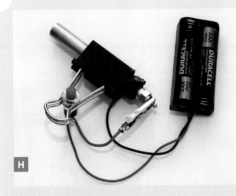

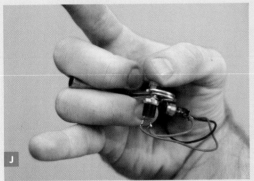

WARNING: Do not look down the pipe, like I do all the time! Someday I'm going to catch a fireball in the face.

4. READY, FIRE, AIM!

4a. Depending on the length and width of your barrel, you'll want to adjust the amount of flash cotton and flash paper used. Remember to unplug the alligator clip from the glo-plug before loading.

4b. Wad a pea-sized bit of flash cotton into a loose ball, tamping it down the barrel with a pencil or screwdriver until it barely touches the glo-plug.

4c. Fold a small square of flash paper into a missile. Remember: The flash cotton is your accelerant, while the flash paper forms the fireball itself. You'll want the paper tight enough to fly a few feet, but loose enough to ignite before it leaves the tube.

4d. Replace the alligator clip.

4e. Yell some grammatically questionable Latin and fire!

Improvement Ideas

Commercially available flash guns sometimes have 2 barrels and 2 separate triggers. If you make the first Orpheus Six-Shooter, please send me video (and I'll send you a soothing hand salve in return).

My body design is simple, made from parts you hopefully have around the house, but the professional flash guns use a metal body that holds the battery and barrel both, making them much more easily concealed. Pro shooters also use a press-on clip instead of an alligator clip to attach power to the glo-plug. Either improvement could be rigged easily by a maker more clever than me.

The Orpheus Shooter is just begging to be integrated into a leather glove or cane, as well.

My next project for the Shooter: wiring it into a HobbyTron R/C Apache helicopter for remote firing. Why bang on your ceiling to quiet the upstairs neighbors when you can fly a chopper into their window and set them aflame?

Joel Johnson is a technology writer living in Brooklyn, N.Y. He writes a monthly how-to column for *Popular Mechanics* and spends his days blogging at gadgets.boingboing.net.

Sucker Bucket

MAKE takes apart an old carnival game to reveal its fraudulent gimmick.

BY MARK FRAUENFELDER

Photography by Ty Nowotny

arnival games seem easy. But anyone who's ever tried to win a prize at a dime toss knows better. They're maddeningly hard to win. You might think the reason is because carnival game equipment contains hidden gimmicks like weights, levers, or magnets to thwart any honest attempt to win, but that's not usually the case. Most of the time, the trick is right out in the open.

For instance, basketball toss games use smaller-than-regulation hoops. Unless you lob a perfect shot, the over-pressurized ball will bounce off the rim like a bullet ricocheting off an anvil at the OK Corral. Next time you visit a cork gun booth, watch the sly old carny load your weapon. He'll set the cork on the end of barrel at an aim-queering angle. (If you want to get screamed at, go ahead and try straightening the cork before shooting.)

But once in a while, you'll come across a carnival game with a secret gimmick that ensures the carny won't have to part with the cheap plush toys strung across the back of his booth. The contraption shown here is one of these. It's called a "scissor bucket" and belongs to Marsee Henon, who works at O'Reilly Media. She inherited it from her grandfather. The object of the game is to throw three balls into the basket without having them bounce out.

Henon was kind enough to allow us to take the game apart to see what was inside. We discovered a round, felt-covered piece of wood attached to a lever (Figure A). The padded wood sphere (Figure C) rests against the basket and tilts away when a ball strikes the backboard at the bottom of the basket.

How Does It Work?

An acquaintance who goes by the moniker Cardhouse Robot saw the photos of the inner workings of the scissor bucket, and explained the mechanism to me:

"There is a damper hidden behind the bottom of the bucket. This is attached to a seesaw mechanism that runs clear down to the bottom of the game. Assuming you have to make three successful throws that hit the bottom and then drop through the hole (Figure B), the first toss hits the dampered bottom; the damper is pushed back; the ball falls through the hole and hits the seesaw, which pushes the damper back into place.

"Same thing for the second throw, except when the carny retrieves the ball for the third throw, he raps the ball against the bottom of the bucket, which kicks the damper away from the bottom.

"The third throw hits the bottom, and without the damper bounces clear out of the bucket. It still falls into the collection mechanism, knocking the damper back against the bottom of the bucket in preparation for the next sucker."

In short, the scissor bucket is an ingenious, albeit fraudulent, money-making machine. Henon told me that "a good operator — or agent, as we call them on the carnival — was so smooth and fast you never had a chance to catch on, and he cleaned you out of 500 bucks or whatever he could."

Fortunately (or unfortunately, depending on how you look at it) the scissor bucket is no longer part of the carnival landscape, because state and county inspectors would seize one the instant they saw it in operation. Today, any scissor bucket that managed to escape being destroyed in a raid is now part of a lucky collector's private museum.

🎥 Videos of the scissor bucket in action:
makezine.com/13/sucker

➕ For more about how carny games work, get a copy of *Carnival Secrets* by Matthew Gryczan.

Mark Frauenfelder (markf@makezine.com) is editor-in-chief of MAKE.

Maker

Darkside Rocketeer

Jack Parsons, the space pioneer history likes to forget.

By Gareth Branwyn

When I was 12, I was vice president of the Chester Virginia Rocketry Society — no great political achievement, as we had all of four members, but the point is, I lived and breathed rocketry. Almost literally. The smell of spent motor casings still triggers Proustian memory, taking me back to farm fields and car batteries sparking Estes motors to life, lofting our latest affront to gravity and aerodynamics into October skies.

Photography courtesy of NASA/JPL/Caltech

Maker

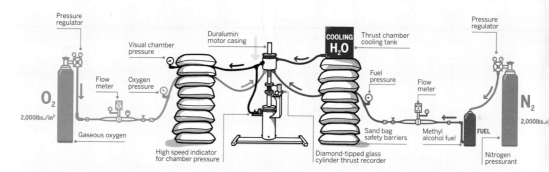

O₂

TOP: Frank Malina's test rig schematic redrawn. OPPOSITE PAGE: The iconic JPL "nativity" scene, taken before the first motor tests on Halloween, 1936, an auspicious date, given Parsons' after-hours interests. Parsons is lying at far right, foreground. Others (L–R): Rudolph Schott, Apollo Smith, Frank Malina, Ed Forman.

I read everything about rocketry and space. I knew all sorts of relevant facts, figures, and historical personalities. And yet, I never bumped into one of the men chiefly responsible for solid-motor rockets. His name was John Whiteside Parsons, but he went by Jack.

Apparently I'm not alone in my ignorance. I took a straw poll of friends and colleagues, and only a few had ever heard of Jack Parsons. Fewer still knew more than "he had something to do with the JPL."

Anyone who knew anything seemed to get it from a recent biography, George Pendle's *Strange Angel: The Otherworldly Life of Rocket Scientist John Whiteside Parsons* (see MAKE, Volume 04, page 177), which is how my ignorance of this space pioneer was finally cured. Turns out it's the "strange" part of this man's life equation that has fouled his scientific legacy.

Marvel Whiteside Parsons, later mercifully renamed John, was born Oct. 2, 1914, in Los Angeles. His parents had recently moved to California to pursue their dreams. When the marriage went south, Jack and his mother moved north, into his well-to-do grandparents' Italian-style villa in Pasadena. Jack enjoyed a charmed childhood, with all the trappings of wealth. Busch Gardens was behind his house, and close by was the Arroyo Seco, a natural playground of rock canyons and chaparral-covered slopes, a

fantasyland right out of the Old West. As Pendle points out in *Strange Angel*, growing up in these sheltered environs, it's no surprise that Jack's imagination developed unconstrained by reality. This freedom to dream was only magnified when, at 12, Parsons discovered Hugo Gernsback's *Amazing Stories*, and, through its pulp sci-fi pages, an intense desire to reach the stars.

Gaga over Rockets

Parsons began trying to build his own rockets, first deconstructing black powder fireworks to pack his own motors. When he reached junior high and found that others didn't share his bookish or geeky interests, things looked grim, until he met Edward Forman, an older student who would become Jack's lifelong friend and fellow rocket pioneer.

Ed Forman was not of Jack's social class. He came from a Missouri farm family who had recently moved to California. The family ended up homeless for a time, living in the Arroyo Seco, until they found a place. The two boys discovered they shared many things. Both suffered from dyslexia, both read science fiction, and both were gaga over rockets. Soon they embarked on a two-man space race, egging each other on with bigger and bolder rockets.

As the boys grew from teens into young men, they continued to raise the stakes on their rock-

Illustration by Damien Scogin

etry experiments. Parsons went to college for a time, while Forman went to work as a machinist. To try and save enough money to continue college, Parsons got a job working at an explosives factory. Here he discovered an uncanny affinity for chemistry, developing an encyclopedic knowledge of chemicals and chemical theory. Parsons and Forman combined their growing expertise to push the envelope even further.

But they soon discovered that, to go any further, they'd need to test the thrusts generated by different fuel mixtures. They didn't have the equipment or the math skills. It was this need for new collaborators that brought them, in 1935, to the doorstep of the California Institute of Technology. There they met Frank Malina, a graduate student also keen on space.

With the chemist Parsons, the machinist Forman, and the mathematician Malina in place, and the resources of Caltech at hand, they were poised for something big. But storming beachheads to the heavens didn't come easily. While they managed to get the attention and enthusiastic blessings of world-renowned aerodynamicist Theodore von Kármán, director of Caltech's Guggenheim Aeronautical Laboratory (GALCIT) — no small feat for two young men without degrees — there was no funding. Supported solely by after-hours Caltech resources, junkyard scores, and their own money, they began years of intense, often harrowing, testing of various solid and liquid fuel mixtures.

Rocketeers Running for Their Lives

The group, dubbed the GALCIT Rocket Research Group, undertook its first serious test, of a gaseous oxygen and methanol motor, on Oct. 31, 1936. Fittingly, they set up the test in the Arroyo Seco. The first test didn't go well (picture the cartoonish image of rocketeers running for their lives, "chased" by a flailing hose of ignited oxygen), but they learned a few things. A photo was taken that day, of the group relaxing before the fireworks. This frozen moment is now considered by the Jet Propulsion Laboratory (JPL), which these men would soon found, as its "nativity" scene.

The team would continue testing through 1936 and into '37. Given their raucous tests in the Arroyo

Maker

Seco, and what von Kármán referred to as the "unnerving explosions of Parsons' rockets" resonating through the campus, the group was given a nickname: the Suicide Squad. Then, in 1938, Uncle Sam paid a visit to von Kármán.

The Army Air Corps had taken an interest in GALCIT's rockets. Specifically, they were interested in using rocket motors to assist heavy bombers taking off from island runways in the Pacific. The Suicide Squad had a job, and a budget, first $1,000, then $10,000. Back they went to Arroyo Seco, this time leasing land from the City of Pasadena (where JPL stands today). Where the group had previously focused on liquid fuels, they now began to seek suitable solid-fuel concoctions that were up to their task. Parsons, the brilliant chemist, set to work.

By 1941, rocket history was about to be made. No one had yet figured out how to achieve a controlled, directed burn of a solid-fuel rocket, one long enough and powerful enough to do something like helping lift an airplane. How could you pack fuel into a motor casing seamlessly enough to form a gas-tight seal so that combustion wouldn't occur through fissures or between the fuel and casing?

Parsons tried many materials, eventually coming up with something he called GALCIT 27 (the 27th formulation), nicknamed "the Goop." As Pendle jokes in *Strange Angel*, the ingredients read like the contents of a schoolboy's desk: amide black powder, cornstarch, ammonium nitrate, and stationery glue, with blotting paper used as the bond between the fuel and the 1'-long steel casing. The Goop was packed into the casing in 1" increments to maximize material density. Static tests showed they could get a controlled burn of 28lbs of thrust for 12 seconds. It was time to strap their motors onto a plane to see what would happen.

On Aug. 6, 1941, the Squad showed up at March Air Force Base with a truckload of motors that Parsons had struggled to keep from exploding in the back as they bounded down bumpy dirt roads. Static tests with rockets bolted to a single-engine Ercoupe airplane worked perfectly, but an in-flight test ended in one of the motors exploding. When the group reconvened two days later, both ground and air tests ended in explosions.

Finally, Parsons figured out that as the motors "cured," fissures formed, and the fuel pulled away

from the case, allowing combustion to race through the fuel, expanding, turning motors into bombs.

The motors would need to be freshly packed. His breakthrough came just in time. The scheduled rocket-powered takeoff was on Aug. 12. With military brass, Caltech students, and others looking on, the tests were a roaring success. A normal 580' takeoff in 13.1 seconds was reduced to 300' in 7.5 seconds. America's first rocket program, the Jet-Assisted Take-Off (or JATO), was underway.

Fading from History

This moment in aerospace history, too, was encoded in a photo. It also perhaps represents the moment Jack Parsons begins fading from history. The image, found in history books and on the website of Aerojet Corporation (the aerospace firm the Squad also founded), shows the team standing around a plane wing, von Kármán in the center, writing equations for the camera. Parsons is there, but for some reason, he's been cropped from the shot. Only the tip of his nose is visible. It's unclear whether this was intentional or not, but it

Courtesy of NASA/JPL/Caltech

is emblematic of the historical cropping to come.

Parsons would go on to make other important advances in rocketry, the most fundamental of which was castable case-bonded solid fuels, first using asphalt (as both binder and fuel) and potassium perchlorate (as oxidizer). This technology is still in use today, in the space shuttle's solid rocket boosters (SRBs). The science of rocketry owes a great debt to Marvel John "Jack" Whiteside Parsons. So why the cold shoulder?

When Parsons wasn't trying to reach the stars in a rocket ship, he was charting a far different course, using the ancient "technologies" of the occult magician. Parsons was a follower of the notorious British occultist Aleister Crowley, aka "The Beast." Parsons was even seen by Crowley, for a time, as his protégé, the person who'd birth Crowley's new religion, Thelema, in the United States. To this end, Parsons ran the Agape Lodge, a Pasadena commune of sorts, known for its wild parties, dark occult rites, drug use, and bed-swapping couples.

As the successes of the Suicide Squad's rockets mounted, and JPL and Aerojet rapidly

AUG. 12, 1941: America's first rocket program lifts off, in a single-engine Ercoupe plane outfitted with rocket motors developed by Jack Parsons and the infamous "Suicide Squad." Parsons, Ed Forman, and mechanic Fred Miller worked through the night to fresh-pack the motors for this flight after Parsons discovered that they tended to explode after curing too long.

expanded — and as rocket science in general grew in respectability — Parsons' private life became an increasing liability to all those involved. He was sidelined, bought out. And things only seemed to crash and burn from there. Parsons' close friend and fellow magician, L. Ron Hubbard (yes, that L. Ron Hubbard) allegedly ran off to Florida with Parsons' girlfriend and money from his shares of Aerojet to start a yacht sales business. Parsons was disowned by his "magical father," Crowley, who died soon after. He worked in the film industry doing pyrotechnics and dreamed of starting his own explosives company in Mexico. He was likely packing for a trip there when, in June 1952, an explosion in his home lab killed him.

Given Parson's chemistry knowledge and his decades of handling volatiles, some suspected foul play, or suicide, or otherworldy forces. But as Pendle tells MAKE, "The simplest solution tends to be the best — and the simplest solution is that a can of fulminate of mercury slipped out of his hand during an experiment. Parsons had worked for so long and with such success with chemicals that he no longer saw them as being particularly hazardous."

Parsons embodied the heart and soul of independent science. One of the reasons von Kármán invited young Jack and Ed into the hallowed halls of Caltech was that he saw in them the type of untarnished dreamers that make novel discoveries. Unfortunately, it was that same dogged determination, that same deep desire to stretch human horizons, that led Parsons down a darker, more serpentine path in his inner life.

But have history's authors intentionally sought to sideline Jack Parsons? In the internet age, his marginalization is due partly to the sensational side of his life: a net search finds the few fragments about his rocketry buried amongst the occult, the Hollywood Babylon, the Scientological. Yet even official histories of rocketry, the space program, and World War II aviation barely mention him.

Aerojet, the company he co-founded, doesn't mention him at all; the picture on their history web page is the famous cropped one. JPL's site also has few references. Pendle claims that when JPL's archivist, the late Dr. John Bluth, tried to gather material on the Suicide Squad, he discovered that most of their papers, drawings, and notes had been used as insulation, to plug up holes in leaky building walls.

Pendle neatly sums up why Parsons frequently is found under the rug of history:

Rocketry underwent fundamental change within Parsons' lifetime, transformed from sci-fi fantasy to an integral part of the military-industrial complex (where it remained until recent private space endeavors). A lightness of

OPPOSITE PAGE: The day of the first successful Jet-Assisted Take-Off tests, Aug. 12, 1941, with Theodore von Kármán (center), Frank Malina, and others posing for the camera. Parsons only makes it into the picture by a nose (seen on the left). ABOVE: One of the few honors Parsons has received is his own crater on the moon (37.3° N, 171.2° W). Fittingly, it is located on the "dark side."

Jack Parsons' Adventures in Inner Space

The life of Jack Parsons was colorful, to say the least. He lived equally in a world of science and science fiction, ancient magick and modernism. He recited hymns to the great god Pan before his rocket tests and liked to perform his magic rituals underneath high-intensity power lines in the Mojave Desert.

Artist Howard Hallis captures the crazier dimensions of Jack's world in this faux comic cover. It depicts an alleged scene from Parsons' life. Scientology founder L. Ron Hubbard is said to have run off to Florida with Parsons' girlfriend and his life savings, money Parsons got after being bought out of Aerojet to save them from the embarrassment of his sex-drugs-and-rock-n'-roll (OK, romantic classical) lifestyle.

When Parsons showed up, Hubbard tried to flee a Florida marina in his yacht. As the story goes, Parsons evoked the Martian demon Bartzabel from his hotel balcony. A freak squall suddenly blasted Hubbard's boat, ripping off the sail and forcing him back to shore. Parsons was waiting for them when they made port. That's Hubbard in the boat with Betty Northrup, Parsons' ex-girlfriend (um … also his sister-in-law), and that's the fiery hand of the sacred whore "Babalon" attacking the boat.

spirit was lost in this transition; a certain sense of humor and individualistic attitude, which Parsons and the Suicide Squad encapsulated, all but disappeared. The space race, despite being built on the ultimate boy's fantasy of exploring outer space, came to be treated as a curiously nationalistic form of science. And nothing could undermine JPL's seriousness more (nor weaken its ability to attract investment) than to declare that its founder was a sci-fi-inspired occultist communist who had never been to university.

Perhaps it is those private space endeavors, and the resurging interest in the DIY ethos in general, that will rekindle interest in Jack Parsons, so that the next generation of rocket geeks will recognize his name alongside those of Goddard, Oberth, von Braun, Tsiolkovsky, and Rutan.

Gareth Branwyn is a contributing editor to MAKE and "Cyborg-in-Chief" of Street Tech (streettech.com).

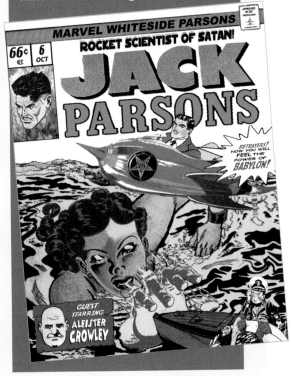

ALL-PURPOSE SWAHILI BED

By Tim Anderson

In Kenya, the most common and most useful piece of furniture is the rot- and bedbug-resistant Swahili bed.

Small islands dot the coast of Kenya near the Somali border. Once there were powerful city-states on these islands. They traded as far as China. They were centers of Islamic learning, and scholars came from far and wide to study here. Now they're mostly villages surrounded by fortified ruins, located far up winding channels through mangrove swamps.

In most houses, you find only one type of furniture: the Swahili bed. It's used as a couch, bed, table, and everything else. It's comfortable and perfect for the hot, humid climate. And it's quite similar to the Shaker bed once used in the United States.

Step 1. Make the frame.
It takes at least two people to weave a bed, both to get it tight enough and to socialize. The frame is very simple, with horizontal beams mortised into the vertical posts. The tension of the straps holds the frame together. The frames shown here are made from the local mangrove wood, which is very hard and rot-resistant. Mangrove wood exports used to be a major source of wealth for these Swahili city-states.

Step 2. Weave the bed.
The palmetto straps used are a plain flat braid, just

like braiding hair but with more strands. I've seen 5-, 7-, and 8-strand braids used. Villagers weave these to sell in the markets.

It takes about 400 feet of strap to weave a bed. The end is tied to a leg to start. Then it's wrapped from one end of the bed to the other, head to foot, about 15 times. Next the cross-weaving starts, threading the web over and under through the long rows.

Step 3. Tighten the bed.
When the weaving is done, the straps are left long to make it easier to tighten the bed. After the web stops stretching, the ends are tied off and cut short.

Step 4. Prevent bedbugs.
I often saw beds left underwater in the mangrove channels, held down by rocks. My local friends told me that salt water kills bedbugs. I wish I'd known that years ago. A friend of mine in the U.S. had a bedbug problem and tried every product on the market without success. Eventually he had to throw out the bed and half his possessions.

Tim Anderson (mit.edu/robot) is the founder of Z Corp. See a hundred more of his projects at instructables.com.

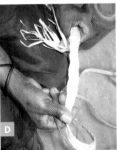

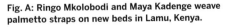

Fig. A: Ringo Mkolobodi and Maya Kadenge weave palmetto straps on new beds in Lamu, Kenya.

Fig. B: Palmetto leaves are soaked in seawater to soften and make them easier to weave. Salt water also deters bedbugs.

Fig. C: Mkolobodi has reached the end of a strap and is splicing it to the next one, by weaving the strands of the first strap into the braid of the next.

Fig. D: The finished splice. Next he'll trim off the protruding strands.

Fig. E: Everyone likes a Swahili bed. Here a cat takes a siesta on a Swahili bed in an alley in Lamu.

Fig. F: An unusually fancy bed in the Swahili House Museum, located in Lamu. The four posts are used to suspend a mosquito net.

Quick Bits

Tips and tools for digital diversions.
By Charles Platt

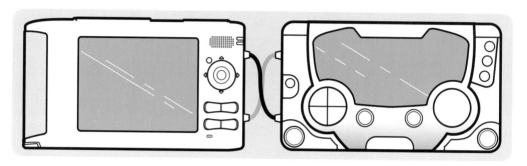

SERIOUS MEDIA PLAYER

For geeky people (like me) who want really serious hardware that looks really serious, the Wolverine ESP media player ($329 and up, wolverinedata.com) is about as serious as you can get.

Seemingly styled by engineers for the pocket-protector set, you'll certainly need a pocket protector for this hefty 10-ounce package. The 3.6" display has a retro look, with monospaced fonts and icons reminiscent of Windows 3.1, and the controls include an Escape key.

Still, if you put function ahead of style it's a killer, with up to 250GB of storage on an industry-standard hard drive that you can upgrade one day if a quarter-terabyte isn't sufficient for your nerdy needs. The battery likewise is swappable, and is a cheaply available Sanyo item.

The ESP plays MP3, WMA, AAC, WAV, OGG, and CDA, audio files, and displays MPEG-1, MPEG-4, XviD, and WMV9 video formats. It also recognizes numerous photo formats, from JPEGs to the RAW versions used in high-end digital cameras such as Canon, Nikon, and Olympus. When you're shooting a lot of photos while traveling, you can back them up by inserting your CompactFlash or Secure Digital card in one of the slots in the ESP and review them at your leisure. When you get home, a USB cable uploads them to your desktop computer.

With 50 times the (current) storage of a Gmail account, the ESP has room for more than 50,000 songs, or thousands of photographs, or dozens of full-length movies. Alternatively, with so many megabytes to spare, you can eschew the audio compromises of MP3 compression, rip your CDs into lossless WAV format, plug your ESP into your stereo, and enjoy old-school high fidelity. That's how I'm using mine; its battleship-gray case fits right in beside my vintage 1978 Apt Holman preamp.

SOUND GRABBER

As an increasing number of radio stations stream their programs, here's a cheap and simple way to capture and save webcasts. Audio Mid Recorder (tucows.com/preview/360842) taps any audio passing through your SoundBlaster-compatible sound card and saves it to a file, allowing you to select the sound format and the level of compression.

If you use VoIP, it can record your phone conversations. You can also play a protected WMA file, capture the sound, and save it in unprotected mode, although this may degrade the quality slightly, since you'll be re-sampling the stream.

Other options include automatic shut-off after a preset time, automatic start, and voice-actuated record.

The free download version imposes a 60-second limit on each recording, but for 25 bucks you can get the unlimited version. This is a basic tool to grab anything from sound effects to spoken word, ideal for anyone who's into sampling.

Illustration by PARS/E design

Make Your Own Sun

Create dramatic back-lighting effects with image editing software.
By Charles Platt

Taking photographs directly into the sun can create dramatic effects, but typically causes lens flare and tends to disrupt the color-balance circuitry in a digital camera (Figure A). How can we keep the highlights on the rocks and the backlighting of the cactus spines, while eliminating solar effects and restoring the blue sky? The technique described here won't salvage any pictures that you've taken already, but it will help you to avoid the problem in the future.

1. BLOCK THE REAL SUN

When you're taking the picture, hide the sun, simply by sticking your fingers into the frame (Figure B).

2. ERASE YOUR HAND

After taking the picture, open it with a photo-editing application and replace the fingers with blue sky, using the Clone tool followed by the Gaussian Blur filter (in Photoshop) or any other technique that creates a smooth result (Figure C). If you're on a budget you may find that Photoshop LE is affordable, especially on eBay.

The foreground looks unreal without any source of light, so with the next step let's make our own sun, which we can keep under control so that it doesn't ruin the picture.

3. INSERT A FAKE SUN

If you have Photoshop, use the Marquee tool to select the upper two-thirds of the sky, and use the Feather option to soften the edges of your selection. Now go to Filter ⇒ Render ⇒ Lens Flare. A little flare will help to make the picture look realistic.

4. ADJUST THE BRIGHTNESS

Make a circular selection, centered on the fake sun, and feather the edges a lot. Increase the brightness of this area. You can make repeated selections of different sizes and adjust their brightness until everything looks right (Figure D).

Some will say this is cheating, but old-school photographers used all kinds of fakery with an enlarger in a darkroom. The difference is that digital processing is quicker, cheaper, easier, and a lot more fun.

Photography by Charles Platt

The Incredible Shrinking DVD

Back up multiple movies on a single disc.
By Richard Kadrey

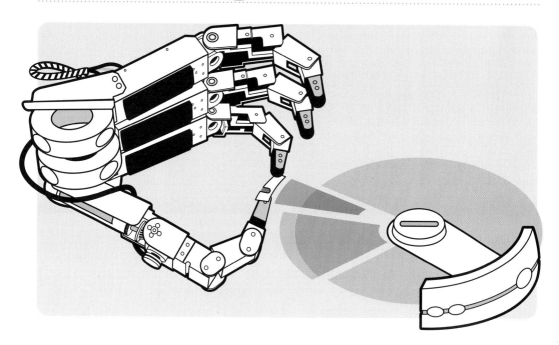

I own a lot of DVDs, and like all expensive pieces of software, I like to back them up. Even though copyright law allows you to create a backup for personal use, movie companies don't want you to do this, which forces you to sneak in through the back door. Here are a few ways to get started, if you own a Mac.

To do anything with your DVD, you have to get the data onto your hard drive. Since most DVDs are copy-protected, you'll need software that can read all of the disk's content. MacTheRipper is incredibly good at doing just that. Not only can it copy most disks, but it can also remove such pesky roadblocks as region codes and Macrovision, old-school copy-protection code.

In the rare case when a disk's copy protection is too complex, try FairMount. This clever piece of software tricks your computer into seeing a DVD as an external drive and allows you to copy the contents of that "drive" to your machine. FairMount is slow, so you'll want to try MacTheRipper first.

Now that your DVD is on your hard drive, there are several things you can do with it. The first and simplest is to copy the data back onto a recordable DVD. You can also convert the movie portion of your disk into an iPod format or an *.avi* file, playable on almost any computer. Converting formats is a nice option since it can take an 8GB DVD and reduce the movie portion (but not the extras) to around 700MB and still leave it perfectly watchable. If you're traveling and don't want to carry a pile of discs, at 700MB, you can burn several movies onto a single data-formatted DVD.

VisualHub is a great tool for converting the movie portion of your DVD into iPod or .avi format. Just drag the *Video_TS* folder from the DVD on your hard drive to the VisualHub menu, choose the file type and image quality you want, and press Start. The reformatted file will appear in the DVD's main folder. You can now drag the converted file into iTunes to load on your iPod, or use Roxio Toast or the Mac's Burn folder to burn several movies onto a single DVD.

Unfortunately, if you use VisualHub to convert a subtitled film to another format, it won't automatically add the subtitles to the converted file. The simplest way to add subtitles is to use ffmpegX. You simply drag the .avi file onto the ffmpegX menu. Then click the Filters button followed by Load Subs, and browse for the .srt (SubRip) subtitle file from your hard drive.

Where does the .srt file come from? There are a number of sites on the web that specialize in nothing but burnable subtitles. Simply download the file you need, load it into ffmpegX, and it will burn the subs to your movie.

NOTE: To run ffmpegX you need 3 UNIX applets. They are mpeg2enc, mencoder, and mplayer. All are free and easily downloadable from sites like **versiontracker.com**.

These aren't the only tools or methods to back up and convert DVDs on a Mac, but they work well and are the simplest ways to get started. Once you get comfortable working with these tools, you should try others. Movie studios are getting more clever about stopping you from backing up your discs. To protect yourself and remind them that it's not nice to treat their customers as criminals, you should check out new backup tools as they become available online.

➕ RESOURCES

MacTheRipper: mactheripper.org
FairMount: metakine.com/products/fairmount
VisualHub: techspansion.com/visualhub
Roxio Popcorn and Toast: roxio.com
ffmpegX: homepage.mac.com/major4
mencoder and mplayer in a single .zip file: makezine.com/go/m2zip
mpeg2enc: mjpeg.sourceforge.net
Downloadable subtitle files: opensubtitles.org

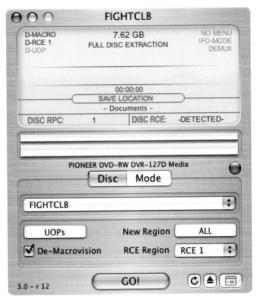

Bagels are good, pirating is wrong. Think twice before you copy a DVD...

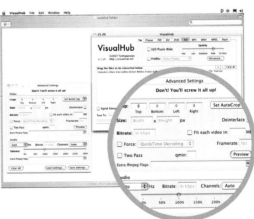

FORMAT IT YOUR WAY:
VisualHub lets you convert video files — including DVDs you've ripped to your hard drive — into several different formats for viewing on a television, computer, iPod or iPhone, PSP, and Tivo. Although VisualHub uses a simple drag-and-drop interface, its Advanced Settings menu lets you customize file size, bitrate, aspect ratio, and audio settings. You can also add tags and then preview your creation in a new screen.

Music Control System

Set up a cheap wireless server for your song collection. By Andy Seubert

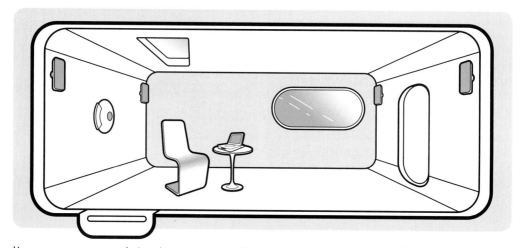

It was easy enough to rip my music CDs onto my hard drive. The problem was how to access all those songs conveniently from wherever I happened to be in my house. The answer is to use an old computer as my music server, configure it as a web server, and access it via a wi-fi connection from my laptop.

THE HARDWARE

To make things simple, I'll assume you can scrounge a bare-bones PC that you'll use only as your music server. You don't need much computing power to play music and serve a web page; I used a very old Packard Bell. It must run Windows XP with all the updates, and must have an Ethernet jack.

I'll also assume you have a wireless-enabled laptop, and a wireless router with at least one empty port. Plug your server into that port using a standard Ethernet cable. Now plug the output from the sound card on your server to any unused input on your regular stereo receiver, probably using an audio cable with RCA jacks on one end and a mini-jack plug on the other. RadioShack sells these cables.

Copy your music collection onto the hard drive of your server, and we're ready for the setup.

1. CHECK YOUR SYSTEM

To let your laptop find the server, the server needs a static IP address. We have to pick one that won't cause a conflict with other devices sharing the router.

On your server, click Start ⇒ Settings ⇒ Control Panel, double-click Network Connections, double-click Local Area Connection, click the Support tab, and then the Details button. Write down the numbers for your IP Address, Subnet Mask, Default Gateway, and DNS Server. (Don't worry if you don't know what all these numbers mean.)

2. SET UP AN IP ADDRESS

Close the top 2 windows to get back to the Network Connections window. Right-click Local

Illustration by PARS/E design

Area Connection and select Properties. Highlight Internet Protocol (TCP/IP) and click the Properties button. Click the radio button beside "Use the following IP address." Now, for your IP address, very carefully type the first 3 numbers from the original IP address you found in Step 1 (often, they will be 192.168.0) but enter a fourth number that is *different* from the fourth number of your original IP address.

You've created a new IP address for your server. Make a note of it!

Now enter the Subnet Mask, Default Gateway, and Preferred DNS Server, using exactly the same values that you found for these items in Step 1, *without* making any changes. Click OK twice to close the windows.

3. SILENCE XP

Since you're going to connect your stereo to your server, you won't want to hear every bonk and chime that Windows plays when it wants you to know something. Open Control Panel and double-click Sounds and Audio Devices. Click the Sounds tab, pull down the menu under the Sound Scheme heading, and choose No Sounds. This refers only to the sounds generated by the operating system. Sounds that come from your music player are controlled separately. Click OK to close the window.

4. INSTALL WINAMP

We'll use Winamp software to play the music because it's a very nice, full-featured media player with a free plugin named AjaxAMP, which will let us control the music remotely through a web page. Download and install the software from winamp.com and ajaxamp.com.

During installation, Winamp wants to install some "extras." We don't need these, so unselect the Winamp toolbar, free extras, and free music.

After installing Winamp, run it. It will prompt you to add music the first time you run it. Click "Don't show this again" and click the Cancel button. Close Winamp.

Install AjaxAMP, then open Winamp again, pull down the Options menu, and select AjaxAMP Preferences. Change the server port to 80. Click Library, and then Add Directory, and select the topmost folder containing your music collection.

Fig. A: AjaxAMP screen with the controls and library listing easily accessible. **Fig. B:** You don't have to leave the table to change the tunes.

5. PLAY THE MUSIC

Open a browser window, and in the Address bar, type the new IP address you assigned to your server in Step 2. Bookmark it for future use. If everything went as planned, you should see the AjaxAMP web page with the controls and the play-list on the left side of the screen and your library on the right side. Choose a song, click Play, and music should start playing.

I implemented this system using Linux originally, and the Windows version can be tweaked with additional features such as auto logon. Check makezine.com/13/upload_musicsystem for details.

My family uses our music control system all the time. It actually encourages my kids to explore our whole music library instead of just their favorite CDs. We also have spoken-word recordings, so we can listen to books while we do chores or prepare meals. When friends visit, they can click their favorite songs from several albums. And, the system is great for parties. Rock on!

When not fixing servers, Andy Seubert fires up the retort in his backyard to make homemade charcoal for blacksmithing.

Songs to Go

Enhance your music for playing in the car.
By Charles Platt

Most factory-installed car stereos are mediocre, and mine is no exception. I was contemplating a major upgrade, but didn't feel like spending all that money. Instead I decided to adjust the music to compensate for the limitations of the stereo. By boosting the low end and the high end while lowering the shrill frequencies around 2kHz, I could make it sound considerably better.

Since this required more precision than was allowed by the simple bass and treble controls built into the stereo, I thought about installing a graphic equalizer — but those available for cars are limited by space constraints. My ultimate answer was to preprocess the sound at home, then burn CDs optimized for the car listening experience.

1. MAKE AUDIO FILES

I made audio files from my CDs. Countless utilities will do this, but I like Express Rip (nch.com.au/rip), a piece of Australian freeware that offers more options than Windows Media Player and claims to be faster. After you install it and launch it, choose *.wav* as your output format for this project, to avoid losing quality through compression. Click the Encoder Settings button and select 44100Hz, 16 bits

stereo, which is the same format used on music CDs. Insert a disc, click the Rip CD button, and the software works in the background while you use your computer for other things such as checking email.

2. DOWNLOAD AND INSTALL AUDIO EDITOR

To edit your files you can use Wavosaur, a powerful but free virtual-studio program from wavosaur.com. It doesn't include a graphic equalizer, because it expects you to use plugins from third-party vendors. You can install any that conform with the audio standard known as VST (Virtual Studio Technology), and there are thousands online.

In my very first search I found 32 free graphic equalizers! The one I liked best is Electri-Q by Aixcoustic, available free from aixcoustic.com. Download and run the installer, and it places an

Illustration by PARS/E design

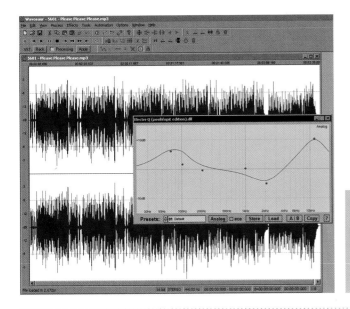

BOOST MOBILE: I use Electri-Q (yellow window) to boost low frequencies, cut the high midrange, and boost the very high frequencies, to compensate for my lousy car stereo. The bigger window shows the sounds ready to be edited in Wavosaur.

instruction manual and a *.dll* file in a folder named *C:\Program Files\Aixcoustic\Electri-Q*. Locate that folder with Windows Explorer and drag a copy of the *.dll* file to your Wavosaur folder to make it more easily accessible.

3. LAUNCH EDITOR AND EQUALIZER

Launch Wavosaur and open one of your *.wav* music files. Now activate your graphic equalizer. Choose Tools ⇒ VST ⇒ VST Rack from the menu bar, and in the VST Rack window that opens, click the Load VST button, and find the Electri-Q plugin in your Wavosaur folder. Still in the VST Rack window, click the View button to display the equalizer. You can now close the VST Rack window.

4. APPLY EQ

You're ready to apply EQ to your sound. In Wavosaur click the Play button and the little Processing check-box just under the main menu bar. You hear the music while processing it through the equalizer, which lets you boost or cut any frequencies, in a wide or narrow range. Finally, use Tools ⇒ VST ⇒ Apply VST to apply the EQ to the whole file. You can also use Tools ⇒ VST ⇒ Batch Processor to apply the same EQ to all the files in one folder — a very convenient and powerful feature.

5. BURN A CD

Burn your adjusted sound onto the CD-R that you'll play in your car stereo. I used Express Burn (nch.com.au/burn), another free program from the same source as Express Rip.

6. PLAY

Try out your new sound. You may have to go back to your computer and tweak it a couple more times, but once you have your ideal EQ settings, you can apply them to all the music in your collection to make "car listening versions."

THE AUDIO TAKE-HOME MESSAGE

The VST concept has been almost as significant for audio as the PostScript language was for graphic arts. You can put together an entire rack of audio processing modules to apply reverb, repeat echo, flanger, vocal remover, acoustic space modeling, tape hiss suppression — any effect you can imagine.

VST isn't so popular on the Mac, but Apple offers an equivalent system known as Audio Units. Whichever system you use, it will enable effects that used to entail power-hungry hardware costing thousands of dollars.

Candy Alert
By Cy Tymony

Devise sneaky uses for high-tech candy packaging and other small toys.

You will need: Gummy candy with light-up tongs, R/C car transmitter, and a noisemaker (such as one from a candy toy cellphone)

Candy makers are including innovative extras with their products that sneaky scavengers can reuse for projects. A cursory look around the candy aisle reveals spring-loaded containers, light- and sound-producing cellphone toys, battery-powered fans with amazing light shows, even tongs that light up when you squeeze them to grab gummy candy. The batteries, switches, LEDs, and motors included in just these 4 packages would cost about $10 if purchased separately. Here's how to easily modify some of these useful parts for sneaky projects, in this case an intruder alert.

1. Tape the toy tongs' switch to a door.
The light-up tongs include a watch battery, an LED, and a pressure switch that activates when you squeeze the tongs. This switch can be removed to act as a security trigger when it's positioned with tape to a door, window, cabinet, or drawer (Figure 1).

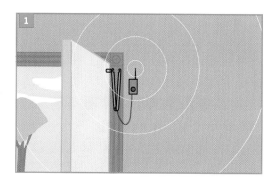

2. Wire the switch to an R/C car transmitter.
Connect the tong switch's 2 wires to an R/C car's transmitter activator button (*see MAKE, Volume 05, page 113*) so that it can alert you when doors or windows have been breached (Figure 2).

3. Wire the R/C receiver to a noisy alarm.
Now connect the R/C receiver's output contacts to a noisemaker — such as the candy toy cellphone.

You can also wire the tong switch directly to the toy cellphone (Figure 3).

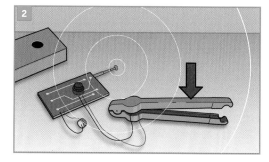

Going further:
A candy fan toy can be converted into a motorized car. A spring-loaded candy stick makes a great sneaky security device, triggering the toy cellphone alarm like a Rube Goldberg contraption.

Magazines sometimes include high-tech inserts to promote products, and these too have parts ripe for the reusing. NBC recently placed *Bionic Woman* TV show promotional inserts in major magazines. These inserts included 2 watch batteries on a printed circuit board, connecting wire, and a slide switch that lit a super-bright LED when you turned the page. If purchased separately these parts would cost nearly $10, and you can easily put them to use as alarms, educational quiz testers, and more.

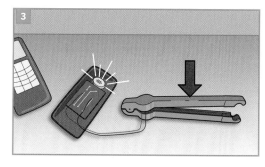

Cy Tymony is the author of the *Sneaky Uses for Everyday Things* book series. He lives in Los Angeles. sneakyuses.com

Illustrations by Tim Lillis

BUSINESS REPLY MAIL

FIRST-CLASS MAIL   PERMIT NO 865   NORTH HOLLYWOOD CA

POSTAGE WILL BE PAID BY ADDRESSEE

Make:

PO BOX 17046
NORTH HOLLYWOOD CA 91615-9588

BUSINESS REPLY MAIL

FIRST-CLASS MAIL   PERMIT NO 865   NORTH HOLLYWOOD CA

POSTAGE WILL BE PAID BY ADDRESSEE

Make:

PO BOX 17046
NORTH HOLLYWOOD CA 91615-9588

Make: Projects

Create the shock felt 'round the block with our Boom Stick air cannon and start any party with a bang! Next in sequence is a babytronic beatbox, perfect for toddlers, but challenging enough for a big kid like you to build. Feeling out of control? Kill the buzz (or ride the waves) by making a smart structure that's an active vibration-damping system.

Photograph by Garry McLeod

BOOM
STICK
By Edwin Wise

DECOMPRESSION THERAPY

The super-loud Boom Stick is a PVC air cannon that delivers maximum bang for the buck. It assaults the startle reflex of any nearby victim, adding an instant rush of physical terror to haunted houses, art pieces, pranks, and performances.

I work in haunted houses during the Halloween season, as an actor, guide, technician, makeup artist, and effects creator. Some of my effects instill fear through foreshadowing or complex storylines, but the most effective way to scare people is often just a simple, brute-force startle.

The air cannon is a great and safe device for such scares. In its simplest form, it consists of an air reservoir, a quick-exhaust valve (QEV), and sometimes a resonating chamber. Haunted house suppliers and special-effects houses sell commercial models with large-gauge QEVs, but these cost hundreds of dollars. Home projects that rely on a standard air compressor typically use smaller, cheaper water valves from washing machines or sprinklers, but for me, these designs have yielded only a disappointing "poof-hiss."

Inspired by the PVC-based designs of spud gun enthusiasts (but leaving out the potato), I've found a better approach: a two-stage, chamber-sealing, quick-exhaust, piston-valve air cannon that you can build out of common plumbing components for about $100. I call it the Boom Stick.

Set up: p.117   **Make it:** p.118   **Use it:** p.123

Edwin Wise is a software engineer with more than 25 years professional experience developing software during the day and exploring the edges of mad science at night. He can be found at simreal.com.

Photograph by Garry McLeod

BUILDING BOOM

The Boom Stick creates a pressurized volume of air and releases it very quickly, generating a loud shockwave.

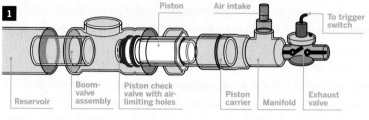

1

Piston   Air intake   To trigger switch

Reservoir   Boom-valve assembly   Piston check valve with air-limiting holes   Piston carrier   Manifold   Exhaust valve

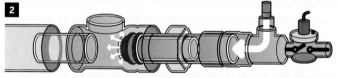

2

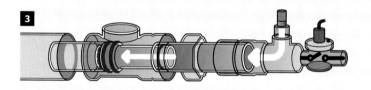

3

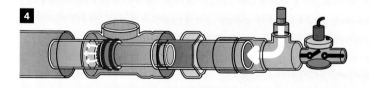

4

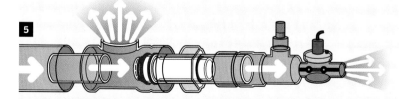

5

HOW IT WORKS

1. The piston rests in the piston carrier, and the entire system is at ambient air pressure. Small holes in the piston allow limited airflow through from behind; a rubber washer inside the piston acts as a check valve, passing air in only one direction and increasing efficiency.

2. When air flows in behind the piston faster than it leaks out of the holes, pressure builds up in the manifold.

3. Pressure behind the piston pushes it into the boom valve tube, sealing the pathway between the air supply and reservoir.

4. Pressurized air slowly fills the reservoir through the holes in the piston. The cannon is loaded once the pressures between manifold and reservoir balance.

5. To fire the cannon, a small exhaust valve opens and releases air pressure behind the piston, drawing the piston back into the manifold. As soon as the piston clears the boom valve tube, the pressurized contents of the reservoir release into the atmosphere with an impressive bang.

Illustration by Damien Scogin

SET UP.

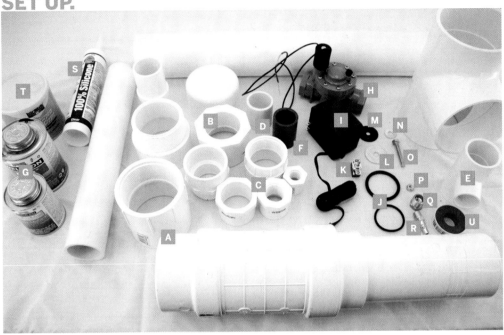

MATERIALS

[A] 3" diameter PVC parts:
» 18"–24" long pipe
» Tee fitting with female pipe thread (FPT) stem
» Repair coupling
» FPT to slip adapter
» Male pipe thread (MPT) to slip adapter
» End cap

[B] 2" diameter PVC parts:
» 15" long pipe
» FPT to slip adapter
» MPT to slip adapter
» Insert coupling
ProPlumber model #PPFC200. Only carried at Lowe's.

[C] PVC reducing bushings:
» 3" to 2" slip (2)
» 2" to 1½" slip
» 1½" slip to 1" FPT
» 1" slip to ½" FPT

[D] 1½" PVC pipe, 2" long

[E] PVC reducing tee fitting, 1½"×1"×1½"

[F] 1" repair coupling, Schedule 80 PVC **must fit inside 2" insert coupling**

[G] PVC primer and medium-thickness glue

[H] Irrigation valve, 24V solenoid with 1" MPT ends **A cheap one ($10) is fine.**

[I] 24V power supply **Look in the irrigation aisle next to the valves.**

[J] 2" O-rings, ³⁄₁₆" thick (4)
» 1¾" O-rings, ⅛" thick (4)

[K] On-off switch, SPST

[L] Fender washers, 1⅝" with ⁵⁄₁₆" hole (2)

[M] Neoprene washer, 1½" with ⁵⁄₁₆" hole

[N] ⁵⁄₁₆" washers (2)

[O] ⁵⁄₁₆" bolt, 2" long

[P] ⁵⁄₁₆" lock nut with nylon insert

[Q] Brass pipe adapter, ½" MPT to ¼" FPT

[R] Quick-release pneumatic coupling, ¼" MPT

[S] Silicone caulk

[T] Lithium grease

[U] Teflon pipe tape

TOOLS
[NOT SHOWN]

Plumber's epoxy putty (optional)

Air compressor that can produce 40–60psi **An air tool compressor is best.**

Tape measure

Hacksaw or pipe cutter

Crescent wrenches **at least 2**

Vise **capable of clamping the flange of 3" bushing**

Gloves and goggles

Sandpaper **coarse and medium grits**

Electric drill with grinding stone bit

Drill press or lathe

Popsicle stick

File (optional)

NOTE: All PVC pipe and fittings should be NSF-rated Schedule 40, unless otherwise specified. Try your local home improvement or plumbing supply store. If you can't find the exact parts indicated, you can improvise endlessly in the plumbing aisle, or else try Grainger (grainger.com) or MSC (mscdirect.com).

MAKE IT.

BUILD YOUR OWN BOOM STICK

START >>>   Time: **A Day** Complexity: **Medium**

1. MODIFY THE PVC FITTINGS

1a. Take two 3" to 2" bushings and grind out the ridge inside them with a drill using a grinding stone bit, so that the 2" pipes can slide firmly through.

1b. Sand down both sleeves of the 2" insert coupling so they slide easily into 2" pipes. You can bolt the part between 2 fender washers, chucking it into a drill press, and sanding carefully on both sides to keep it from flying off. This will be our moving piston body.

NOTE: Don't let the PVC get hot or it will melt and deform. Use light pressure and moisten it occasionally to keep it cool. Start with coarse-grit sandpaper and finish with medium-grit.

> ⚠️ **CAUTION: DANGEROUS PROJECT** At normal temperatures, standard Schedule 40 PVC has a working pressure of around 150psi, but heat, sunlight, solvents, scratches, and time make the material lose strength, and even at the 40–60psi used for this project, it will eventually fail. When it does, it will break into fragments that will be thrown with great force by the compressed air. Always operate your Boom Stick inside a solidly built plywood box or wall, so that shrapnel cannot reach anyone's tender flesh.
>
> ABS plastic does not shrapnel like PVC, but the common type used for DWV (drain/waste/vent) applications is not pressure-rated, so it may or may not hold up. Foam-core PVC or ABS is even more lightweight and MUST BE AVOIDED AT ALL COSTS.
>
> Pressure-rated ABS such as Duraplus from Ipex (www.ipexinc.com) is the perfect material for this project, but it costs 10 times as much as Schedule 40 PVC. Copper and other metal pipes are similarly expensive.

Photography by Edwin Wise

1c. Cut the pipe pieces down to size. For the reservoir, cut an 18"–24" length of 3" pipe. For the boom valve and piston carrier tubes, cut 2 lengths of 2" pipe, one 6" and the other 8". For the air fittings, cut a 2" stub of 1½" pipe.

1d. Cut the 1" Schedule 80 repair coupling into a 1¼" section and a 1" section. There may be ¼" or so of scrap left over.

1e. Cut the sanded insert coupling into 3 pieces by trimming a ⅜" ring off one end and chopping enough of a sleeve off the other end to leave a ¹¹⁄₁₆" stub.

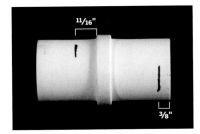

NOTE: The measurements need not be exact, but look at the photos for Steps 2c–2e on the next page to see how this piece is used.

1f. File or sand the ends of the pipes smooth. File or sand a bevel on one side of the ⅜" coupling ring and the boom valve (2"×6") pipe. These bevels will correct minor alignment errors during operation.

2. ASSEMBLE THE PISTON

2a. Drill four ⅛" or smaller holes in one fender washer, just outside the radius of the regular ⁵⁄₁₆" washers that will be mounted over them. Drill four ¼" holes in the other fender washer, also outside the radius of the smaller washers.

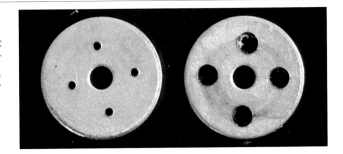

2b. Run the bolt through, in order: a small washer, the neoprene washer, the small-drilled fender washer, the 1¼" Schedule 80 PVC segment, the large-holed fender washer, another small washer, and the lock nut. Tighten the lock nut just enough to hold the assembly firm, but not so much so that the neoprene distorts.

NOTE: The neoprene washer limits airflow, which lets pressure push the piston forward into position. When the pressure balance reverses, it seals the piston as it travels back in order to put all the air into the boom.

2c. Fit two 2" O-rings onto each end of the main piece of the sanded insert coupling. Then test-assemble the entire piston. Using the other 2 pieces of the insert coupling and two 1¾" O-rings, enclose the 1" Schedule 80 PVC segment and the piston valve assembly as shown.

NOTE: Pipe fittings are tapered, which makes it harder to get the parts to fit together nicely when they're cut. Use epoxy putty or gel to reinforce the construction as needed.

2d. Use PVC glue or epoxy to glue the piston together. First, glue the ¾" Schedule 80 segment into the ⅜" ring, on the side opposite the bevel. Place a small O-ring as a spacer on the segment, and glue this subassembly into the body of the insert coupler.

2e. Glue the piston valve halfway into the assembly, with the neoprene washer facing in. Then glue the remaining insert coupler piece around the outside half, with another small O-ring spacer in between. Reinforce the connections with epoxy.

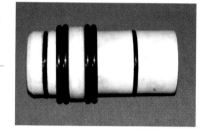

3. FIT THE O-RINGS

The large O-rings are bumpers that protect the PVC during operation. The small O-rings form the piston's seal inside the piston carrier and boom valve cylinders. The long end of the piston must mate with the 2"×8" pipe, and the short end with the 2"×6" pipe. The goal is for the piston to be able to fit into the pipe and seal via the O-rings. These can be tricky to get right. With the PVC parts I bought, the perfect-sized small O-ring would be 5/32" thick. But I only found them available in ⅛" and 3/16", so I used the ⅛" size and pushed them out with a layer of silicone caulk underneath.

3a. Glue flowed onto the small O-rings in previous steps. This isn't good for them, so once the glue dries, cut or pry them off and discard. Replace with the remaining 2 small O-rings.

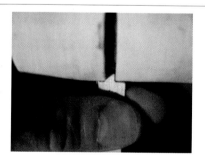

3b. Glue the large O-ring bumper pairs together with silicone caulk. This keeps them from jumping off. (You can also try one thicker O-ring on each side.)

3c. Out of a popsicle stick, make a small tool that fits a groove ⅛" deep and ⅛" wide. Fill the piston grooves with silicone caulk, and use the tool to remove all but the thin layer that it can't reach. This will help the small O-rings make a seal.

NOTE: You may need to do this several times before the O-ring seals and the piston slides. Even with everything fitting and well greased, the difference between success and jamming or leaking is subtle.

4. ASSEMBLE THE BOOM VALVE AND PISTON CARRIER

4a. For the boom valve assembly, use PVC glue to weld one of the slide-through-modified 3" to 2" bushings into one end of the 3" tee fitting, and the 3" female adapter into the opposite end. Weld the unmodified 3" to 2" bushing into the 3" repair coupling. Wait for the glue to dry, and then dry-fit each end of the 2"×6" pipe into the 2 bushings, with the beveled end in the tee assembly.

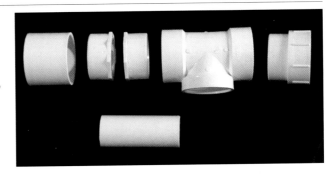

4b. For the piston carrier, PVC-weld the other modified bushing into the 3" male adapter. Let the glue dry, and then test-fit the 8" piston carrier pipe into the bushing.

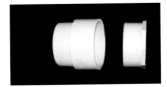 

4c. Slide the long end of the piston into the carrier pipe and screw the piston carrier male adapter into the boom valve assembly female adapter.

4d. Adjust the 2 pipes in their bushings until the piston (without its O-rings) travels freely between carrier pipe and boom valve assembly. The small O-rings should tuck inside both tubes when the piston is extended, and you can see a gap between the piston and the valve pipe when the piston is retracted. Proper alignment is key. Mark the position of the 2 tubes, remove them (and the piston) from the bushings, and then weld the tubes back into place at the marks.

4e. Mark the positions of everything. Then remove the piston, unscrew the 2 assemblies, and glue in the tubes. Apply primer and glue only to the 2" pipes inside the marks and not the bushings, or else you'll foul the ends of the pipes.

4f. Weld the unmodified bushing and repair coupling assembly to the other end of the valve pipe, and the 2" male adapter to the free end of the carrier pipe. Alignment isn't so important with these.

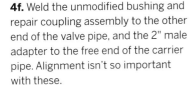  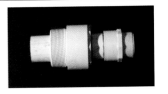

5. ASSEMBLE THE RESERVOIR AND MANIFOLD

Unlike the valve/piston system, the reservoir and manifold are low-precision designs that will tolerate variation.

5a. For the reservoir, weld the 3" end cap onto one end of the 3"×18"–24" pipe, and weld the other end into the repair coupling on the boom valve assembly.

5b. For the manifold, weld the short piece of 1½" pipe into one side of the 1½" tee fitting and weld its other end into the 2" to 1½" reducing bushing. Weld the 2" female adapter to the bushing.

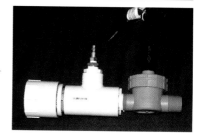

5c. Screw the inlet port of the 1" irrigation valve into the 1½" slip to 1" female threaded bushing, using Teflon tape to seal the threads. The flow arrows should point away from the bushing. Tighten firmly. This is the exhaust valve.

5d. Weld the exhaust valve subassembly into the other side of the manifold tee fitting, orienting the wiring connections as desired. For the trigger, connect the on-off switch to either of the 2 wires.

5e. Weld the 1" slip to ½" female threaded bushing to the center port of the tee fitting. Wrap Teflon tape around the brass adapter and thread it into the bushing, and then Teflon-tape the quick-release coupling into the adapter. This is the air intake.

6. FINAL ASSEMBLY

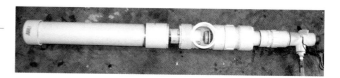

6a. Allow 24 hours for all of the PVC solvents and glues to cure. Remember, patience is a virtue.

6b. Lather up the piston and all the O-rings with lithium grease. Insert the piston into the piston carrier with its valve aiming toward the reservoir.

6c. Screw the piston carrier back into the boom valve assembly. This connection does not need to be airtight, but the carrier pipe and valve pipe must be aligned.

6d. Wrap several layers of Teflon tape around the 2" male adapter on the piston carrier, and screw it into the air manifold. You're done!

FINISH

NOW GO USE IT »

GO BOOM

BOOM STICK OPERATION

1. Attach an unpressurized air hose to the quick-release fitting on the air intake.
2. Attach the 24V power supply to the exhaust valve and trigger switch.
3. Test the exhaust valve to make sure it works.
4. Put the entire system in a sturdy box or solid wall, or at least behind a blast shield.
5. Pressurize the manifold to about 40psi. The piston should snap into the valve tube and the reservoir should fill with a hiss. If the piston doesn't fit into the valve tube, the small O-rings may be pushed out too far. If the air leaks around the O-rings, they are not out far enough. If the tubes are misaligned, you may have to rebuild the piston carrier.
6. Activate the trigger switch for about half a second. The pipe behind the piston will lose pressure and the piston will slam back into the carrier pipe, exhausting the reservoir.
7. Jump for joy at the loud bang!
8. Repeat.

FIXES

The hard part in this design is getting the O-rings to seal firmly without jamming the piston's motion. If you just can't get them to seal, never fear; add a second irrigation valve to the air inlet, and only let air in just before you want to set off the device. The effect won't be as clean, but you'll lose less air during operation.

The piston carrier is modular for a reason: you can remove it easily and experiment with different piston designs (of which there are many), and you can replace the piston if it breaks. Also, if you glue the piston carrier into place with bad alignment to the valve tube, you only have to throw away a few inexpensive pieces to try again.

To keep stuff from falling into the Boom Stick, cover all openings in its box with hardware cloth.

RESONATING CHAMBERS AND CONFETTI

Once you get the basic Boom Stick working, create a resonating chamber by gluing a 3" male adapter onto some 3" pipe, and screwing it into the cleanout port on the boom valve's tee fitting. Try constricting the exhaust, putting a 3"×2" or even smaller bushing into the base of this chamber. Try long ones and short ones. Stuff confetti into the chamber and make a mess of your workshop. But never, ever launch anything directly at anyone!

ACTION VIDEO

See Wise's Boom Stick in action at makezine.com/go/boomstick. But note that the boom sound is mostly lost. Microphones can only do so much.

RESOURCES

Huge list of haunter how-tos:
halloweenmonsterlist.info

O-Ring Handbook:
dichtomatik.us/products/o-ring-handbook

Generally useful site with size and pressure specs for PVC: engineeringtoolbox.com

OSHA warning memo on pressurized PVC:
makezine.com/go/oshapvc

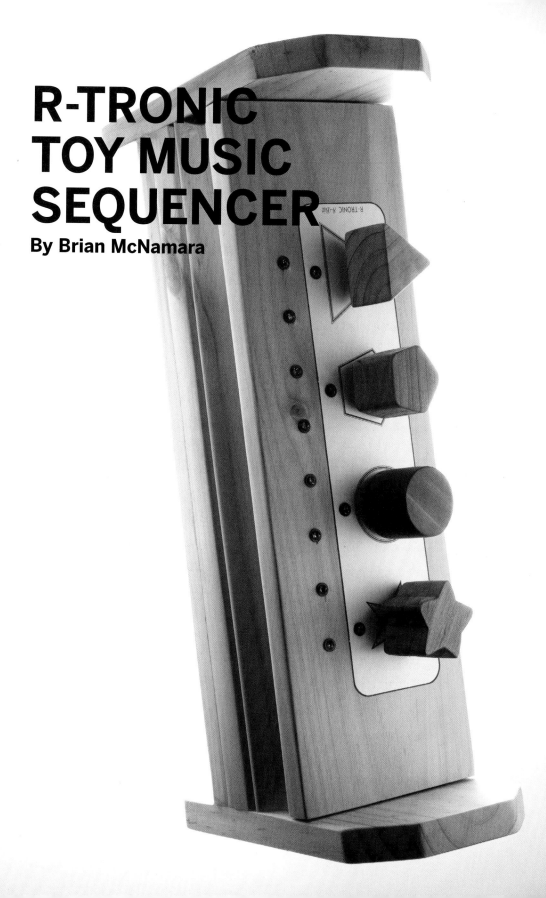

R-TRONIC
TOY MUSIC
SEQUENCER
By Brian McNamara

BABY BEATS

This simple sequencer lets babies play with shapes, sounds, and lights, while it also teaches older kids the basics of electronic music — and secretly you'll have lots of fun with it yourself.

I wanted to make a unique present to give my daughter for her first birthday, a musical toy that she could sit down and play with immediately but that would also become more educational for her in a few years. So I built her the R-Tronic 8-Bit, a simple music sequencer that lets you build up, play back, and edit musical patterns. It uses wooden shapes as buttons and LEDs instead of fancy displays.

I started on the project 3 months before my daughter's birthday, programming a Picaxe microcontroller with a speaker on a breadboard, using just enough software to make the sequencer's 4 noises. Then I added 4 switch inputs to trigger the sounds, followed by 12 LED blinkies. I ported the tangled breadboard circuit to a neat printed circuit board, and finally built the wooden frame and fit the electronics. The final wiring was completed the night before my daughter's birthday party.

If I had any worries that she wouldn't like the R-Tronic, I needn't have. As soon as she saw it, she knew just what to do.

Set up: p.127   Make it: p.128   Use it: p.133

Brian McNamara (grandtippler@hotmail.com) lives in a small town near Canberra, Australia. By day he works at a university designing and repairing biological research equipment; by night he designs, hacks, and bends kids' toys and musical instruments.

ANATOMY OF A SEQUENCER

The R-Tronic loops sounds in sequences that are 8 beats long. LEDs along the top flash in series to show which beat it's on.

Push one of the shape pegs, and it adds its corresponding sound into the repeating sequence, at the current beat, overwriting other sounds (or erasing it like a toggle if the same sound is already there).

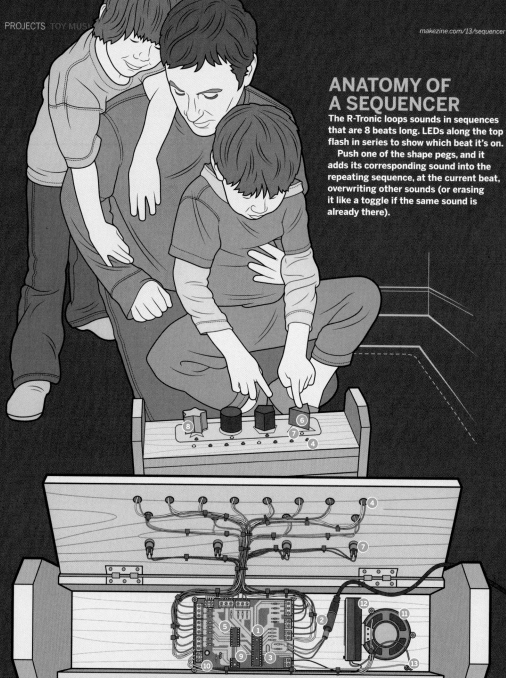

(1) Picaxe-28X microcontroller programmed in BASIC to read input from shape pegs and generate output to LEDs and speaker.

(2) Audio jack provides microcontroller programming port.

(3) Crystal generates oscillations used by microcontroller for sounds and timing.

(4) Sequence LEDs show your place in the 8-beat sequence.

(5) A 3-to-8 decoder lets 3 microcontroller pins run all 8 of the sequence LEDs.

(6) Wooden shape pegs push switches to trigger 4 sounds.

(7) Shape peg LEDs indicate the shape peg associated with the current sound.

(8) The microcontroller has only 3 input pins available for the 4 pegs, so the star (4th) input combines the triangle and pentagon inputs. (The chip's 4th input pin is needed as a general interrupt.)

(9) 8-pin operational amplifier (op-amp) boosts sound output from the microcontroller to drive the speaker.

(10) Multi-turn potentiometer adjusts the audio volume.

(11) Speaker plays sounds.

(12) Three AA batteries in a holder power everything.

(13) On/off switch

Illustration by Timmy Kucynda

SET UP.

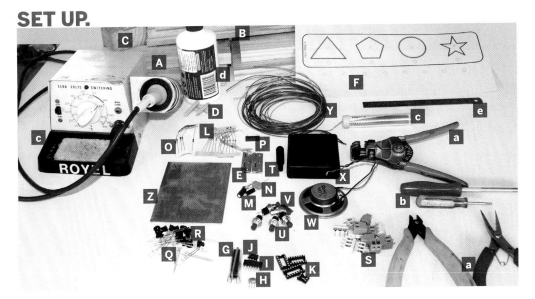

MATERIALS

[A] Lumber, 5"×¾"×48" or similar size **I used pine.**

[B] Wood molding, 2½"×½"×32" long

[C] Wood block, 1⅜" thick **to cut 4 different-shaped blocks. Or substitute pre-shaped blocks.**

[D] Wood dowel, ¼"×4" long **to make four 1" pegs**

[E] Hinges (2) **with screws**

[F] Silver foil label paper, 8¼"×10¾" **$8 from** desktopsupplies.com, **#68000-10**

ELECTRONICS

[G] Picaxe-28x microcontroller **$9 from** world-educational-services.com

[H] Crystal 4MHz resonator **comes with microcontroller**

[I] 74HC138 3-to-8 line decoder **from** mouser.com, **part #512-MM74HC138N**

[J] LM386 power amp **RadioShack #276-1731**

[K] IC holders: 16-pin, 8-pin, 14-pin (2), and 3-pin strip (optional)

[L] ¼W resistors: 10Ω, 330Ω (12), 4.7KΩ (2), 10KΩ (5), and 22KΩ (2)

[M] 0.1µF capacitors (2)

[N] 250µF electrolytic capacitor

[O] 1N4001 diodes (5) **RadioShack #276-1101**

[P] Potentiometer, 10KΩ multi-turn

[Q] Colored LEDs: white, amber, red (4 each)

[R] LED holders (12) **RadioShack #276-079**

[S] Terminal block connectors: 2-pin (5), 3-pin (6)

[T] Stereo jack, 3.5mm

[U] Momentary button switches (4) **RadioShack #275-1571**

[V] SPST switch **for on/off switch**

[W] Small speaker **Mine came from an old computer.**

[X] 3×AA battery holder and clip, with 3 AA batteries

[Y] Stranded wire, 22-gauge **Multiple colors make it easier.**

[Z] R-Tronic printed circuit board **Use the Gerber files at** makezine.com/13/sequencer **to make one, or send it to a fabrication shop. If someone coordinates a shared bulk order in the discussion area, they'd be much cheaper. You can also email me, and if I have extras I can sell you one for about $18.**

[NOT SHOWN]

Self-tapping mounting screws (7) **for PCB, speaker, and battery**

Screw **for securing lid**

Cable ties

Beeswax

Food dyes **or other nontoxic paints or stains**

Heat-shrink tubing, ⅛" and 1/16"

TOOLS

[a] Wire cutters, strippers, and pliers

[b] Screwdrivers

[c] Soldering iron, solder

[d] White glue

[e] Ruler

[NOT SHOWN]

Saw, hobby knife

Chisel with mallet or hammer

Drill with 1/16", 7/32", ¼", and 5/16" bits

C-clamps

Pencil, marker, paper, tape

Small brush and bowls

Picaxe serial programming cable **$7 from** sparkfun.com, **#PGM-08313**

PC with serial port

Photography by Brian McNamara

MAKE IT.

BUILD YOUR BABYTRONIC SEQUENCER

START ⟫⟫ Time: **3–4 Weekends** Complexity: **Moderate to Difficult**

1. MAKE THE WOOD FRAME AND PEGS

I used a 5"×¾"×48" plank and some 2½" molding, but your box can differ, as long as the electronics fit.

1a. From the plank, mark and saw two 8" lengths (for the ends) and two 16" lengths (top and bottom). From the molding, mark and saw two 16" lengths, for the front and back. Trim the 2 top corners of each end piece: mark 1" in and 1" down from each corner, rule a line between them, and cut to shape.

TIP: The molding's cut-away profile allows you to open the top of the finished box easily. Instead of molding, you could use a router to make your own pattern on the front piece.

1b. Mark a line 2½" up from the bottom of each end piece. Align the bottom edges of the front and back pieces with the ruled lines, and the outside surfaces of the front and back with the ends' edges. Glue and clamp the 4 pieces together. Allow glue to dry before removing clamps.

1c. Glue and clamp the bottom piece onto your frame, flush with the front and back pieces. Let dry before removing clamps.

TIP: Wipe off excess glue with a damp cloth; it's much easier wiping it off now than sanding it off later.

1d. On the top of the back piece, mark 2" in from each end then mark the width of your hinges farther in. Saw and chisel between the marks to make notches for the 2 hinges.

1e. Hold the hinges in place to mark the screw holes on the back piece. Drill 1⁄16" pilot holes and screw the hinges on. Hold the top piece (lid) against the frame, then mark and drill pilot holes and attach the hinges.

1f. Make sure the lid moves up and down freely, then remove it with the hinges attached. Sand all edges of the lid and frame, removing any excess glue, then seal or paint the wood with something nontoxic (I rubbed it with beeswax). Reattach the lid, and your frame is finished.

1g. Mark and cut 4 shapes out of wood. I made a triangle, pentagon, circle, and star from a block 1⅜" thick.

NOTE: I cut my own shapes, but you can also use pre-shaped wooden blocks.

1h. Paint and seal shapes with nontoxic products. I used food dye to stain, then beeswax to seal.

1i. Drill $7/32$" holes in the center of each shape, about halfway through, then glue a 1" piece of ¼" dowel into each. Allow the glue to dry.

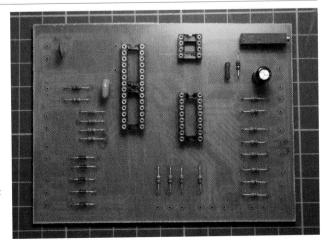

2. POPULATE THE CIRCUIT BOARD

2a. Fit and solder the resistors and diodes to the board. Be sure to fit the diodes in the correct direction.

2b. Solder on IC sockets for the 28-pin microprocessor (I used two 14-pin holders end-to-end), for the 16-pin 3-to-8 decoder, and for the 8-pin audio op-amp. Add the capacitors, potentiometer, and crystal (in an optional 3-pin socket strip).

NOTE: I designed and used a custom circuit board. You can also use plain breadboard and follow the schematic, but the wiring will be dense. Either way, refer to the diagrams at makezine.com/13/sequencer.

2c. Attach the terminal block connectors around the perimeter of the board and plug the microprocessor, op-amp, and decoder chips into the IC sockets.

Solder the 3 wires for the programming port onto the 3.5mm audio socket. Now solder the wires to J1 on the PCB. The tip of the socket is soldered to the lower pin on the PCB, and the ring (middle) of the socket is soldered to the middle pin on the PCB. The sleeve (inner contact) on the socket is soldered to the top pin on the PCB. Screw the backshell onto the 3.5mm audio connector.

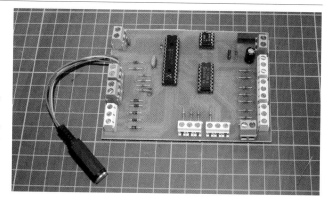

3. DRILL THE FRAME

3a. Print the lid template from makezine. com/13/sequencer. Unscrew the lid. Trim the template, center it on the lid panel, and tape it in place. Then drill ¼" holes through the panel for each of the 4 shape pegs and the 12 LEDs, as marked on the template.

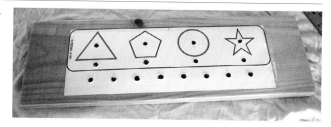

3b. Using a ⁵⁄₁₆" bit, drill back up from the underside of the panel most of the way through the 12 LED holes, leaving a thin fillet of wood. This lets the LED holders latch correctly.

3c. For the speaker, drill four ¼" holes through the bottom of the frame on the right-hand side. Drill another ¼" hole in the bottom-right corner for the on/off switch.

3d. Drill a ⅛" hole in the right end piece, in line with the lid. This is where we'll add a screw later for securing the lid closed.

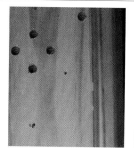

3e. Print the template from Step 3a again, this time on silver foil label paper, using a laser printer. Use a hobby knife to cut out the outline and the holes for the 4 shape pegs and their 4 LEDs. Peel off the sticker backing and affix the label to the panel.

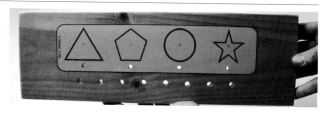

4. POPULATE THE TOP PANEL

4a. Solder 14" lengths of 22-gauge wire onto the legs of each of the 4 button switches, then insulate the connections with heat-shrink tubing.

4b. Trim the legs of all 12 LEDS to about ¼", then solder 14" lengths of wire onto each, insulating with heat-shrink. Use different colors for the anodes and cathodes so they're easy to identify later. The anodes (+) customarily have longer legs.

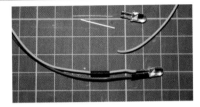

TIP: Heat-shrink tubing strengthens the mechanical connection as well as guarding against short circuits.

4c. From the top side of the lid, fit the 12 LED holders into the LED holes. From the underside of the panel, clip the LEDs into the holders. You may need to use a small screwdriver to snap them into place. I mixed white, amber, and red LEDs to look nice, following no particular pattern.

4d. Continuing on the panel underside, screw the momentary switches into the ¼" holes behind the shape template. Use a black marker to mark each switch's wires so you can tell which is which when you connect them later.

4e. Arrange cable ties around the wires to form a neat loom. This will feed down into the bottom of the box, where the circuit board sits.

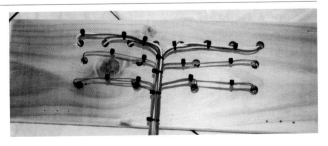

5. FIT THE ELECTRONICS AND FINISH THE WIRING

5a. Center the PCB in the bottom of the box. Mark and drill mounting holes for it in the bottom panel, but don't mount it yet. You can also drill the board itself, but I positioned the holes so that 4 screws would hold it at the edges. Position the battery holder clip and speaker next to the PCB, then mark and drill mounting holes for those.

5b. Solder the red wire from the battery holder onto one side of the on/off switch. Solder a free wire onto the other side of the switch. Glue the switch into its hole, and clip in the battery holder.

5c. Connect wires from the speaker, battery holder, and on/off switch to the screw terminals on the PCB (refer to TB1 and TB7 on the wiring diagram).

5d. Screw the lid back onto its hinges. Follow the wiring diagram and split the loom into 3 parts, routing connections to each terminal row. Work your way around the board, trimming, stripping, and terminating all the wires. Use additional cable ties to keep things neat. Note that for the LEDs' positive connections and the peg switches, 2 wires go into each screw terminal.

5e. Have a good look at your wiring to confirm that everything is in place, then mount the circuit board with the screws and load 3 AA batteries into the holder.

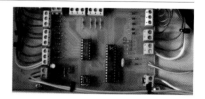

6. PROGRAM THE MICROCONTROLLER AND TEST

Finish the project by programming the microcontroller and testing the sequencer, following the instructions at makezine.com/13/sequencer.

FINISH ☒

USE IT.

PLAY, BABY, PLAY

The 8 sequence LEDs represent 8 time slots that can hold sounds. When one of the LEDs is lit, if a sound is triggered using one of the shapes, it will be repeated each time that LED lights up.

Each of the 4 shapes represents a different sound. When you press a shape, the sequencer will remember what slot number (1–8) you were up to and which sound was triggered, and it will play that shape's sound each time that slot is cycled through. This lets you build up a sequence of sounds one at a time, up to a maximum of 8 in the sequence.

You can change the sequenced sounds by pressing a different shape during any time slot, overwriting the previous choice. Individual sounds can be cleared from the sequence by pressing the same shape during that slot, a bit like a toggle switch. Or you can clear the entire sequence from memory and start from scratch by turning the R-Tronic off and on again.

SUGGESTED MODIFICATIONS

This project is just asking to be hacked. The programming for the Picaxe microcontroller is in BASIC, so you can easily edit the file *R-Tronic 8-Bit.bas* to change the sound effects for each shape. You could also associate additional sounds for when more than one shape is pressed at the same place in the sequence. And the wooden case simply holds the electronics, so you can be as creative with it as you want.

The shape pegs on my R-Tronic are interchangeable and fit into each other's slots. The sticker is just a guide, and it's actually the position rather than the shape that determines the sound. For kids older than 1 or 2, it would be great to make a version of the R-Tronic that only triggers a sound when the shape matches the sticker underneath. Keyed peg holes with matching peg shapes are an obvious way to do this.

Photograph by Sam Murphy

RESOURCES

▪◀ Watch a short video of the R-Tronic in action at makezine.com/go/rtronic.

SMART STRUCTURE

By Steven Griffin

STOP-MOTION AUTOMATION

Build an active vibration-damping system that uses piezoelectric sensors and actuators to absorb any shocks to an aluminum beam. Then turn a knob and watch the beam vibrate out of control.

Smart structures range from K2's vibration-damping Four skis to the adaptive mirrors in Mauna Kea's Keck telescopes that counter atmospheric aberrations. Someday they might also enable buildings and bridges to counter stresses from traffic, weather, and earthquakes. Here's an introduction to this fascinating technology, a desktop "skyscraper" that uses integrated sensors, actuators, and electronics to cancel out vibrations.

Our skyscraper is a flat aluminum beam, and for the sensors and actuators we'll use piezoceramic wafers, which convert physical bending into voltage and vice versa. Piezoceramics are used in stereo speakers, microphones, accelerometers, and many other devices.

A simple feedback circuit closes the loop between our sensors, which detect the beam's motion, and the actuators, which give it little calibrated pushes. Strike the beam like a tuning fork, switch the circuit on, and the system counteracts the vibrations and stops the motion instantly. You can subtract damping as well as add it: throw the phase switch the other way, give the beam a tiny tap, and watch the vibrations grow to a maximum.

Set up: p.137 Make it: p.138 Use it: p.141

Dr. Steven Griffin, an aerospace engineer living in Albuquerque, N.M., enjoys finding simple solutions to multidisciplinary problems. He has explored the use of smart structures in applications from musical instruments to space vehicles, and is always on the lookout for new opportunities.

Photography by Steven Griffin

NEGOTIATING A STANDSTILL

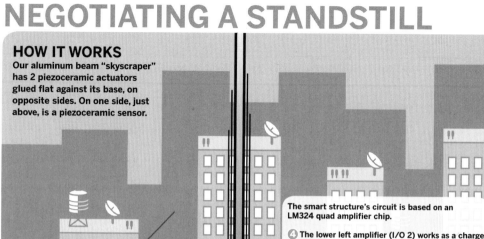

HOW IT WORKS

Our aluminum beam "skyscraper" has 2 piezoceramic actuators glued flat against its base, on opposite sides. On one side, just above, is a piezoceramic sensor.

The smart structure's circuit is based on an LM324 quad amplifier chip.

④ The lower left amplifier (I/O 2) works as a charge amplifier, a circuit routinely used to buffer charge from a piezo onto a capacitor to be measured.

⑤ The upper left (I/O 1) is a low-pass filter that boosts the input's low-frequency vibrations (~24Hz), which match the beam's first resonance. It also converts displacement into velocity by shifting back the phase, as explained below.

⑥ The chip's right side (I/O 3 and 4) forms a bridge amp that powers the tandem actuators 180° out of phase, over a range of ±36V.

① The sensor is smaller and only needs to be on one side because it detects flexing in both directions.

② The actuators are on both sides because they have more work to do. They flex out of phase, with one side shrinking as the other expands. This action applies a moment to the beam that induces bending.

③ The phase switch swaps the signals to the actuators to make them move in the exact opposite direction.

Our beam exhibits *sinusoidal vibration*, which occurs whenever something is pulled back to its resting position with a force that's proportional to its displacement. The sensors measure displacement, but to damp vibrations you need to counter velocity, which is the first derivative of displacement. So our circuit does some calculus, but with sinusoidal vibration this is easy: just shift the phase back 90°.

➕ For complete schematic and wiring diagrams, plus videos of the smart structure in action, see makezine.com/13/structure.

Illustration by Nik Schulz

SET UP.

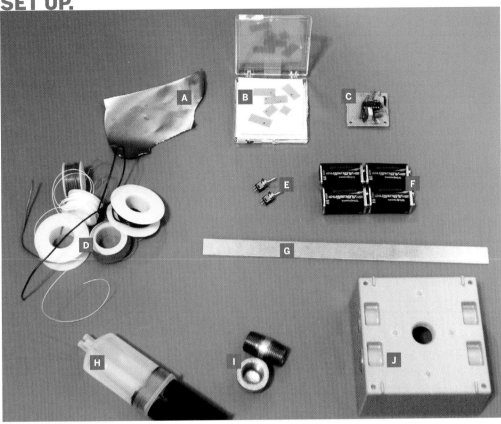

MATERIALS

[A] Copper foil **less than 1" square and ~0.001" thick. I got a roll from** online metals.com**. You can also use copper tape if you can remove all the adhesive.**

[B] Piezoceramic wafer material **at least 2.5"×0.4"×0.0105" thick. I used a 2.85" square plate of type 5A4E lead zirconate titanate (PZT) from** piezo.com. **Some piezoceramic vendors will custom-cut pieces to your dimensions, but I cut my own with a razor knife. For extreme precision you could use a diamond saw, if available.**

[C] Breadboard, 2×2

[D] Wire **Use stranded 22-gauge in multiple colors for circuit board, and solid 30-gauge for connections.**

[E] Sub-mini toggle switches, SPST (1) and DPDT (1)

[F] 9V batteries and snap connectors (4)

[G] Aluminum beam, 11.8"×0.6"× ~0.065"

[H] 5-minute epoxy

[I] 1½" male threaded ½" galvanized pipe **with matching cap from a hardware store**

[J] 5-hole outlet box with ½" inlet **from a home or hardware store**

[NOT SHOWN]

Epoxy putty

Small adhesive plastic feet (3)

[ON BREADBOARD]

M324 operational amplifier chip

Resistors: 100Ω (2), 1kΩ (2), 10kΩ (3), 10MΩ (1)

Capacitors: 4.7µF (2), 22µF (1), 680µF (1)

Trimpot (variable resistor), 1MΩ multi-turn

16-pin IC socket

TOOLS

[NOT SHOWN]

Soldering equipment, flux, desoldering braid

Snap-off knife or hobby knife with extra blades

Small pane of glass or other good cutting surface

Pencil and marker

Ruler and straightedge

Fine sandpaper

Rubber gloves

Multimeter

Hammer and center punch

Drill and drill bits

MAKE IT.

BUILD YOUR SMART STRUCTURE

START ⋙   Time: **2 Days** Complexity: **Moderate**

1. MAKE THE SENSOR AND ACTUATORS

1a. On the poled side of the piezoceramic wafer (usually designated with a small red dot), use a pencil and straightedge to mark cut lines for two 1"×0.4" pieces and one 0.5"×0.4" piece. Use a marker to put pole-side dots on each piece.

1b. Score the ceramic using a razor knife and a straightedge. Make sure that all surfaces are clean and that you apply enough pressure to the straightedge to keep the wafer material in place as you cut.

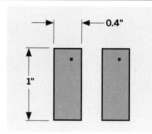

1c. Continue scoring repeatedly over the same lines, gradually increasing pressure each time. The ceramic should break along the score line after 5–25 swipes. Patience is important! It is possible to break piezoceramics along a score line after 1 firm swipe, as in glass cutting, but it takes practice.

1d. Cut three 0.2"×0.1" pieces of copper foil. Tin the pieces with solder on 1 side by heating them with the iron and letting solder melt against them.

1e. Practice soldering on a test piece of piezo. Our wafer has nickel plating that serves as a solder-anywhere electrode, but it's tricky, so most vendors include instructions. I set my iron to ~680°F and apply it to a spot of liquid flux on the wafer for about ½ second before applying the solder. A good foil-to-electrode joint is flat and uniform, which lets you connect to the side of the sensor lying against the beam without creating a stress concentration like a wire would.

1f. On the poled (dotted) side of 1 actuator and the unpoled sides of the other 2 pieces, make solder pads near any edge, for the foil. Make the pads very thin by wicking away solder with a desoldering braid. Then place the tinned side of the foil strips against each pad and apply the iron to the other side for about 1 second to complete the joint. Put a solder dot on the opposite side of each piezoceramic piece as shown here; no need to wick away the excess.

2. ATTACH THE SENSORS AND ACTUATORS TO THE BEAM

2a. Clean the beam and abrade it lightly with fine sandpaper.

2b. Epoxy the actuators, foil side down, to opposite sides of the beam 2.3" from the base end. Mix 5-minute epoxy separately for each, and spread it in a thin layer. Wear rubber gloves, and apply moderate pressure until set.

2c. Glue the sensor to the beam in a similar manner, sandwiching a small, epoxy-soaked square of notebook paper underneath as an insulator. Attach it 3½" from the base end, to the side with the actuator's poled side facing out. This will be the beam's front.

2d. Solder a purple 30-gauge solid wire between the actuators' foil leads, and a blue wire between their solder dots. Solder an 8" purple wire and an 8" blue wire to the front actuator's foil lead and electrode dot, respectively.

2e. Solder an 8" green wire and an 8" yellow wire to the sensor's foil lead and electrode dot, respectively.

2f. Use a multimeter to check resistance and capacitance across each piezo element. Resistance should read as infinite, and capacitance should measure 24nF ±25% for the actuators and 7nF ±25% for the sensor. If not, clean any conductive debris that might be shorting out the electrodes.

3. BUILD THE BASE AND INSTALL THE BEAM

3a. Use a hammer and a center punch to knock an insert out of the outlet box, for the wires to go through (*see page 134*).

3b. Screw the cap onto the pipe section, and screw the other end inside the conduit box far enough so it clears the bottom.

3c. Use a stick to stuff the lower half of the pipe with fresh epoxy putty. Push the beam into the putty until the actuator bottom is 0.1" above the box.

3d. Fill the remainder of the pipe with 5-minute epoxy, until it's flush with the top surface of the box.

4. BUILD THE CIRCUIT

4a. Cut a piece of breadboard to approximately 2" square and solder a 16-pin IC socket in the middle. Following the schematic at makezine.com/13/structure, solder in and connect all circuit components. Wire open "pigtail" leads with the colors shown at the sensor/actuator interface points (designated by arrows) and at the points indicated by plus, minus, and ground signs.

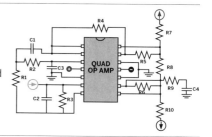

4b. Run the yellow and green wires from the sensor down through the small hole in the base. Connect the yellow to the circuit's yellow lead and the green to circuit ground.

4c. Run the purple and blue actuator wires down through and connect them to one of the switches. This will be the phase switch.

4d. Following the wiring diagram at makezine.com/13/structure, wire the other phase switch wires, plus the wires to the power switch and the series of batteries.

5. SEAL IT UP

5a. Mount the power and phase switches onto the side of the box by drilling through the centers of 2 of the conduit caps. Mount clips for the circuit board and batteries inside the box.

5b. Mount 3 hard plastic feet to the underside of the box in a triangle arrangement, to minimize box wobble. You're done!

FINISH ⊠

NOW GO USE IT »

WAY TO KILL THE BUZZ

TUNING THE CIRCUIT

Open the box and remove the circuit board, lid, and batteries, but keep them connected. Place the handle of a small brush or other round object under the middle of one side of the box, with the rim of the open box supporting the other side. This arrangement will keep the box from wobbling while you tune the beam.

Starting at maximum resistance (100kΩ) on the trimpot, turn the power switch on and flip the phase switch to make the beam vibrate. Turn the trimpot in half-turns in both directions until you find the place where the motion, the system's instability, is greatest.

Switch the phase switch to stable. The motion should stop immediately. Turn the trimpot in quarter-turns in each direction and lightly flick the beam. You should be able to find a point where the beam stops the fastest and added damping is the highest. Now your beam is smart.

INCREASING VISIBILITY

One way to get a closer look at the time and frequency domain behavior of the smart beam is by connecting an oscilloscope or spectrum analyzer to the output of the sensor charge amp, pin 7 on the op-amp chip (and to the ground at pin 11). You can also glue a small dental mirror to the tip of the beam, and position a laser pointer at the base. Project the laser spot onto a distant wall, and you'll see a vivid illustration of the behavior of the beam.

Just imagine how your smart beam could be used in all kinds of structures to cancel out stresses from high winds, rough terrain, earthquakes, and other shocks and jiggles. The sky's the limit.

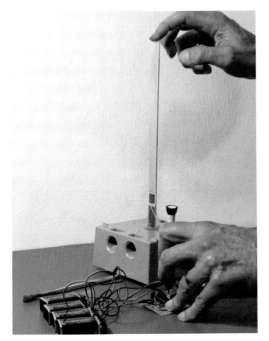

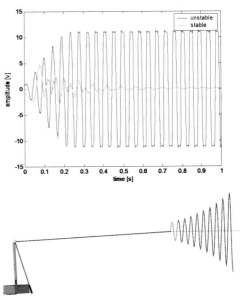

MAKE's favorite puzzles. (When you're ready to check your answers, visit makezine.com/13/aha.)

Radar Date

On October 2, 2001, the date in MM/DD/YYYY format was a palindrome (the same forward as backward): 10/02/2001.

When was the last date before 10/02/2001 that this phenomenon occurred?

Crystal Orbs

You have 2 identical crystal orbs. You need to figure out at what height an orb can fall from a 100-story building before it breaks. You know nothing about the toughness of the orbs: they may be very fragile and break when dropped from the first floor, or they may be so tough that dropping them from the 100th floor doesn't even harm them.

What is the least number of orb drops you would have to do in order to find the lowest floor they break on? In other words, what's the most efficient way you could drop the orbs to find your answer?

You are allowed to break both orbs, provided that in doing so you uniquely identify the correct floor.

Poison Pills

The evil king from an earlier MAKE puzzle sends his own assassin to take care of the evil queen who tried to poison him. Of course, her trusty guards catch the assassin before any harm is done. The queen notices that the assassin is quite handsome, and she doesn't really want to punish him with death. She decides to test his wisdom.

The queen gives the assassin 12 pills that are all completely identical in shape, smell, texture, and size, but 1 pill has a different weight. The queen gives the man a balance and tells him that all the pills are deadly poison except for the pill of a different weight. The assassin can make 3 weighings and then must swallow the pill of his choice. If he lives, he will be sent back to the bad king's kingdom. If he dies, well, that's what he gets for being an assassin.

Only 1 pill is not poisonous, the one that has a different weight. The assassin does not know if it weighs more or less than the other pills.

How can he save his skin?

Michael Pryor is the co-founder and president of Fog Creek Software. He runs a technical interview site at techinterview.org.

Illustrations by Roy Doty

The author with his
repurposed puppet pal.

Photography by Carlos Alejandro

ZIPPY THE RECYCLED MARIONETTE

Build characters from old Zip drives.
By Ian Alejandro

To earn my Showman badge in Cub Scouts, I needed to make some type of puppet. I went to my "invention bin" (a box of things to be repurposed) and found 2 old Zip drives. As I pried them apart and laid out all the parts inside, I realized they would make a cool marionette. And so Zippy was born. Here's how I did it. You don't have to use Zip drives, but they work great.

1. Pry the Zip drives open with a screwdriver, then disassemble (Figure A, on next page), cut the wires away, and keep the following pieces: 2 spinners (eyes), the outer case (body), sliding tray (head), 4 case sides (arms), and 4 case ends (legs).

MATERIALS

Zip drives (2)
Black fishing line
2"×½" wood slat **2' long**
Beads (5)
Eye screws (3)
Krazy glue
24-gauge solid-core wire and wire cutters
Slotted screwdriver and a T6 Torx screwdriver
Dremel tool **or drill with** ¹⁄₃₂" **drill bit**
Sandpaper, clothespin, pipe cleaner, and clamps
A nail and a pencil
Spray paint (optional)

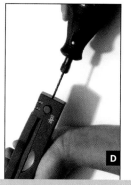

Fig. A: Disassemble the sliding tray from inside the Zip drive. Fig. B: Glue the disc spinner eyes to the tray head. Fig. C: Drill the hole for the lower back string.

Fig. D: Drill the thigh for one of its spring joints. Fig. E: Steps for constructing wire spring joints. Fig. F: Body and leg with 2 completed joints.

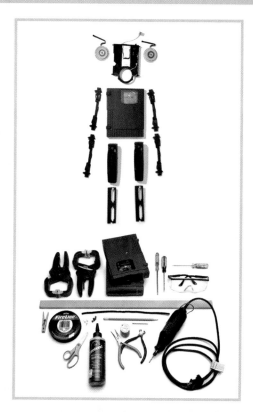

2. For the eyes, glue the 2 spinners to the sliding tray, on the side opposite the spindle hole, which looks like a mouth (Figure B).

3. Clamp and let dry, then drill a vertical hole through the chin. The head is now complete.

4. On the body, drill holes centered at the top and bottom (Figure C) for the neck and back strings, and pairs of holes on the sides and along the bottom for the arms and legs.

5. Drill holes in the ends of all 4 arm pieces and the 2 leg pieces for the thighs (Figure D). For the other 2 leg pieces, the shins, drill only 1 end.

6. Make 8 small arm/leg springs by wrapping the wire around a nail 20 times and 1 large neck spring by wrapping the wire around a pencil 25 times.

7. To make the arm and leg joints, twist-tie wire pieces through 1 side, slide a spring over the wire, then twist-tie the other side and trim any extra wire (Figures E and F). The connections need to be loose enough to let the limbs move freely. Attach the neck in the same way, using the larger spring (Figure G).

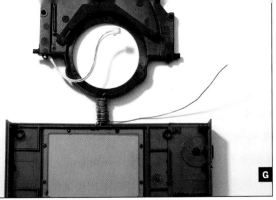

G H

I

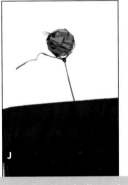

J

K

Fig. G: Thicker wire spring joint for the neck.
Fig. H: Cut a slat for the control bars. Fig. I: Control
bars drilled and glued together with a clothespin.

Fig. J: Beads make it easy to adjust the length of the
strings tied to the bars. Fig. K: Control bars painted
and fully strung to the marionette.

8. Out of the wood slat, cut one 10" main control bar, one 7" leg bar, and one 6" head bar (Figure H). Sand the edges smooth.

9. Drill 2 holes in each end of the head bar, 1 hole in 1 end of the main bar, and 1 hole in each end of the leg bar, all centered along the width. Glue the head bar and the clothespin to the top of the main bar, head bar in the middle, clothespin in front (Figure I). The clothespin holds the leg bar to let you control the entire puppet with one hand. Black spray paint is optional.

10. For a handle, attach a pipe cleaner to the top of the head bar, running it through the inner pair of holes.

11. In the underside of the main bar, place 2 eye screws at the front for the hands, and 1 eye screw at the middle, under the head bar, for the shoulders.

12. Time to start stringing. For the shoulders, tie fishing line to 1 shoulder, thread it through the middle eye screw, and run it down to the other shoulder. The length of this string will determine the distance you want the marionette to be from the control bar.

13. Attach 1 string to each side of the head at the eye, and tie the other ends to the holes at the ends of the head bar. For strings tied to the bar like this, using beads at the ends will make it easier to keep all strings the same length (Figure J).

14. Tie the lower back of the marionette to the back end of the main bar.

15. Tie a line to the hand end of 1 arm, run it through the 2 front eye screws under the main bar, and tie the other end to the opposite hand.

16. Attach strings to each knee, tying the other ends to the sides of the leg bar (Figure K). You're done!

I was right to choose a marionette for my badge project. It was easy to put together, and the end product has been an enjoyable challenge to operate.
    A great resource for stringing and working your marionette is *Marionettes: How to Make and Work Them* by Helen Fling.

Ian Alejandro is a Webelos II in Cub Scout Pack 2 in Newark, Del. He enjoys building with Lego and reading MAKE.

3-IN-1 BASKETBALL TOY

A wooden game uses a familiar cafeteria food-fight launcher. By Bob Pennington

I have 5 grandkids whom I love making toys for. After a friend showed me a crudely made but fun mini basketball toy, I got a better-mousetrap idea: expand the toy into something with 3 game modes that let you shoot the ball into a hoop, through a vertical hole, and longer-distance into a ring.

The toy is mostly wood, and it uses a plastic spoon for the firing mechanism. The spoon is drilled through the handle and clamped in a diagonal-cut block with a bolt and a wing nut, which lets you adjust it. At the other end, a block with a brass-reinforced ⅜" hole holds the hoop and hole posts.

The 1" wooden ball for the hoop and hole games is strung and glued onto a 16" length of nylon carpenter's twine, which runs to an eye screw in the post holder. The ball for the ring game is attached to a 36" string, which is tied to a fishing leader and clipped to an eye screw near the spoon holder.

The basketball-style hoop has a 1½" hole and backboard atop a 10" post. The vertical hole, measuring 1¾", sits on an 11½" post. The rings are just 1" slices of 3" and 4" PVC pipe set on the floor.

I sanded or routed all wood pieces and coated them with varnish. All 3 games require skill and dexterity and are lots of fun.

My grandchildren still practice in my absence so they can beat "Pop" when I show up. Plus, now my son and son-in-law both want one for their office. Big boys need to have fun, too!

Bob Pennington makes toys, percussion instruments, and assemblage-art ray guns called Positrons. He also plays pennywhistle in an Irish band.

Photograph by Bob Pennington

IN-CAR CAMCORDER MOUNT

Rig an onboard camera like the cops and NASCAR, for 15 bucks. By Christophe Caron

Some time ago, the Audi club I belong to held a track day at Infineon Raceway (formerly Sears Point Raceway) in Sonoma, Calif. I wanted to document my fast laps with onboard videos from my HD camcorder. But I needed an in-car camera mount to enable hands-free recording — ideally positioned behind the driver's seat, to show my view through the windshield.

I looked online and found many types of video camera mounts, some that mount on roll bar cages (for race cars) and others that attach to headrests (for everyday vehicles). But while shopping, I realized that I wouldn't receive any suitable mount in time, even if I ordered it right away. So I built one myself. I can see some refinements for it, but it works nicely and the footage it captures is pretty stable. You can watch a sample video at makezine.com/go/infineon.

MATERIALS

You should be able to find all of these at a home or hardware store for less than $15 total.

¾" aluminum or steel square tube about 2' long
U-bolts (2) that will fit around your car's headrest posts
Wing nuts (4) that match the U-bolts
¼"-20 screw, 1" long This should be the standard diameter and thread for camera mounts.

TOOLS

Hacksaw
Metal file
Drill and drill bits
Tape measure or ruler

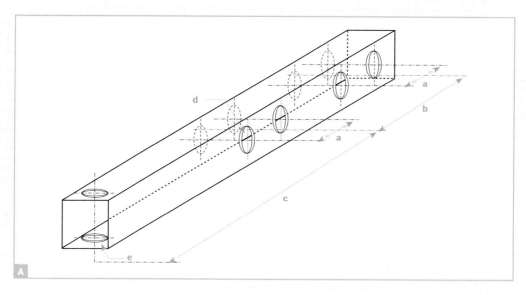

A

Build the Mount

The mount is very simple, and its specific dimensions will depend on your car. At one end of the tube, drill 4 holes spaced to fit the U-bolts tightened around the headrest posts of your front passenger seat. Then drill another hole at the other end of the tube for the mounting screw, running perpendicular to the others and positioned to give the camera an unobstructed view when you attach the mount to the passenger-side headrest.

In Figure A, *a* is the width of the U-bolt, *b* is the distance between the 2 headrest posts, and *c* is the approximate distance between the inner headrest post and the midpoint between the front seats. For the holes to drill, *d* is the diameter that the U-bolts run freely through, and *e* is the diameter that the mounting screw will run through.

Ready for Action!

It's time to take your mount for a test drive. First, bolt it onto the passenger headrest's posts so that it grips tightly to the seat. Attach the camera with the mounting screw. You can make rudimentary adjustments to its pitch angle by playing with the seat-back reclining angle. Then turn on the camera, push Record, fasten your seatbelt, and go!

I suggest that you slide the passenger seat as far back as you can, to keep the tube away from the driver's head. Also, don't let anyone ride in the back. In an accident, the wing nuts and U-bolts could be dangerous to rear seat passengers.

Possible Improvements

Two safety improvements would be to tether the camera with a strap, so it isn't ejected in a frontal collision, and to add end caps to the square tube, most importantly on the side that points toward the driver. Even safer would be to use a longer tube that attaches to both front headrests, but this would make it harder to adjust the pitch.

Finally, you could attach the camcorder using a swivel stand, like the ones that come with webcams, instead of the mounting screw. Then you could adjust the camera's angle in any direction. But depending on the quality of the stand, the car's vibrations might loosen it, even with a lighter camera.

Christophe Caron lives in the San Francisco Bay Area. Curious about just about everything, he enjoys making stuff, the outdoors, and IT. His biggest project to date: a daughter. contact@christophecaron.com

HERE'S THE ESCAPEE:
A 0-80 nonmagnetic
stainless steel
socket-head cap screw.

LOST SCREW FINDER

 An easy vacuum attachment that filters
small nonmagnetic parts. By Frank Ford

Photography by Frank Ford

MATERIALS
Plastic CD-ROM spindle container
  Finally, a use for one of these!
Small wire screen **I cut mine from an old**
  kitchen strainer.
1" diameter PVC plumbing: two 90° elbows,
  one 45° elbow, and 2' of pipe
Silicone glue
A vacuum, plus any adapter needed to fit it
  to the PVC **My shop vacuum's 1½" hose**
  fit the PVC pipe after a bit of filing, no
  adapter necessary.

TOOLS
Hacksaw or PVC pipe cutter
Utility knife
Metal file
Scissors or wire cutter
Stapler or staple gun

Ever drop a screw or other teeny part, look around like crazy, and finally have to give up? Wish you had a magic magnet that could attract plastic or brass parts out of the debris on your shop floor?

Well, that's never happened to me ... but if it ever does, I'll be glad I made this little gizmo. It's a vacuum attachment that captures small bits in a little canister so I can sort through them.

1. Using a knife along with a short piece of PVC pipe as a template, mark and cut 2 holes in the base of the CD spindle. Neatness doesn't count for much here, but the holes should just clear the diameter of the pipe and shouldn't be too irregular.

2. Cut ¼" sections off 1 end of each of the 90° elbows. Again, accuracy isn't important. My

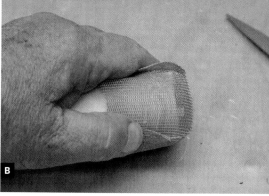

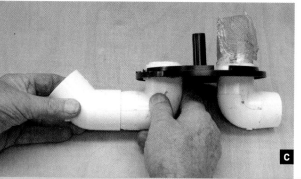

Fig. A: Fit the inlet pipe through one of the holes in the plastic spindle base, and secure it on the inside with more adhesive. **Fig. B:** Fashion a little screen "boot" that slips over the end of the outlet pipe.

Fig. C: Glue a 2" section of pipe into the inlet elbow, and glue the 45° joint onto the other end, angled back down toward the spindle base. **Fig. D:** Screw the CD spindle-cover canister into place.

weapon of choice is a hacksaw, but any saw or pipe cutter will do.

3. Using a file, taper the uncut end of one 90° elbow so that it fits the hose of your vacuum or attachment. This is your outlet elbow. My vacuum takes a 1½" input, but your mileage may vary, so here's where you'll improvise.

4. Cut a ¾" section of pipe and squidge on a bunch of silicone glue as you fit it into the cut end of the second 90° elbow. Fit the pipe through one of the holes in the plastic spindle base, and secure it on the inside with more adhesive and the ¼" ring you cut off. This is the inlet pipe (Figure A).

5. Make your outlet pipe the same way, but use a 1½" section of pipe. It should stick in 1" or so into the CD spindle base.

6. Fashion a little screen "boot" that slips over the end of the outlet pipe (Figure B). I hacked away at my screen with scissors, and trial-fit the shape onto a spare piece of pipe. When I got a form that worked, I stapled around the form to hold the shape in place.

7. Glue the screen boot onto the end of the outlet pipe with a lot of that silicone goo, and use more to seal up its ragged edges.

8. Glue a 2" section of pipe into the inlet elbow, and glue the 45° joint onto the other end, angled back down toward the spindle base (Figure C). Fit in a longer section of pipe, to serve as the nozzle. I didn't glue this last section, so that I could switch to different lengths as needed.

9. Screw the spindle-cover canister into place (Figure D), and it's ready for use!

Putting It to Use

Using the Lost Screw Finder is a simple affair. Sweep the area where the errant part was last suspected, round up everything, and check the contents of the dragnet. Most suspects stick to the screen, right where you'd expect them.

Frank Ford is a founder of Gryphon Stringed Instruments in Palo Alto, Calif., where he has been a full-time luthier since 1969. He's a prolific writer, appearing in books, magazines, and his website, frets.com.

EASY BACKYARD GRAYWATER SYSTEM

 Get a lush garden from your laundry water. By Tim Drew

The typical American household sends the water it's bathed, brushed its teeth, and cleaned its clothes with, called graywater, to the municipal waste facility. Then it waters its lawns and gardens with more fresh water, wasting about 1,000 gallons per month. But you can safely use graywater for irrigation if it's handled by a proper recycling system, and if you use biodegradable detergent and don't wash diapers.

As an avid gardener living in dry California, I wanted a simple and inexpensive way to reuse water to keep my garden green and healthy. In 2004, my wife and I had to retrofit our house's basement, so I moved the laundry machines to the back carport, which is at a slightly higher elevation than our adja-

cent garden and far from a sewer connection. This was my opportunity. At first, I simply let waste water from the washer run into a 3" flexible corrugated pipe, which I moved around to drain near any plants that I wanted to water. Later, after we decided not to move the machines back inside, I built this more permanent underground system.

The basic design involves a 2" ABS standpipe that runs down from the washer and connects to a gently sloping horizontal pipe buried under a garden path. At the other end, the water splits and travels a bit farther in 2 directions, then flows out through perforated pots and bark chip mulch, and into the soil beneath some water-loving plants and trees.

Photography by Tim Drew

Fig. A: Black ABS pipe leads from the carport washing machine standpipe to the watering area via a trench dug under the garden path; white PVC pipe is for an unrelated irrigation system installed at the same time.

Fig. B: Pipes and pots for the double-ell split and right branch of the graywater system laid in the ground before burying. Fig. C: Left branch (with 16° elbow fitting) and irrigation terminal shown before burying.

MATERIALS

2" ABS pipe long enough to run from the washing machine down underground and to irrigation outlets
2" ABS fittings to connect pipe; I used 90° elbows, 16° elbows, and straight junctions.
2" double-ell ABS fitting(s) for each split I used only 1. You might need to get these from a professional plumbing supplier; all other materials should be found at a local hardware store.
5- or 10-gallon plastic pot(s) for each split and irrigation outlet; I used 3.
Concrete stepping stones or pavers
Western red cedar medium chip bark mulch $1–$4 per cubic foot
Shovels
Wheelbarrow
Hacksaw to cut ABS pipe
Torpedo level
Drill with a large drill bit ½" to 1"
Tinsnips
ABS primer and glue

The area to be watered was 40' away and 10' below the washer. First I excavated the path that the underground pipe would follow, making sure that it was deep enough to allow for a downward slope of at least ¼" per foot. I installed the standpipe behind

the washer using pipe straps, and joined it to the underground pipe (as with all joints) using ABS primer and glue. Later, I buried the joint in gravel.

At the other end of the long underground pipe, I installed a double-ell fitting to split the water into 2 streams feeding different locations (Figure B). To make sure the water split evenly, I held a torpedo level against the fitting to ensure it stayed level while I glued it up. To keep the fitting easily inspectable and accessible for repairs rather than buried in dirt, I enclosed it in a plastic pot .

I dug trenches for more 2" pipe to run from the split to the 2 outlets where the water enters the soil (Figure C). At each, I used a perforated 5gal black plastic pot to distribute the water. I used tinsnips to cut a hole high up on the side of each pot for the pipe to enter, and drilled ½" to 1" perforations in the bottom and around the sides for the water to flow out. You can also nest a perforated 5gal pot below a 10gal pot used as a retaining wall (Figure D).

I buried the pots in trenches dug 3'–4' long and 1'–2' deep, filled the trenches back up with medium chip bark mulch, and covered each pot with a paving stone (Figure E). For more height, you can also cover with a trimmed inverted pot (Figure F). The mulch helps distribute the water to the plant roots

Fig. D: Irrigation outlet (for house graywater system, still being built) with the cover off to show workings. Fig. E: Irrigation outlet covered with paving stone (circled) and redwood bark mulch.

Fig. F: Plastic pot cover for irrigation outlet (for house graywater system). Fig. G: New plants near irrigation outlet.

while maintaining good drainage around the outlets.

Finally, I buried the pipes, covering the main pipe run with paving stones and redwood bark mulch to turn it back into a path. I also put a paver over the split point, to allow for easy access later.

Some important considerations: Keep an open space around all the pipe terminals, to let you periodically remove any solids, so they don't build up and block the flow. Similarly, it's important to have an open space around the double-ell, so the split can be inspected. Other systems I've seen have a large hole bored into the top of the double-ell to let you visually inspect the interior of the fitting for clogs and clear it out with a finger if needed.

My garden loves the system, which cost less than $150 in materials, and I've already installed pipe and outlets for another one that will reuse the rest of our house's graywater. Our household of 5 adults does about 6 or 7 loads of laundry per week. At roughly 40 gallons per, that's 260 gallons saved. And it's energy saved as well; around 20% of the energy used in California is related to water use — pumping, treating, disposing, etc.

As far as I know, the type of system I built was originally described (although perhaps not designed) by Art Ludwig of Santa Barbara, Calif.

He calls this type of system a "branched drain to mini-leach field system" and describes it in detail in his book *Create an Oasis with Greywater*, which is available at oasisdesign.net.

GRAYWATER SYSTEMS: A GRAY LEGAL AREA

Graywater systems are legal in California and other states, but depending on your location, you might be legally limited to certain types of systems and required to get a permit.

Obtaining a permit can be a roll of the dice, and many people don't bother because of the expense, hassle, and uncertainty. This creates a Catch-22 situation: local building inspectors are overly cautious and scrupulous because they have little familiarity with graywater recycling, so nobody builds permitted systems and the inspectors stay in the dark. The more graywater systems people build with permits, the more experience building inspectors will have with them, and the easier it will be to build them and get inspectors to sign off on them.

But I haven't gotten a permit yet for my system — so you go first. Luckily, a permit isn't required in my city to hang my super-efficient clothesline.

Tim Drew is an energy efficiency program analyst with the State of California and an obsessive gardener who constantly strives to live a life that is free of oil and plastic.

GROW GIANT VEGETABLES

Extreme sports meet 4H.
By Carl Malamud

At the Half Moon Bay Great Pumpkin Weigh-Off last year, Thad Starr took first place with his 1,524-pound Atlantic Giant pumpkin.

The 40-year-old Oregonian, who took home $9,144 in prize money, had been growing giant pumpkins for just two years, proving that dedication, passion, and lots of chicken manure are more important than experience in the exciting hobby of competitive vegetable growing.

Would you like to grow a pumpkin to beat Starr next year? You'll need some land, money, and serious dedication.

While pumpkins are the fruit of choice in many growing competitions, they're not the only mutants on the planet. In England, growing giant marrows (zucchini) is a ruthlessly competitive sport, with specimens topping more than 100 pounds.

In the South Pacific islands and parts of West Africa, growing giant yams has a long tradition. In the United States, you'll find 30-pound carrots in Alaska and 100-pound watermelons in Arkansas (Bill Clinton has been known to go on endlessly about his home state's huge fruits).

People go to extreme lengths for extreme vegetables, but perhaps none are more extreme than the Chinese Commission of Science, Technology, and Industry for National Defense, which recently sent seeds of 2,020 plants up into space to expose them to low gravity and high radiation, which they claim changes the seeds' genetic makeup.

These seeds are now showing up in Chinese markets, where sellers tell customers they'll be able to grow peppers, tomatoes, and other plants 30% larger than normal.

Photograph by Sam Murphy

Fig. A: Plow the field and fertilize the soil. Fig. B: Plant the germinated seedling in the garden; cover during early development to ensure a successful start. Fig. C: Put in an irrigation system. Your pumpkin will drink 100 gallons of water a day at its peak. Fig. D: Build a greenhouse using tarp and PVC pipe (or whatever materials you choose). Be sure to cover your prize at night to protect against critters and the cold.

Photography by Carl Malamud (Figs. A–F). Sam Murphy (Figs. G–H)

MATERIALS

2,500 square feet of arable land the size of a typical suburban backyard

A choice seed from your local pumpkin club Be prepared to pay up to $700. You might get a free seed with a slightly less impressive pedigree by asking nicely.

4–6 spare hours a day applied toward growing a super-vegetable*

*Technically, pumpkins and squashes are fruits, of course, but they're "eat-your-vegetables" vegetables, just like the tomato.

A Lean, Mean Growing Machine

Growing giant pumpkins requires obsessive tending of a vine, forcing it to direct all its energy to one single fruit. Every step of the process is super-charged, from the choice of seeds to the last crucial weeks on the vine.

1. Prepare the soil. Pumpkin people swear by lots of organic material added to the soil. The pros have intricate regimes, planting winter rye to plow under for nitrogen, adding compost from mushrooms or kudzu, and layering all sorts of loamy additives to gives those roots a nice, easy path to grow down to their nutrients.

2. Germinate the seeds. Germinate indoors, using seeds that have had their edges carefully filed down to give the early leaves an extra chance to break through. Grow them in peat pots until the true leaves appear, and then bring them outside as early as possible after the last frost to maximize the growing season.

3. Plant. Dig a 3' hole so the taproot has plenty of room to grow. Fill it with a super-rich mixture of nutrients. Your plant is going to snake out 25 feet to the left and right and 25 feet straight ahead, so clear lots of area and keep it free of weeds that want to ingest all that good nitrogen intended for your pet gourd.

4. Build beds and sheds. The longer the growing season, the bigger the pumpkin. Build raised beds and heat them up so the plants get in just a little bit earlier. Then, of course, build a greenhouse around your vines to protect them from harsh elements.

5. Tend. Vines want to spread forever. Fool your

Fig. E: Obsessively prune tertiary vines, or bury them to fool the plant. Fig. F: Critters love the taste of pumpkins. One bite can ruin your prize, so do everything you can to protect your baby.

Fig. G: In October, use a forklift to load your pumpkin into the bed of a pickup truck. Fig. H: Take a gander at the competition.

pumpkin by burying the vine so it throws down roots instead of crawling forward. You want a main vine with secondary vines going out to the left and right to form a Christmas tree pattern.

6. Pollinate. No birds and bees for pumpkin people. Put wire-ties on female flowers or pantyhose over the buds to keep stray pollen from coming in. Pinch off any flowers not in an optimal location on the main vine. Hand-pollinate those that remain, and when you've got a good one that's set, get rid of every other pumpkin on the vine so all the energy gets concentrated on your future prize-winner.

7. Grow. Here's the amazing part: In August, when your vine is down to one pumpkin, start feeding the vine 100 gallons of water per day, and you'll see your pumpkin take on 25–50 pounds a day. You can sit in your garden and watch the thing expand.

8. Deter rodents. A 1,000-pound fruit is a magnet for woe and pestilence. Woodchucks love pumpkins. Build electric fences, scarecrows, or traps, or play Hunter Thompson and sit on your back porch watching over your vine with a .22 and a case of grapefruit and gin, but be careful not to shoot your pumpkin.

9. Feed nutrients. When your pumpkin is doing the big swell, you have to continually feed it. Calcium makes the skin nice and strong, and growers are not above injecting fresh cream into the shell to strengthen it. Others swear by mixtures of fish parts and molasses to give your pumpkin a real training table meal as it reaches sumo size.

It all ends the first week of October, when all across the country people haul up their pumpkins with a forklift, nestle them in their 4×4s, and bring them to the weigh-offs in hopes of fame and glory.

After the contest, you must choose your pumpkin's fate. Do you want to bring it to the Peace, Love & Giant Pumpkins festival in Elk Grove, Calif., home of the Pumpkin Regatta, where your gourd becomes a boat in a race around the lake, or to the Punkin Chunkin competion in Bridgeville, Del.(*see MAKE, Volume 11, page 30*), where you hoist your fruit up 100 feet and let it fly down on an automobile?

➕ For additional resources, including websites, books, and DVDs, visit makezine.com/13/diyhome_pumpkin.

Carl Malamud is the president of public.resource.org and a writer on food science topics.

BACKYARD HENS

Feathered friends and fresh eggs.
By Terrie Miller

Photography by Terrie Miller

Chickens have been genetically engineered for millennia to be friendly, no-fuss food-making machines. Keeping a small backyard flock of these charming birds may be easier than you think, and the eggs you'll get are tastier and more nutritious than what you buy in the store.

Before you start, you might want to check local ordinances. Many municipalities allow some number of hens, but forbid roosters. Don't worry, you don't need roosters for egg production.

Choose the Breed(s) and Flock Size

For most backyard flocks, you'll want a docile, friendly temperament combined with good egg production. Some high-producing breeds, like White Leghorns, have a reputation for being

ONE-TIME MATERIALS

Chicks
Large cardboard box
Plastic packing tape
Incandescent lamp with reflector
Thermometer
Chick feeder and waterer
Chicken coop with nest box and roosting area
Feeder and waterer **for adult chickens**

ONGOING SUPPLIES

Chicken feed **age-appropriate formulas**
Pine shavings **or other litter for chicks**
Straw **for adults**
Water
Calcium and grit supplements

Fig. A: Cardboard-box brooder provides food, water, bedding, and shelter for two Plymouth Rock and three Light Brahma chicks, 2 weeks old.

Fig. B: Incandescent lamp with reflector keeps the chicks warm, and a framed wire screen protects them.
Fig. C: The 5-week-old chicks huddle near the light bulb when they're a bit chilly.

flighty and skittish. If you want to consume more than the eggs, you can choose a breed that's also known for its meat quality. Good dual-purpose breeds for the backyard include Rhode Island Reds, Barred Plymouth Rocks, and the big, friendly Brahmas.

If you have a local feed store that sells chicken raising supplies, ask for their advice on breeds that do well in your area. They'll also have good advice on what to feed your chicks and adult chickens.

Many feed stores also sell chicks, or you can buy them online (see makezine.com/go/eggs for sources). Chicks typically ship via Priority Mail when they're 1 day old, in a perforated cardboard box and in groups large enough to keep warm. The last bit of yolk sac that a chick absorbs as it hatches supplies it with enough nutrients for 72 hours, so a fast trip through the mail is no problem.

Once you've chosen a breed (or breeds; mixed flocks are fine), estimate how many eggs per week you'll get from each hen and decide how many you'll need. You might want to start out with 1 or 2 extra, in case you get a rooster by mistake. I'm told that chick sexing is only about 90% accurate.

Raise The Chicks

Before getting your chicks, you need a "brooder," essentially a large box with a heat source and a secure top to keep pets and vermin out. I used a cardboard box, after lining its bottom with packing tape to make it water-resistant and cleanable (Figure A). To cover it, I put a framed wire screen on top.

For warmth, you can use an incandescent lamp with a reflector. A 60-watt bulb is fine for a small indoor brooder. Hang it so you can adjust its height (Figure B), and make sure the box is large enough to have a "cool" side away from the bulb that the chicks can move to if they get too warm.

In their first days, chicks need a temperature of about 95°F, but you can reduce the heat by a few degrees each week. Monitor the temperature with an adhesive thermometer (check the reptile section at a pet shop), and also watch the chicks themselves. If they crowd under the light, they're probably cool (Figure C); if they avoid it, they're too warm.

I used a chick feeder and waterer for their food and water (Figure D). You definitely need a waterer designed specifically for chicks. These ensure that the little birds have fresh water at all times, but aren't deep enough for them to walk through and become wet and chilled (or worse, drown). The

Fig. D: The 4-week-old chicks eating from feeder. The waterer is set in an old cake pan to minimize wet bedding from spills. Fig. E: The 6-week-old chicks, almost ready to move to the coop outside.

Fig. F: The final flock of three (Bubble, Trouble, and Hecate Hen) in the backyard coop. The other two were returned to the feed store (sorry, roosters!).

chicks will also need litter; pine shavings (not cedar or hardwood) will work fine for this.

Chicks grow fast (Figure E) — it's astonishing! — and at about 6–8 weeks should be feathered out and ready to move into unheated outdoor quarters (Figure F). You may find, as I did, that one of your "hens" starts crowing in the morning. In this case, you have a few options. Our feed store buys back any chicks it has mis-sexed. Otherwise, you can sell or give him away, keep him (local laws and neighbor relations permitting), or have him for dinner. Since my chickens are like pets to me, I won't do the latter.

Move to the Coop

You can buy a chicken coop, build one, or do a little of both; refer to makezine.com/go/eggs for coop plans. Your hens will need a sturdy, protective enclosure at night, and maybe during daytime, too, to defend against the elements and keep out raccoons, dogs, rats, and other predatory wildlife.

One option if you have room is a "chicken tractor," a pen that you can move from place to place to provide the ladies with fresh foraging opportunities.

If you let your hens range freely during the day, it's usually easy to coax them back into their coop before sunset. They're highly trainable, so you can teach them to come to a call or whistle. They also seek high places to spend the night, so they'll be naturally drawn to an elevated roost inside the coop. Hens also love kitchen scraps, and soon you'll have them eating out of your hand — literally, if you like. You'll also want to offer them grit and calcium supplements like oyster shell (see makezine.com/go/eggs for info).

Your coop should have food, water, shade, good ventilation, straw or other bedding, and a nest box for egg laying. Used bedding can be great for your compost pile.

For egg laying, your hens will want a dark nest box just big enough to sit inside. You can buy or make these; one example I've seen is a covered plastic cat litter box trimmed down and turned on its side.

Laying is stimulated by daylight, so if you get your chicks during late summer or fall, you probably won't see any eggs until the days start getting longer. You can also make them lay more out of season by exposing them to artificial lighting.

Chickens will make any backyard more fun!

Terrie Miller is the online manager for MAKE and publishes crittergeek.com and citizensci.com. She and her husband live in Sebastopol, Calif., with one dog, two cats, two snakes, and some friendly chickens.

IGNITION

WARNING!!!
HIGH VOLTAGE!!!

DIY SCIENCE

EXPLOSION ENGINE

DIY internal combustion using Home Depot parts. By David Simpson

A few months ago, some of the cadets in my Civil Air Patrol squadron were stumped by the chapter we were reading on internal combustion engines. The pictures failed to convey what really happens, and even the word "combustion" sounds like what a candle does. Engines are all about explosions, front and center! So we needed to make some explosions and show the students how these blasts get turned into the power that runs cars, airplanes, and weed whackers.

I thought it would be fun to make my Internal Explosion Engine entirely out of parts available at Home Depot, and I did it (almost), basing my design on the classic PVC spud gun. The result has all the parts of an engine and shows how they work together. After building this project, you'll feel a lot more knowledgeable talking to your mechanic.

Overview

Our combustion cylinder is 2" PVC pipe, and the fuel is butane, which you squirt in manually. The ignition spark comes from a piezoelectric grill starter wired to 2 pairs of screws inside the cylinder. A 12V electric air pump blends fresh air with the butane and flushes out the exhaust.

The explosion forces down a PVC piston and its dowel connecting rod, turning the galvanized pipe-and-flange crankshaft, which rotates 4 or 5 times until balance weights on the flywheel pull it back for the next firing. I made the frame from a PVC composite board that tools like wood, but looks spiffier. A complete list of materials and tools is on page 164.

Construction

Keep everything as square as possible, so linkages

Photography by David Simpson

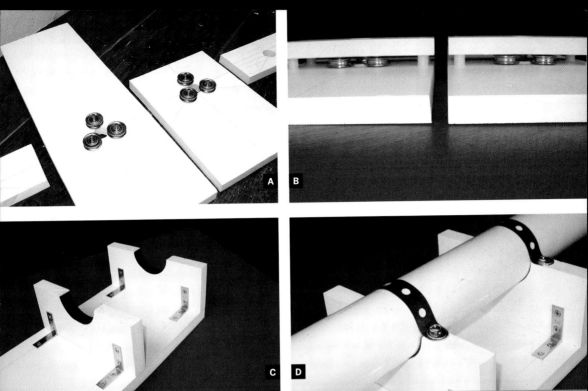

Fig. A: Crank supports with bearings installed, and smaller "sandwich" blocks, ready to assemble.
Fig. B: Side view of finished crank bearing assemblies. Bearings are made from metal patio door rollers.

Fig. C: Cylinder saddles mounted to front bearing block and lined with adhesive tread. Fig. D: Cylinder test-mounted in saddles with brass pipe strapping hold-downs.

work smoothly. If you don't have a drill press, monitor your drilling angle, and after making a pilot hole, slide the bit back in to make sure it's straight. If not, correct it, using the next larger bit.

1. Cut the crankcase and base boards.

Cut 3 lengths of ¾"×7¼" (referred to as 1×8) Veranda or Azek trim board: 25" for the base, 23" for the forward crank support, and 11" for the rear crank support. I attached 6 rubber feet to the underside of the base, but you can also do this at the end.

2. Build the crank bearing assemblies.

For each crankcase bearing, we'll use three 1¼" patio door roller bearings spaced evenly around the crankshaft. (If it didn't violate "available at Home Depot," I'd have simply used 2 sealed ball bearings.)

Mark a point on each support centered 7½" up from the bottom, and use a compass or template to draw a circle the width of your crankshaft pipe (mine was ¹³⁄₁₆") around each point. Use a protractor to mark 3 evenly trisecting lines around each point.

Using the roller bearings as guides, mark the points where you can mount a bearing along each line so they'll cradle the crankshaft on all sides. Drill a ¼" hole ¼" deep at each point, then drill out

the center to 1" (slightly larger than the crankshaft). To allow the top bearings some play, use the Dremel router bit to extend each top hole up about ¹⁄₁₆", making them oblong.

Cut two 3½"×7¼" blocks of trim board; these will hold the other sides of the bearing shafts. Mark and drill the positions of 3 bearing mount holes and 1 big center hole, just as you did with the supports. Mark, drill, and countersink 4 more holes on each block, ½" in from each corner and large enough for 1⅝" drywall screws to drop through.

Time to assemble. Lay the bearing support blocks flat, drilled side up. Sandwich each bearing in its holes (Figure A) with the smaller blocks on top, fitting ¼" nylon flat washers over the shafts on each side. Mark the support blocks below each corner hole, and drill pilots for drywall screws. Screw the blocks together, threading 4 stacked ¾"×½"×⅛" nylon washers onto each, in between as spacers (Figure B). The bearings should spin freely, and each top bearing should have a little up/down play.

3. Make the cylinder saddles.

On a long piece of the 7¼" trim board, mark 2 lines, 3" and 6" in from one end, then mark the center point of the first line. Cut a 2" hole around the point

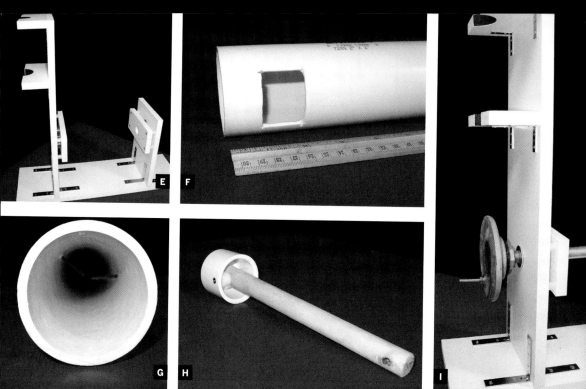

Fig. E: Crank bearing assemblies mounted onto the base.
Fig. F: Exhaust port cut into the bottom of the cylinder.
Fig. G. Spark points (drywall screws) form a spark gap inside the cylinder.

Fig. H: PVC end cap piston connects to the dowel connecting rod with wrist pin and nylon spacers.
Fig. I: Galvanized pipe crankshaft and pipe flange crank with a bolt running through the connecting rod.

using a hole saw. Using clamps and a straightedge as a fence, cut along each line to create 2 identical arch-shaped pieces.

Mount the 2 saddles to the forward crank support, on the opposite side from the bearing, using 1½" corner braces. Position one flush with the top and the other 7" down. For traction, line the arches with 1" adhesive tread (Figure C).

For the cylinder hold-downs, use 2 lengths of ¾" brass pipe strap. Drill ¹⁄₁₆" pilot holes on either side of each saddle for mounting screws, and do a "dry run" securing the 2" PVC in place (Figure D).

4. Mount the crank bearing assemblies.

Mount the 2 crank bearing assemblies to the top of the base, 6" in from each end, with the bearing sides facing each other. Use a square to make sure the supports are vertical and parallel, and secure them with pairs of 3" corner braces on each side. Offset the braces by ½" so their screws don't clash (Figure E).

5. Make the cylinder.

Use the Dremel to cut an exhaust port in the 2" PVC pipe about 1⅛" high by 1½" wide, and ⁵⁄₁₆" from the end (Figure F). Chamfer the inside bottom of the cylinder to give clearance for the connecting rod.

6. Insert the spark points.

Mark the circumference of the cylinder at 11½" and 20½" from the bottom. Through each line, drill 2 pilot holes spaced 120° straight into the center. Screw in 4 drywall screws until the tips of each pair lie ¼" to ⅜" apart inside the pipe (Figure G).

Test the points by linking one from each pair together with an alligator clip jumper, then run leads from the 2 free points to the grill igniter. Push the igniter button, and you should see 2 sparks. If not, disconnect, tighten the screws to bring the points closer together, and try again.

7. Mount the cylinder head.

Fit the PVC end cap, or adapter with screw plug, onto the cylinder (the end cap makes a "hemi" style head, while the adapter and plug let you examine the sparking more easily). Secure with 3–4 screws.

Marking PVC Pipe Straight Across
One way to mark a pipe evenly for cutting is to lay it in the corner of a box or drawer, hold a pencil down at the measured marking point, and rotate the pipe underneath until the pencil mark goes all the way around.

Find more tools-n-tips at makezine.com/tnt.

K

J   L

Fig. J: Cylinder and moving parts installed: piston, rod, crank, crankshaft, and flywheel (not shown).
Fig. K: Fuel and air injection: Holes for canned butane and an air pump with a basketball inflation needle.

Fig. L: Ignition system: Piezo grill igniter in the project box with holes on either side to keep the leads safely separated.

8. Assemble the piston and connecting rod.

Drill two ¹⁵⁄₆₄" holes centered through the 1¼" PVC end cap, ⅜" from the bottom. Precision is important here. The 2" tension pin, which acts as the wrist pin, should fit through and move without binding. Drill a ⁷⁄₃₂" hole for the pin, ½" from the top of the 9" dowel; it should fit snugly. Drill a ¼" hole for the crank, ½" from the bottom of the dowel, parallel to the top hole. Attach the piston to the rod using the pin and two ⅜"×⅝" nylon spacers (Figure H).

9. Make the flywheel and crank.

Tightly screw each of the 2 pipe flange adapters onto the flanges. Thread a 2" flat-head bolt, washer, lock washer, and nut out through one of the mounting holes in one of the flanges. Slide the metal pipe through both bearing assemblies, and slide a ¾" steel washer and ⅞" external tension retaining ring onto each end. Screw on the flange assembly with the bolt (the crank) and attach the other flange assembly (the flywheel) onto the other end (Figure I).

Link the connecting rod to the crank by threading a washer, the rod, another washer, and 2 nuts locked against each other onto the crank bolt. The crankshaft should turn freely and rock the connecting rod and piston. At this point, it's a floppy mess!

10. Secure the stationary engine components.

Slide the cylinder over the piston and strap it down loosely. Position it so that the exhaust port faces sideways and half of the wrist pin drops below the cylinder at the bottom of the stroke (Figure J). Tighten the hold-downs, but not enough to distort the cylinder.

11. Mount the air injection system.

Remove the guts of a 12V car-trunk air pump and attach a basketball inflating needle to the hose. Drill a ⁵⁄₆₄" hole into the cylinder roughly ⅝" below the head, slide the needle into the hole, and fabricate a small saddle out of board that you can zip-tie between the hose and cylinder to keep the needle in place (Figure K). Mount the compressor to the back of the forward crank support using screws, coupling nuts (as standoffs), washers, and rubber grommets. The air hose should lay flat against the support.

12. Mount the ignition system.

To keep a safe distance from the explosions, I made extra-long leads for the igniter using alligator clips and 9' lengths of hookup wire. And to avoid the risk of zapping myself, I mounted the igniter inside a small project box. Drill holes for the wires in opposite ends of the box (Figure L) and keep them apart as they snake over to the spark points so the spark doesn't jump too soon. Connect the wires the same way as when you tested the spark points in Step 6. Your ignition system is now "armed and dangerous." Label the housing with appropriate safety lingo.

13. Drill the fuel injection port.

Drill a ⅛" hole in the cylinder about ⅝" below the head. This is where you'll inject bottled liquid butane into the explosion chamber. Slip a small washer over the bottle's nozzle to prevent it from sticking to the cylinder.

14. Counterbalance the flywheel.

Weight the flywheel assembly with a bolt, washer, lock washer, and nut combination, so that the piston naturally comes to rest just past the top of the stroke — the optimal position for power delivery.

15. Lubricate the piston.

Using a squeeze ketchup bottle, squirt the thickest clear shampoo you can find into the exhaust port so that it runs around the piston. This helps with compression and lubrication. Catch the overflow in a plastic container below the connecting rod — the engine's "oil pan."

Fire It Up!

With all the fanfare of a shuttle launch, follow this sequence:

1. Set the piston to the just-over-top position (the counterbalance weight should take care of that).
2. Plug the air compressor into a car lighter jack and switch it on.
3. Fire a 1-second shot of butane into the cylinder.
4. Wait 15 seconds to let the air and fuel mix.
5. Fire! You should get a good explosion and at least 5 rotations of the crank. Wait 15 seconds for the compressor to replace the exhaust with fresh air, then repeat Steps 3 and 4. Periodically lube the piston with a squirt of shampoo.

Experiment with the duration of the fuel burst and the air/fuel mix time. Slightly shorter or longer may yield a more efficient blend and a better bang!

David Simpson teaches aviation to teenage cadets as aerospace education officer for the Civil Air Patrol in Morristown, N.J. He is also a private pilot, and he began building and flying model airplanes at the age of 11.

MATERIALS

1×8 (actually ¾"×7¼") white PVC trim board, at least 6' I used Azek. For Steps 1–2, cut 7 pieces to these lengths: 25", 23", 11", 3½" (2), and 3".
2" Schedule 40 PVC pipe, 2' long for cylinder
½"×18" galvanized pipe for crankshaft
1¼" Schedule 40 PVC end cap for piston
2" Schedule 40 PVC female adapter and male plug, or end cap for cylinder head
Nylon spacers, ⅜"×¼" ID (2) and ¾"×½"×⅛" (32)
Nylon washers, flat, ¼" diameter (12)
¼"×2" tension pin for wrist pin
Grill igniter I used Weber Igniter Kit 7510
Patio door roller kits (3) 6 rollers total, for bearings
Bernzomatic butane 60g cylinder (2.1oz)
Corner braces: 3" (8) and 1½" (4)
¾" hardwood dowel, 9" long for connecting rod. Sight down it to make sure that it's straight.
¾" brass pipe strap, 18" long
Hookup wire, red and black I used 9' of each.
¾" adhesive clear polyurethane bumper pads (6)
11" plastic cable ties (2) from RadioShack
Wood or sheet metal screws, with various washers for braces, straps, cylinder head, and standoffs
¼" flat-head bolts with nuts and lock washers (2) one 2" long, the other 2¾" long
Pipe flanges, 5½" OD, 2¼" ID (2)
Pipe flange adapters, 2¼" OD (2) for ½" pipe
¾" SAE washers with oversized ID (2) for ½" pipe
⅞" retaining rings (2)
Alligator clips (4)
2' test jumper lead
3"×6"×2" project box from RadioShack
1" adhesive tread, 8½" long I used 3M brand.
12V air compressor and 12V power supply
Basketball inflating needle
11" cable ties (2) to secure air hose to cylinder
3/16" coupling nuts (2) standoffs for air compressor
½" rubber grommets (2) to anchor air compressor
1⅝" fine-thread drywall screws (12) for spark points and bearing assembly fasteners
Condiment squeeze dispenser
8oz thick, clear, unscented shampoo for lubricant
4"×4"×2½" plexiglass container for the "oil pan"

TOOLS

Table or circular saw that can cut PVC
Dremel tool with router, cut-off, and grinding bits
Drill and drill bits: 1/16", 5/64", ⅛", 7/32", 15/64", ¼"
Hole saws: 1" and 2"
Metal shears
Screwdrivers
Steel spring clamps (2)
Compass, or circle template and protractor
Straightedge, carpenter square, and ruler
Label maker, or marker and labels
Pencil

For more information, contact David Simpson at dsimpson@hydroflightsim.net.

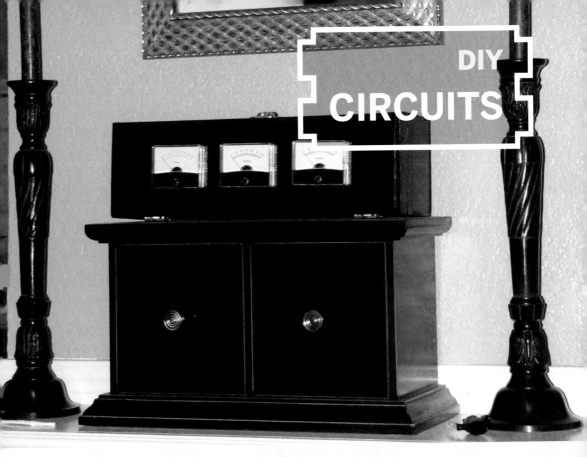

ANALOG AMP METER CLOCK

Elegant timepiece marks the hours with needle meters. By Gene Scogin

Photography by Gene Scogin

Several years ago I had the idea of making an analog clock that used voltmeter-style needle gauges rather than a standard dial. A few weeks ago I finally made one, using an Arduino board and 3 current meters from a local electronics store. I built it up in stages, starting out with a single meter that displayed just seconds, then adding hour and minute meters, adding buttons and programming to make the time settable, and finally building it into a nice box. Here's how I did it.

Feeding the Meter

The Arduino board has 6 outputs that can drive analog values using pulse width modulation (PWM). This means they simulate output voltages lying in between binary high and low (0V and 5V) by cycling rapidly between the two for varying time ratios; for example, a 2.5V output would be simulated by being on for exactly half the time. I found that the Arduino's pulse frequency was fast enough (490Hz) and my meters were slow enough that you could drive them directly from the board's outputs without the needles vibrating; you don't need a capacitor to smooth out the signal.

I was only able to find ammeters and not voltmeters, so I needed to put a resistor in series with the meter to limit the current. Ohm's law states that to get 1mA of current with a voltage of 5V, you need $5,000\Omega$ of resistance. To allow for normal variations in components, I assembled this resistance by putting a $4,750\Omega$ resistor in series with a 0Ω to 500Ω potentiometer. To set the range for each meter, you first zero it with the adjustment screw on the meter itself, then adjust the pot to set its high point.

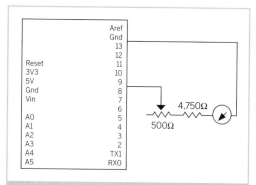

The microcontroller output pin runs through adjustable resistance and then to the seconds meter.

The breadboard carries 3 identical circuits running in parallel, for the hours, minutes, and seconds meters.

MATERIALS

Arduino microcontroller board I used an Arduino Diecimila I bought at Maker Faire. You can order one from store.makezine.com.

1mA current meters (3) Make sure your board delivers enough current to drive the meter's needle over its whole range; I originally tried a 50mA meter, but that wasn't scaled right for the Arduino.

4,750Ω resistors (3)

500Ω potentiometers (3) aka variable resistors

Button switches, momentary SPST (3)

Solderless breadboard

Computer with printer and paper

Spray adhesive

Nice wooden box and paint

Original ammeters showed a scale between 0 and 1 milliamps.

Making It Tick

Once we have our meter hooked up, we can write a simple C program to make it count 60 seconds over its full range every minute. The analogWrite() function takes a value between 0 and 255 and the index of an output pin, and sets the output for the specified pin to a PWM value between 0V and 5V.

To track the seconds, the program runs a continuous loop that calls millis(), a built-in Arduino function that returns the number of milliseconds since the board was last powered up. The value returned is compared with the millis() value from the previous loop, and the difference is added to the running total of seconds, which in turn updates the display.

When the seconds wrap around, the code resets the running total to 0 and adds the remainder. The code also handles another special case, when the

value returned by millis() itself rolls over, after about every 9 hours of uptime.

I used the Arduino's pin 11 to drive my newly programmed seconds meter. Then I went on to programming and driving the hours and minutes meters in a similar fashion, using pins 9 and 10. The wiring for each meter is exactly the same: the microcontroller output pin connects to the potentiometer in series with the resistor, which then leads to the meter. All the code for this project, along with wiring diagrams, is available at makezine.com/13/diycircuits_clock.

Setting the Time

To make our clock useful, we need a way to set the time after we power it up. To do this I used 3 switches. One cycles the clock through its 4 modes (normal, set, all-low, and all-high — explained later), one

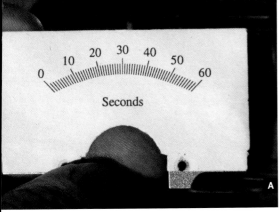

Fig. A: The seconds meter scale displays 60 with an input of 1 milliamp. Fig. B: Paper template for cutting holes in the box.

Fig. C: Holes in the box, with some holes sawed out into slots to fit screws. Fig. D: The meters with their new scales fit into the box.

increments the hours, and one increments the minutes. To get a proper reading from digital inputs, we need a pull-up resistor between each input pin and +5V. The Arduino's microprocessor has these conveniently built in, but you need to explicitly activate them by declaring the pin as input with `pinMode(b1pin,INPUT)` and then calling `digitalWrite(pin,HIGH)`.

Because the program runs through its main loop many times each second, we assume that a single push of the button will be read multiple times. To handle this, I have a variable for each button that keeps track of its state. Also, when the program first detects that a button's state has changed, it delays for 20 milliseconds to wait out any signal bounce from the switch.

The mode switch moves the clock between 4 modes: normal, set time, all meters low, and all meters high. Normal mode shows the time, set mode lets you change it, and the all-low and all-high modes set the 3 output pins to 0V and 5V, respectively, for calibrating the meters. The code continues to keep track of the current time in all modes, unless it's reset. I am considering adding additional modes to the clock, such as alarm, stopwatch, and timer.

Making the Scales

The scales on the meters as purchased read from 0mA to 1mA, but for the clock to be readable, we need scales that go from 0 to 24 for the hours and 0 to 60 for the minutes and seconds. Doing this ended up being one of the hardest parts of the project.

I started by disassembling one of the meters and scanning the printed panel with the scale. Then I used the measuring tools in the Unix drawing program Xfig (xfig.org) to measure the image's distances and angles. One complication was that the scale isn't based on a simple circle arc; it's compressed vertically so that the ends of the scale lie farther away from the needle's pivot point than the middle.

To generate the new scales, I wrote a program in Tcl (tcl.tk) that takes a set of distances and angles that describe a scale, calculates its component lines and curves, and outputs an image file in Xfig's native format. I read this file into Xfig and used it to generate a printable PostScript file.

The only problem was that the finest line that Xfig could draw was thicker than I wanted, so I edited the PostScript by hand to make the line thinner before printing it. Once I printed out the new scales, I cut them out and used spray adhesive to stick them on the plates (Figure A).

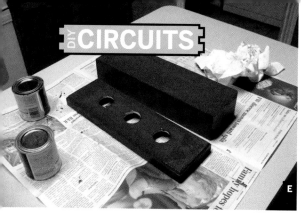

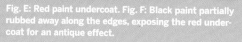

Fig. E: Red paint undercoat. Fig. F: Black paint partially rubbed away along the edges, exposing the red undercoat for an antique effect.

Fig. G: Finished amp meter clock with the lid open to show the circuitry. Fig. H: Clock displaying the analog to a blinking 12:00.

To help line up the scales on the plates, I printed extra marks where the screw holes were. And so that the original scales would not show through the paper, I put the new scales on the backs of the plates, which were blank (and symmetrical).

Boxing It Up

This is the type of project that needs a good box, to display the meters and conceal the wires and such. My wife suggested that a nice wooden box would look good on the mantle, and we chose one at a local craft store.

Mounting the meters meant drilling a wide central hole for the back of the meter itself, surrounded evenly by 4 small holes for the mounting screws. I made a paper template as a guide (Figure B, previous page) and drilled accordingly, but it was hard to get the mounting holes accurate enough, so I used a larger bit and a keyhole saw to clear out enough space for them to fit (Figure C). The meters all fit tightly in the central holes, so I didn't bother putting nuts and washers on the mounting screws (Figure D).

For the power source, I considered putting batteries in the box, but the Arduino pulls 20mA–30mA, so even with D cells, they would need to be changed about every 5 weeks. Instead I decided to use a wall wart and ran the cord through a hole in the back of the box. The buttons for setting the clock and changing modes I left on the breadboard inside.

Finally, I wanted the box to be an aged black, to match our furniture. I accomplished this effect by first putting down a coat of red paint and allowing it to dry (Figure E). I then followed it with black and lightly wiped the wet paint off the edges, exposing small amounts of red underneath (Figure F).

The end result is a unique clock and a great conversation starter that can be displayed prominently in my home, and now in yours, too!

Gene Scogin is a computer programmer who enjoys a variety of hands-on projects.

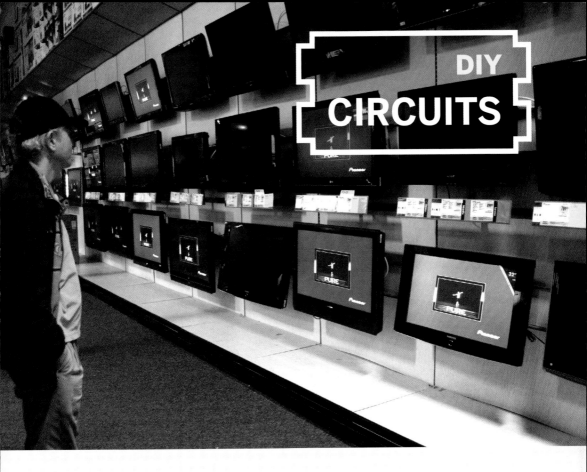

TV-B-GONE HAT

Turn off TVs by just looking at them.
By Mitch Altman

"Hey, you mind turning that thing off?" Simple enough question, but I got tired of people looking at me like I'm from Mars. When a TV is on in the room, I can't think. I just stare at the thing and drool.

So I invented TV-B-Gone, a key chain that stealthily turns off just about any television. When the TVs turn off, people turn on, engage in conversation, read, eat, and perform all sorts of human activities. Peace happens.

I recently teamed up with prolific kit maker Limor Fried to create a $20 kit version of the original TV-B-Gone key chain. This version works up to 40 yards away, and it's totally hackable; the entire project is open source and documented at ladyada. net/make/tvbgone. Here's how I built one into a baseball cap that lets me look at almost any TV, touch the top, and watch with glee as it shuts off.

MATERIALS

TV-B-Gone kit available from Limor Fried's site or the Maker Store (store.makezine.com)
Baseball cap or any other hat with a visor
Tactile switch, SPST momentary Jameco part #119010 (jameco.com)
1" heat-shrink tubing, 2" long Jameco #419291
1/16" heat-shrink tubing, 3/4" long Jameco #419127
30-gauge solid-core wire-wrap wire, about 2' matching hat color
Permanent marker or paint matching hat color
AA alkaline batteries (2)
Needle and thread
Hot glue gun and glue
Hair dryer, heat gun, or lighter
Needlenose pliers

Photograph by Sam Murphy

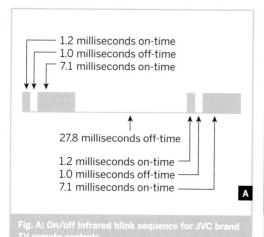

1.2 milliseconds on-time
1.0 milliseconds off-time
7.1 milliseconds on-time

27.8 milliseconds off-time

1.2 milliseconds on-time
1.0 milliseconds off-time
7.1 milliseconds on-time

A

Fig. A: On/off infrared blink sequence for JVC brand TV remote controls.

B

Fig. B: Pull wire-wrap wire through the cap's fabric to connect the switch on top.

How TV-B-Gone Works

TV remote controls all work the same way: by transmitting coded patterns of 940nm wavelength infrared to the television's remote control receiver, somewhat like sending Morse code with a flashlight. The receiver watches for blinking IR, and when it sees patterns it recognizes, performs the corresponding functions on the TV. To avoid accidental triggering by reflected light in the room, receivers only respond to IR light that pulses at a specific carrier frequency.

For our TV-B-Gone, we don't care about couch-surfing functionality; all we need is the code for turning a TV off. (Because remotes have just one on/off button, this is the same as the code to turn it on, and the TV's current state determines which new state to toggle to.)

For example, to turn off a JVC TV, you blink the pattern shown in Figure A using a carrier frequency of 54kHz. The entire sequence lasts only a tiny fraction of a second, so there's no perceivable delay.

Different manufacturers' IR standards vary, but they all use rapid blinking of an even faster carrier frequency. TV-B-Gone transmits the on/off button codes for most TVs, one right after the other. So it works like other remotes, but with just one button.

1. Assemble the kit.

First I built the TV-B-Gone kit itself. I already knew how to do this, but you can follow the excellent instructions at ladyada.net/make/tvbgone.

2. Install the switch.

Take out the batteries and unsolder the battery leads from the board. Then bend the 4 legs of the tactile switch apart so they're flat, and hot-glue the switch to the button on top of the cap (Figure B).

Use needlenose pliers to push some of the wire-wrap wire through the hat fabric near the button. Pull enough wire through on the underside of the hat to reach the end of the visor. Repeat using a second piece of wire, then solder the wires to 2 of the switch's legs on the same side, clip off the other 2 legs, and cover the soldered joints with ¹⁄₁₆" heat-shrink tubing.

If you use a lighter, be careful not to place the tubing (or the hat) directly in the flame. Hold the flame just above the tubing and move it around slowly until it's fully shrunk.

Use a needle and thread to sew the 2 wires to the inside of the hat. I used 5 loops for each, tying them off with a square knot (Figure C). Alternatively, you can also use hot glue.

Position the assembled TV-B-Gone at the edge of the visor of the hat, with the IR emitters just inside the brim, pointing outward. Cut the wires from the hat-top switch so they extend just past the switch button on the circuit board (Figure D).

3. Install the battery pack.

Center the battery pack under the cap's dome with its 2 wires facing forward, toward the visor. Hot-glue the battery pack in place, then sew (or hot-glue) its wires to follow the same paths as the switch wires.

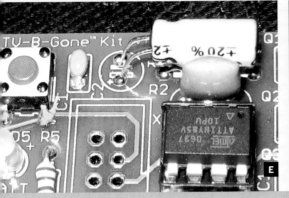

Fig. C: Sew the switch wires along the inside seam from the top button to the brim where the circuit board is glued. Fig. D: Trim the wires to just reach the board switch terminals.

Fig. E: Solder the switch wires to the onboard switch terminals. Fig. F: TV-B-Gone and battery pack installed, insulated, and ready to increase the peace.

4. Install the TV-B-Gone.

Trim and solder the wires to the battery terminals on the circuit board (BATT), red to + and black to -, covering the connections with $\frac{1}{16}$" heat-shrink tubing. Trim and solder the 2 wires from the tactile switch and solder them to the 2 connected terminals for the onboard switch (S1). It does not matter which wire goes to which terminal (Figure E).

5. Test.

Insert 2 batteries into the holder. The visible LED (LED5) should start blinking. If not, immediately take the batteries out and check that the battery leads aren't reversed. You can also confirm that all 4 of the TV-B-Gone's IR emitters are blinking by watching them through a digital camera (most cameras can see IR).

After the TV-B-Gone turns itself off, pushing the button on top of the hat should restart the transmission sequence. If not, double-check the wires running from the hat switch to the board.

6. Final assembly.

Remove the batteries, then cover the circuit board with a 2"-long piece of 1" heat-shrink tubing and shrink it in place. After shrinking, cut little pieces

out of the tubing to expose the visible light and the onboard switch.

Hot-glue the covered board to the underside of the visor with the IR emitters facing forward, as before. Finally, use a colored marker or paint to conceal the silver parts of the hat switch (Figure F).

A Real-Life TV Story

We walk into a restaurant. Nice place — except there are 3 huge-screen TVs blaring from different corners. No one is watching any of them, so off they go. None of the customers even seem to notice, yet the waiter feels obliged to turn them back on.

No problem — off they go again. The waiter calls the manager, who grabs the remote control and turns them on again. Triumphant, they start to walk away. Off go the TVs once more. While they're standing there, dumbfounded, I switch them all on. Then off. Their shoulders slump in unison, admitting defeat. We enjoy our meal and conversation.

I love my TV-B-Gone hat.

Among other projects, Mitch Altman is currently working on TV-B-Gone Pro, which will turn off TVs from 100 meters, and an open source, commercial version of the Brain Machine he wrote about in MAKE, Volume 10.

Photography by Mitch Altman

TRANSISTORIZE YOUR IPOD
Get vintage sounds from time-warp radio.
By Nick Archer

Hearing "Monday, Monday" on giant stereo speakers doesn't pack the emotional wallop of listening to it through the 2¼" speaker of my childhood transistor radio. When the iPod shuffle came out, it hit me: I could wire one of them into a vintage radio and recreate that experience.

I got an old radio from eBay, hooked it up, and it worked! Then I loaded up the iPod with old airchecks from DJs of my childhood, plus old songs and commercials from the same era, and now I can listen just like when I was 12. Everyone I've played it for says it's spooky, like the radio just arrived from the 60s.

Rewiring It

The idea is to route the output from the iPod to the audio input and to the radio's volume control. Open up the old radio (Figure A, on next page) and

MATERIALS

Old transistor radio
iPod shuffle
3.5mm stereo mini plug
3.3kΩ resistors (2)
Insulated wire
Jeweler's screwdrivers
Soldering equipment
Wire cutters/stripper
Rubber cement **if radio speaker cone is damaged**

remove the guts. Stick the tiny screws to a piece of tape for safe storage. My speaker had a hole in it that caused a buzzing sound at high volume, but here's an old trick: layer rubber cement over the hole until it's covered (Figure B). No more buzz!

Photography by Nick Archer

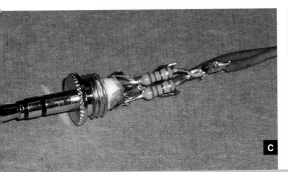

Fig. A: Transistor radio from eBay with the case back removed. Fig. B: Repair a buzzing, damaged speaker with rubber cement.

Fig. C: Convert stereo to mono by adding resistance to channels and connecting them together. Fig. D: The iPod connected and the radio ready for reassembly.

Now, prepare the plug that goes into the iPod (Figure C). After unscrewing the back, solder 1 wire to the terminal that connects to the plug's sleeve; this is ground. Solder two 3.3kΩ resistors to each of the other 2 terminals, and then join the other ends and solder them to another wire. This converts the stereo signal to mono. I put a piece of paper inside the plug to prevent shorting before screwing the shell back on.

Drill a hole in the back of the radio case and thread the 2 wires through from the plug. Solder the wires to the 2 exposed tabs on the radio's volume control.

Attach a 9V battery to the radio's clip, plug into the iPod, and turn both on (Figure D). The iPod's sound should come through the radio speaker, and the radio's volume control should work, but if it works the wrong way, unsolder, and reverse the 2 wires.

Carefully replace the radio guts back into their case, tuck in the new wires, and reassemble. I hung the iPod on the back of the radio's leather outer case so I can still take it off to go to the gym, but yours might fit inside the case, at the top, in place of the ferrite antenna. My radio already had a broken antenna wire, so I left it alone.

Programming It

Now go to reelradio.com and airchexx.com, and grab some vintage airchecks from your favorite childhood station. I've loaded Bill Berlin from WKDA Nashville, Tenn., Dr. Don Rose from WQXI Atlanta, and various jocks from WKBW Buffalo, N.Y., WEAM Arlington, Va., and WOWO Fort Wayne, Ind. Make an iPod playlist with airchecks, your fave songs, and some old commercials.

Load it up and enjoy! Even the old-school earphone works! Will Apple build these for us oldsters? I hope so, but why wait around?

♪ You can hear the radio in action at makezine.com/13/diycircuits_radio. Keep the volume low, and you can really hear how songs sounded in the 60s.

Nick Archer has been a radio DJ, program director, and disco DJ, and now owns a recording studio in Franklin, Tenn., that does radio commercials, internet audio, and books on tape. His transistor radio has been on non-stop since January 1965. archerproductions.com

Gardner's Mathemagic
By Donald E. Simanek

Martin Gardner has had a long career writing about recreational mathematics, which includes games, puzzles, and magic tricks based on mathematical principles (*see MAKE, Volume 12, page 80, "Mathemagician"*). Gardner generously agreed to share with MAKE readers a few that can be described briefly and performed with no sleight-of-hand skills.

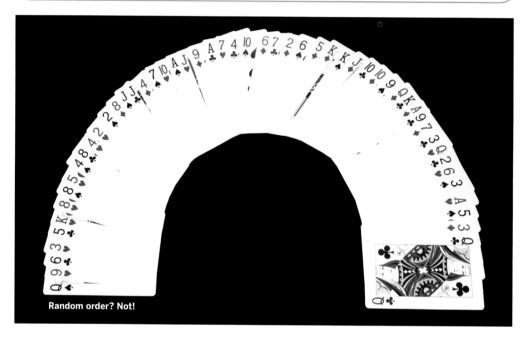

Random order? Not!

The Gilbreath Principle

A number of card tricks are based on a principle that magician Norman Gilbreath introduced to magic. It's an application of combinatorial mathematics (which we will spare you here). Gardner discusses it in his books *New Mathematical Diversions from Scientific American*, Chapter 9, and *Mathematical Magic Show*, Chapter 7. We'll describe here the simpler versions.

Prepare the deck ahead of time with the cards in black/red alternation. No other order is necessary. When you start this trick, you can do any false shuffle that doesn't change the card order. But if you don't have those skills, don't bother.

Have a spectator cut the deck and riffle shuffle the two parts together just once. Tell him to fan the cards and look at their faces to confirm that they are well mixed. Say, "Look near the middle of the

deck and find two adjacent cards of the same color. Don't tell me the color, but cut the cards between those two, and complete the cut."

The dirty work has been done. The deck is now ordered as a sequence of pairs, and each pair has one red and one black card. The spectator doesn't know this and wouldn't likely notice even when looking at the card faces.

Some versions of this trick suggest you take the deck under the table and pretend to be searching for red and black cards by touch, then bring them out and show them as pairs. But people become suspicious when the deck is out of their sight. (I can't imagine why. Don't they trust magicians?) The following method keeps the deck in full view.

Take the deck, facedown, and explain that when red and black cards are adjacent to each other, as many must be, their opposite polarities give off radiation that you can sometimes sense, using your enhanced psychic powers.

Peel off cards from the top of the deck, ignoring an *even* number of cards: two, four, six, etc. Then say, "Aha! Here's a pair." Show that the next two are a red/black pair, laying them on the table. Keep doing this, each time laying the ignored cards in a separate facedown stack on the table, or moving them to the bottom of the deck.

Don't skip the same number of cards each time — make it look as if you are really searching for the radiation from paired cards. Do this until you have ten or more pairs, or enough to convince everyone that you really can do it. It's good to leave some of the deck in the discard pile.

If someone is still not convinced, do the same procedure on the discard pile, for it still has the same ordering. But don't run the entire deck, or else your spectators will become bored or realize that the deck already had complete ordering of red/black pairs.

Of course you must be able to reliably count off an even number of cards. If you bungle this, you may still get a red/black pair, but eventually you won't. Oh well, no one is perfect. When this happens, count off an odd number the next time and you'll be back on track.

Gardner says, "The point is that one riffle shuffle doesn't destroy all order in the deck. In this trick it leaves the cards in red-black pairs. At least eight riffle shuffles are necessary and sufficient to destroy all order in a deck. That was first proved by a good friend of mine, Persi Diaconis, now a prominent statistician."

Two decks together require nine shuffles, and six decks require 12 shuffles. The riffle shuffle looks pretty, but it's not a good mixer. It merely interleaves two runs of cards. The order within each run is preserved.

Here's another example. Use a brand-new deck that has its factory ordering of cards. In a new deck, the cards are ordered by suits and numerically within each suit. Don't shuffle the deck. Have someone select a card. Cut the deck and give it one riffle shuffle. It now has two interlaced ordered sequences. Return the chosen card to the deck. Fan the deck so you can see the faces, and find the selected card. It's highly unlikely the card will go into the original sequence, so the card out of sequence will be obvious.

Steps in rotating the Permuting Cards, four-card version.

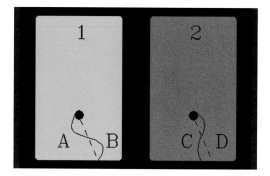

Gardner recently told me of an extension of this idea. Take two fresh, sealed decks of the same kind. Remove the jokers and advertising cards. Turn one deck upside down and riffle shuffle the two decks together. Now count out 52 cards from the top, and you will have two decks of 52, and each one will have all the cards a deck should have. But they will have two interleaved orderly sequences of cards. Actually, you don't need new decks. Any two decks that have the same order will give the same result.

The Permuting Cards

Gardner showed me a version of another trick, using four playing cards bolted together so they are in order, alternating red and black. "The bolt keeps them in order," he said. Indeed, it is hard to see how they could possibly get out of order, since the bolt has a locking nut. Yet with one flourish, Gardner rotated the rightmost two cards all the way around the bolt, and the cards magically rearranged to red, red, black, black. It seems to defy physics, and mathematics, too.

When I figured it out, I wondered whether the principle could be made to work with a larger number of cards, since this version doesn't lend itself to anything but a short magical surprise.

As usual, there's a mathematical (topological) principle underlying the trick. The cards are cut and interleaved, but that fact is hidden by the bolt. The trick is in how you cut the cards — with razor blade or scissors.

Use a paper punch to make holes in all four cards, carefully positioned so all four are aligned. Only the middle two cards are cut, along the S-shaped solid lines as shown above (ignore the dotted lines for now). Then hold card 2 above and to the right of card 1, and slide tab D under tab A. Now card 2 is both above and beneath card 1, and when card 2 is rotated clockwise, it will slide through and under

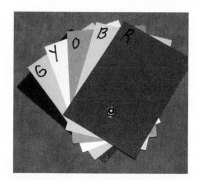

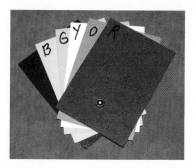

Steps in rotating the Permuting Cards, six-card version.

card 1. Add the uncut cards on top and bottom, then align the holes, and bolt them all together. Use a bolt that fits the holes snugly. A larger-diameter hole and bolt work best, though I've gotten away with ¼" bolts when using thin cards. The rotation may be repeated, restoring the cards to their original order.

There are other ways to make the cuts, but after extensive research in the TTT laboratories, we have concluded that this is the most foolproof.

A six-card version requires two pairs of cards to be cut as described above. Slide the right tab of card 2 under the left tab of card 1. Then slide the right tab of card 3 under the left tabs of both 1 and 2. Finally slide the right tab of card 4 under the left tabs of 1, 2, and 3. Add the uncut cards on top and bottom, align the holes, and bolt them all together.

How about going for broke? Prepare three sets of two cut cards, interleave them, and sandwich them between two uncut cards, for a total of 8 cards. Can it possibly work? Yes, quite well, but with so many cards it's best to use thinner cards, such as 3"×5" file cards. You can number them, or use different colors, and develop your own presentation routine.

Note, as you play with this, that the "cut" cards undergo a cyclic permutation when you rotate them 180°. The top and bottom cards stay put and serve to hide the surgery you did on the others. You can "cut" the fanned cards at any point before rotating, but cutting next to the end cards does nothing interesting. Of course the action may be repeated, cutting at different points. When you wish to restore the cards to the original order, cut between the cards that were originally next to the end cards.

Yes, the idea can be modified to an odd number of cards. A five-card version with three inner cut cards is a good start, which we leave as an exercise for the reader. *Hint: Look at the dotted line in the diagram.*

The photos at left show a version I made to tease my physics students. Students should know the order of colors in the spectrum, first studied by Newton. They are: red, orange, yellow, green, blue, and violet. But some can't remember them. I show them this arrangement that I call "Newton's crutch." I tell them that by bolting the colors together, we ensure they can't get out of order. Then I do "the move" and the colors are disordered.

Donald Simanek is emeritus professor of physics at Lock Haven University of Pennsylvania. He writes about science, pseudoscience, and humor at www.lhup.edu/~dsimanek.

SCIENCE MAGIC TRICKS

NATHAN SHALIT

Automagic
Science Magic Tricks
by Nathan Shalit
$4, Dover Publications

This 120-page book of simple magic tricks will show you how to make a paper clip that defies gravity, a balloon that doesn't burst when you poke it with a needle, a cup of tea that turns into water at your command, a handkerchief that burns without scorching, and other objects that appear to do the impossible.

All the tricks in the book can be prepared and performed by a 10-year-old, but many of them will fool even keen-eyed adults. I remember trying out the Magic Glass Rod on my parents' friends, and they were mystified as to how a solid glass tube was able to flip some words upside-down, but not others. (To strengthen the effect, I used a red pen to write the words that flip and a blue pen for the words that don't and told them that the inks reacted differently.)

The nice thing about Shalit's inexpensive book is that all the tricks rely on science, not sleight of hand, to do their magic. Your job, as the magician, is to present the tricks and pretend the special powers are emanating from you, and not the chemicals, magnets, static electricity, or other natural phenomena that make them work.

—Mark Frauenfelder

THE MAGICAL MÖBIUS STRIP!

UM...

HEY... PSSST... CELINE, WE'RE ON.

GOOD EVENING, I AM TUCKER THE PECULIAR. COADJUTANT TO...

THE GREAT CELINIE!

BEHOLD! FOR TONIGHT I BRING YOU THE MYSTICAL MÖBIUS STRIP!

AHEM... TUCKER, THE PAPER PLEASE!

USING AN ORDINARY NEWSPAPER, RIP A 3-INCH STRIP!

TUCKER! CAN YOU ATTEST THAT IT IS JUST REGULAR PULP?

I CAN!

NOW IF YOU WILL, CAN YOU PLEASE TWIST ONE END OVER AND CONNECT IT TO THE OTHER SIDE USING TAPE?

WITNESS, LADIES AND GENTLEMEN, THE CURIOUS MÖBIUS STRIP!

IT IS CHIRAL, A SURFACE WITH ONLY ONE SIDE, AND ONE BOUNDARY!

HOWTOONS.COM

Project Orion: Deep Space Force
By George Dyson

The Moon was in; Saturn and Mars were out.

The first part of this article, "Project Orion: Saturn by 1970," appeared in MAKE, Volume 12. It detailed the development in the late 1950s of Project Orion, an interplanetary spaceship to be powered by nuclear bombs. This portion of the article covers the envisioned deployment, closer to Earth, of a Deep Space Force. Orion was never built. Adapted from the book Project Orion, *with new material.*

"Although the ORION propulsion device embraces a very interesting theoretical concept, it appears to suffer from such major research and development problems that it would not successfully compete for support," wrote NASA administrator Richard Horner to ARPA director Herbert York in February 1960. The Moon was in; Mars and Saturn were out.

Following NASA's rejection of Project Orion, a small group of officer-physicists at the Air Force Special Weapons Center in Albuquerque, N.M., kept the project team at General Atomic on life support. But continued Air Force funding, without a NASA mission, would require military applications that could justify advancing from a million-dollar feasibility study to the tens of millions it would take to begin development, starting with nuclear tests.

Possible military applications began with Freeman Dyson's original suggestion that "to have an observation post on the Moon with a fair-sized telescope would be a rather important military advantage for the side which gets there first," and grew more ambitious from there. "Space platforms should be examined also, as well as the movement of asteroids and the like," suggested future Secretary of the Air Force Lew Allen in October of 1958.

"After NASA was formed, the Air Force had to justify supporting Orion on the grounds that it had military significance," remembers Ted Taylor, one of the designers of Project Orion. "So I spent a lot of time thinking about that and really got carried away on crazy doomsday machines — things like exploding bombs deep under the Moon's surface and blowing lunar rocks at the Soviet Union. There were versions of Orion in which the entire retaliatory ICBM force was in one vehicle, which was very hard, and any time anyone tried to fire at it, it would turn around and present its

rear end at the bombs coming at it. We were doing something for the project that we didn't want to do but had to, to keep it alive, we thought."

A May 1959 Air Force briefing revealed some "possible military uses of the Orion Vehicle," including reconnaissance and early warning, electronic countermeasures, anti-ICBM, and "ICBM, orbital, or deep space weapons." Finally, there was "The Horrible weapon — 1,650-ton continent-buster hanging over the enemy's head as a deterrent."

The problem was how to distinguish the defensive from the offensive when deploying weapons in space. "Only delicate timing would determine whether satellite neutralizations were offensive or defensive," explained a secret telex on "Global Integration of Space Surveillance, Tracking, and Related Facilities," marked "For Eyes of the USAF Only," from the commander in chief of the Strategic Air Command in Omaha, Neb., on May 31, 1959.

"There presently exist no military requirements beyond cis-lunar space," a classified Air Force summary expounded. "However, one must note that one reason there are no military requirements for a deep space vehicle is simply that no one has ever before seriously considered sending a large, manned, useful payload to this area for military purposes."

Was it crazy to imagine stationing nuclear weapons 250,000 miles deep in space? Or is it crazier to keep them within minutes of their targets here on Earth?

Air Force Capt. Donald M. Mixson stepped in to fill the gap. "He'd have been the first man on board," says his partner, Col. Don Prickett. Mixson and Prickett saw Orion as a way to sustain the type of creative, fast-moving effort that the proliferation of peacetime bureaucracy was bringing to an end.

"Mixson and Prickett were fed up with the Air Force system and Orion was a way to put a burr under the Air Force saddle blanket," explains Orion's lead experimentalist, Brian Dunne. Mixson shuttled

	Recoverable Test Vehicle	Orbital Test Vehicle	Interplanetary Ship	Advanced Interplanetary Ship
Gross Weight	50 - 100 tons	880 tons	4000 tons	10,000 tons
Propulsion system empty weight (Pusher, shock absorbers, storage and delivery)	45 tons	370 tons	1700 tons	3250 tons
Specific Impulse	variable up to 3000 sec	3000 to 6000 sec	4000 sec	12,000 sec
Diameter	40 ft	80 ft	135 ft	185 ft
Height	50 ft	120 ft	200 ft	280 ft
Average total acceleration of ship	2 - 4 g	2 g	variable up to 2 g	variable up to 4 g
Vacuum yield per charge	.1 - .5 KT	.8 - 3 MT	~ 5 KT	~15 KT
Sea level yield per charge	3 tons	.03 KT	.15 KT	.35 KT
Number of explosions to reach 125,000'	100 - 200	200	200	200
Total yield to 125,000'	~2 KT	~ 20 KT	~ 100 KT	~250 KT
Total number of explosions to reach 300 mi orbit	--	800	800	800
Total yield to reach 300 mi orbit	--	.450 - 1.8 MT	3 MT	9 MT
Payloads	(I_{sp} = 3000 sec)			
300 mi orbit (V = 10 km/sec)	--	300 tons	1600 tons	6100 tons
Soft lunar landing (V = 15.5 km/sec)	--	170 tons	1200 tons	5700 tons
Soft lunar landing and return to 300 mi orbit or Mars orbit and return to 300 mi orbit (V = 21 km/sec)	--	80 tons	800 tons	5300 tons
Earth's surface to Venus orbit to Mars orbit to 300 mile earth orbit (V = 30 km/sec)	--	--	200 tons	4500 tons
Earth's surface to inner satellite of Saturn and return to 300 mi Earth orbit. ~3 year round trip (V = 100 km/sec)	--	--	--	1300 tons

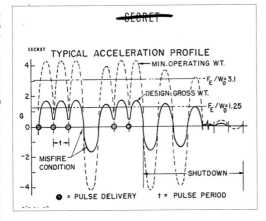

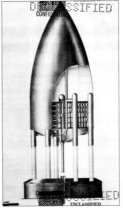

ABOVE: Proposed Orion vehicle parameters, 1958. LEFT: Crew compartment acceleration, 4,000-ton vehicle: pulse interval is 0.86 seconds, with normal acceleration below 2g. RIGHT: Proposed 200-ton test vehicle, 1962: 30-foot diameter, 0.78-second pulse period, 75-foot separation distance, 1.9g acceleration, 220-pound charges, yield unknown.

back and forth between Albuquerque, Washington, D.C., and La Jolla, Calif., intermediating between the physicists who saw Orion as a way to visit Mars and the generals who saw Orion as a way to counter the Soviets on Earth.

Military Implications of the Orion Vehicle appeared in July of 1959 and was, according to a declassified Air Force summary, "largely the work of Mixson, aided by Dr. Taylor, Dr. Dyson, Dr. D.J. Peery, Maj. Lew Allen, Capt. Jasper Welch, and First Lt. William Whittaker. The study examined the possibilities of establishing military aerospace forces with ORION ships and these were conceived as: 1) a low altitude

force (2-hour, 1,000-mile orbits), 2) a moderate altitude force (24-hour orbits), and 3) a deep space force (the Moon and beyond). The report recommended that the Air Force formally establish a requirement for the ORION vehicle in order to prevent the 'disastrous consequences' of an enemy first."

Gen. Thomas S. Power, who had succeeded Gen. Curtis LeMay as SAC's commander in chief, initiated Air Force QORs (Qualitative Operational Requirements) for a "Strategic Aerospace Vehicle," a "Strategic Earth Orbital Base," and a "Strategic Space Command Post" with Orion in mind. Prickett flew out to General Atomic with Mixson for a briefing

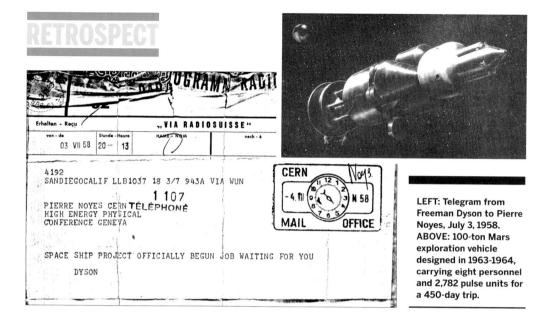

LEFT: Telegram from Freeman Dyson to Pierre Noyes, July 3, 1958. ABOVE: 100-ton Mars exploration vehicle designed in 1963-1964, carrying eight personnel and 2,782 pulse units for a 450-day trip.

with the general. "It was a wide-open discussion on potential, and what we were going to do with it when we got it," says Prickett. "And Power of course didn't have any problem knowing what to do with it."

By 1960, the world's nuclear stockpile was estimated by John F. Kennedy at 30 million kilotons, whose primary mission was to deter a first-strike attack. Orion offered an alternative to keeping all this firepower — some 10,000 times the total expended in World War II — on hair-trigger alert. A declassified summary incorporates Mixson's description of Deep Space Force:

Once a space ship is deployed in orbit it would remain there for the duration of its effective lifetime, say 15 to 20 years. Crews would be trained on the ground and deployed alternately, similar to the Blue and Gold team concept used for the Polaris submarines. A crew of 20 to 30 would be accommodated in each ship. An Earth-like shirt-sleeve environment with artificial gravity systems, together with ample sleeping accommodations and exercise and recreation equipment, would be provided in the space ship. Minor fabrication as well as limited module repair facilities would be provided on board.

On the order of 20 space ships would be deployed on a long-term basis. By deploying them in individual orbits in deep space, maximum security and warning can be obtained. At these altitudes, an enemy attack would require a day or more from launch to engagement. Assuming an enemy would find it necessary to attempt destruction

of this force simultaneously with an attack on planetary targets, initiation of an attack against the deep space force would provide the United States with a relatively long early warning of an impending attack against its planetary forces. Furthermore, with the relatively long transit time for attacking systems, the space ships could take evasive action, employ decoys, or launch anti-missile weapons, providing a high degree of invulnerability of the retaliatory force.

Each space ship would constitute a self-sufficient deep space base, provided with the means of defending itself, carrying out an assigned strike or strikes, assessing damage to the targets, and retargeting and restriking as appropriate. The space ship can deorbit and depart on a hyperbolic Earth encounter trajectory. At the appropriate time the weapons can be ejected from the space ship with only minimum total impulse required to provide individual guidance. After ejection and separation of weapons, the space ship can maneuver to clear the Earth and return for damage assessment and possible restrikes, or continue its flight back to its station in deep space.

By placing the system on maneuvers, it would be possible to clearly indicate the United States' capability of retaliation without committing the force to offensive action. In fact, because of its remote station, the force would require on the order of 10 hours to carry out a strike, thereby providing a valid argument that such a force is useful as a retaliatory force only. This also provides insurance against an accidental attack which could not be recalled.

Photography courtesy of H. P. Noyes (left); artist unknown, courtesy of General Atomic and Thomas Macken (above)

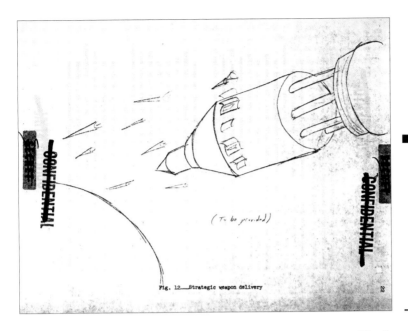

(To be provided)

Fig. 12—Strategic weapon delivery

PRELIMINARY SKETCH:
Orion Deep Space Force. Multiple independently targeted warheads are launched by a 4,000-ton Orion vehicle that has deorbited from its station in deep space and entered a hyperbolic Earth encounter trajectory to perform a retaliatory strike.

"Such a capability, if fully exploited, might remove a substantial portion of the sphere of direct military activity away from inhabited areas of the opposing countries in much the same manner that seapower has," another General Atomic study concluded, echoing the argument that had struck such a responsive chord at SAC. Mixson, according to Freeman Dyson, "had read Admiral Alfred T. Mahan's classic work, *The Influence of Sea Power upon the French Revolution and Empire*, and his imagination had been fired by Mahan's famous description of the British navy in the years of the Napoleonic Wars: 'Those far distant, storm-beaten ships, upon which the Grand Army never looked, stood between it and the dominion of the world.'"

Was it crazy to imagine stationing nuclear weapons 250,000 miles deep in space? Or is it crazier to keep them within minutes of their targets here on Earth?

"Orion would be more peaceful and probably less prone to going off half-cocked," says David Weiss, an aeronautical engineer and former test pilot who shared Mixson's enthusiasm for Deep Space Force. "We were looking at a multinational crew, the same sort of thing that's going on in NATO, and we would have had safeguards — a two- or three-key system in order to launch anything."

The deterrent system we ended up with, instead, depended either on B-52 crews kept under constant alert, or on missile crews stationed underground in silos, or underwater in submarines, waiting, in the dark, for a coded signal telling them to launch.

"At SAC, this was always the weak point," continues Weiss. "You were sitting there listening to your single side-band and it would come through either on a cell-call frequency, which is assigned to you, or on a barrage broadcast, and it would tell you to open up your target packets." There were about 20 minutes available to verify the extent of an enemy attack — or false alarm — before launching an irrevocable response.

The Blue and Gold Orion crews would have spent their tours of duty on six-month rotation beyond the Moon — listening to 8-track tapes, picking up broadcast television, and marking time by the sunrise progressing across the face of a distant Earth. With one eye on deep space and the other eye on Chicago and Semipalatinsk, the Orion fleet would have been ready not only to retaliate against the Soviet Union but to defend our planet, U.S. and U.S.S.R. alike, against impact by interplanetary debris.

Once Orion ships were in deep space orbit, the outer planets would be within easy reach. The temptation would have been impossible to resist. "When you would go out privately with people in the Air Force, here in La Jolla, and talk about what's Orion for, it was to explore space, no question about that," remembers Taylor.

The 1960s might not have become the Sixties had events unfolded as envisioned by Taylor, Mixson, and Prickett. The Fifties might have just kept on going, thanks to Deep Space Force.

George Dyson, a kayak designer and historian of technology, is the author of *Baidarka*, *Project Orion*, and *Darwin Among the Machines*.

Where makers tell their tales and offer praise, brickbats, and swell ideas.

Thanks for making the MAKE video podcast. Your enthusiasm and love for making is inspiring. I've been a crafty person all my life; I actually co-own a yarn store (raesyarnboutique.com) in Lansing, Mich. I've always been interested in electronics, but thought the task of learning how to make something would be too daunting.

Then last summer someone suggested the MAKE podcast to me and I was inspired. I picked up a RadioShack electronics learning lab from eBay, which came with a great collection of extra ICs, relays, switches, resistors, etc. A little while later I picked up my first PIC microcontroller, a PICAXE-08M. It's a great, cheap chip and as a bonus, it is programmed with BASIC, which I know already. I still have a lot to learn, but because of the MAKE video-cast and makezine.com, I am learning electronics instead of dreaming I could. —*Nick Blacklege*

It might seem gracious of Mitch Altman not to have patented his TV-B-Gone remote control, but the fact is that this device isn't patentable.

For a device or process to be patentable, it must be non-trivial and non-obvious. TV-B-Gone is neither. The statement of the problem, "I want to be able to shut off an annoying television," instantly defines the solution: build a remote control that automatically transmits every known TV power-cycling code.

Of course, had Mr. Altman applied for a patent, he would likely have received one, simply because patent analysts no longer pay attention to the rules they're supposed to apply. —*William Sommerwerck*

It was with a fair amount of concern that I read the most recent Heirloom Technology column about cutting down a tree [*MAKE, Volume 12, page 152, "The Widowmaker: Cutting Down A Tree"*].

I know that part of the fun of MAKE is the element of surprise and learning lessons by doing, but I suspect the surprise of a tree kicking back and seriously injuring or killing the reader is not one that most would welcome.

In Step 2, the second cut is described as "just a single cut straight toward the big notch." It is vital that the second cut be above the initial cut by a few inches — this piece of information is missing from the article. This will create a backstop for the tree to press against when the hinge snaps, preventing the tree from kicking back at the base and falling in a completely random direction.

I'm pretty sure that the advice in Step 1, to create the first notch "more than halfway through the tree" is bad as well, although I don't know that it's as dangerous as leaving out the different heights of the two cuts.

I encourage anyone interested in felling trees to check out *The Ax Book* by Dudley Cook, or watch the series of videos at expertvillage.com/interviews/felling-trees.htm. —*Josh Larios, great-grandson of an old-school lumberjack*

Tim Anderson responds: Josh, you're mostly right about the second cut, and I'm doing it that way in the photos. But if you make the second cut too high, it can kick back the other way and fall the wrong direction. Experiments with bananas will reveal how it works.

There's certainly a lot that can be said about felling trees, and even the people who know how to do it get killed pretty regularly.

I'd like to start by saying how much I love MAKE magazine and its website. I just launched an environmental site that tries to capitalize on the same DIY spirit that you folks incite in your audience. I liked the blog piece about energy vampires (makezine.com/go/vampire) and I am glad you brought it up for your readers. I am linking on my site as well.

I would like to make a request. Could you do more to emphasize the use of rechargeable batteries in your electronics projects? I notice in the photos of most of the electronics tutorials that you use standard batteries. Getting the tech and DIY communities to use non-throwaway batteries in their projects would be a welcome victory against electronic waste and pollution.

Keep up the good work and inspiration!
—*Ian Gunsolley, ecoevolution.org*

Mister Jalopy's article "Orange Crate Racer" [*MAKE, Volume 11, page 172*] was most nostalgic for me; my friends and I built a number of these back in the 50s. Mister Jalopy may rest easy regarding

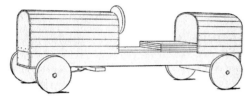

> "Orange Crate Racer" was most nostalgic for me; my friends and I built a number of these back in the 50s.

the use of cable for the steering; it works very well. We used both cable and clothesline rope at various times, and the cable worked best; rope tends to stretch over time and needs to be tensioned. The cable, once properly tensioned, winds evenly on the steering column and rarely needs readjustment during the life of the vehicle.

By the way, these are the first plans I've ever seen for one; we based our designs on intuition and experience. There were never any drawings.

—John Ward

Thanks for your unbelievable publication. I hadn't been moved to subscribe to a periodical since my subscription to *The Amazing Spider-Man* lapsed in 1995. For the record, I get waaay more use out of my MAKE back issues than my *Spider-Man* ones.

I was particularly inspired by "The $5 Cracker Box Amplifier" [*MAKE, Volume 09, page 105*] and ended up making an installation spiraling out from that project. When I made my first one of these amps (the day that Volume 9 arrived in my mailbox, incidentally), I didn't have a cracker box handy to house the amp, so I hollowed out a 1945 copy of *The Bobbsey Twins at the Seashore* that I happened to pick up at a local thrift store.

From that one amp I was inspired to create a series of sound books that eventually grew into an installation. The books were presented in a makeshift library that was lit with throwie-sized LEDs built into arrays and housed in other books. *The Noise Library*, as I titled it, was part of a larger installation show that happens every year on Peaks Island, Maine, called The Sacred and Profane.

Anyway, I just wanted to take the time to thank you guys for your wonderful publication and the initial spark for this project.

—Galen Richmond
Portland, Maine

⌃ My meter information station (meterproject. googlepages.com) is an implementation and expansion of the "Net Data Meter" project from Tom Igoe [*MAKE, Volume 11, page 133*]. I will admit ... this is shameless self-promotion. :)

—Leland Sindt

Thanks, Leland! The MAKE staff enjoys and appreciates the effort put forth by our readers, both in their projects, and in the sharing of those projects. Other readers can send us theirs at editor@makezine.com.

MAKE AMENDS

Hey ... love the newest issue of MAKE. As always, it's chock-full of projects and ideas that I can't wait to sink my teeth and mind into. The one project that especially caught my eye in Volume 12 was the fabrication of the "20-Watt Solar Panel" (*page 158*).

One small but very disappointing wrinkle with the project is the price listed for the DIY20W solar panel kit from Silicon Solar Inc. That kit is listed in the article as costing about $49. In actuality, the cost is $85 and evidently has been since late September. Silicon Solar does offer an 8W kit for $49.

While it's not quite a deal-breaker for me, the price difference does shift the project from the "can't wait" category to the "maybe one day" category. When you get back to that new workbench of yours, could you please torque the editorial screws a lb-ft or so? Maybe that'll prevent similar situations from occurring in the future. ;-) Thanks,

—Steve Borgstrom

Editors respond: **We apologize for our error. Silicon Solar changed its website shortly before we went to press, so that a search for part #DIY20W pulled up the 8-watt kit, which costs $49. A member of the MAKE staff interpreted this as a price change and made the erroneous change to the article.**

Interested readers can order the 20-watt kit for $84.95 at siliconsolar.com/Build-Your-Own-Solar-Panel-Kits-p-16188.html. In the pull-down order form, select model DIY20W.

MakeShift

By Lee D. Zlotoff

The Scenario: You and a buddy arrange to go trout fishing on a favorite isolated stream. You load up your two-wheel-drive wagon with all your fly-fishing equipment, a cooler full of canned soda, food, and ice, and a second cooler of ice for the fish you plan to catch. The spot you're after is about 25 miles off the highway, down a drivable but pitted and rocky dirt road. But it's worth the trek, as the stream itself is a shallow meandering slice of paradise, with perfect sand and gravel bars punctuated by whitewater zones of stream-polished boulders that always make for the best fishing. And, as expected, the day of fishing goes great — at least, that is, until your friend slips on a wet rock and falls hard, breaking his arm.

The Challenge: The immediate swelling, pain, and developing bruise tell you it's a nasty fracture that needs real medical attention. But your friend is still able to walk back to the car, and you assure him that help is only a short drive away. When you get back to the car, though, you discover that one of the front tires has gone flat, with a tear in its side, probably from a sharp rock. Like most people, you haven't checked your spare tire in as long as you can remember — and then you realize that you took it out to check it ... *and never put it back.*

   You know the vehicle will never make it out on this road on only three tires. And the sun is getting low, meaning night will be here soon. Your friend trusts you to get him out of here, but he's looking more pained and concerned by the minute — and you're worried that if left alone for too long, he might go into shock. So what are you going to do?

Here's what you've got: In addition to everything mentioned above, you have a sharp and sturdy fishing knife among your gear, as well as a basic tool kit in the car: hammer, screwdrivers, wrenches, Swiss Army knife or Leatherman tool, duct tape, etc. And, though you don't have a spare, you do still have the jack and wrenches needed to change a tire. Do you have a cellphone? Of course. Does it work this far out? Of course not.

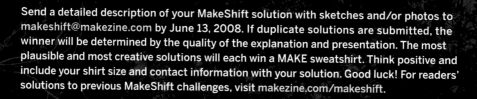

Send a detailed description of your MakeShift solution with sketches and/or photos to makeshift@makezine.com by June 13, 2008. If duplicate solutions are submitted, the winner will be determined by the quality of the explanation and presentation. The most plausible and most creative solutions will each win a MAKE sweatshirt. Think positive and include your shirt size and contact information with your solution. Good luck! For readers' solutions to previous MakeShift challenges, visit makezine.com/makeshift.

Lee D. Zlotoff is a writer/producer/director among whose numerous credits is creator of *MacGyver*. He is also president of Custom Image Concepts (customimageconcepts.com).

Photograph by Jen Siska

Mister Jalopy's
BLAST FROM THE
FUTURE!

今年も知りたい! だから!

破壊
試験

If Snap-On doesn't want to sell to amateurs, somebody else will.

● **If a department-store screwdriver** has a lifetime warranty, why would you ever spend 10 times as much on a prestige brand? After all, if the screwdriver breaks and it is replaced for free, then it's the last screwdriver you'll ever have to buy, assuming you plan to live just a single lifetime.

As a tool snob, I will argue the case for exquisite hand tools for as long as the beer holds out. I will defend the superior finish and perfect balance of professional-grade tools for the entirety of an Elks Lodge all-you-can-eat spaghetti dinner, and will make my closing arguments only after the spumoni has been eaten and the carafe of burgundy has been drained.

When the crickets stop chirping and the sun begins to rise, I will stress the importance of knowing that the tool in hand is at least as reliable as the mechanic using it. And as our friendship is strained to the brink and you have long abandoned your dedication to the dime-store screwdriver, I will wish you no harm and hope that you forever avoid the despair of breaking a ⅜" ratchet at Yellowstone National

Park. With a hailstorm approaching, the buffalo are not likely to lend you one of theirs.

My grandfather, father, and stepfather all relied on Snap-On tools, but my dedication to fine hand tools is not based on blind dedication to a brand. With the precision of surgical instruments, Snap-On continues to engineer tools that immediately feel as if you have been using them for your entire life.

However, since I am not a professional mechanic, I no longer buy Snap-On tools. Sure, they will sell to us amateurs through the Snap-On website, but we are not extended the same warranty that professional mechanics enjoy.

Nonprofessionals are required to send a letter to Snap-On describing planned purchases and then wait for a reply for nonprofessional warranty information. And, if the tool breaks, there is no practical path for repair, as that is handled by the Snap-On franchisees. Try calling a franchisee and tell them you need a tool repaired that you purchased from their website. With a warranty that can't be used, Snap-On has made it clear that they are not interested

新時代TOOL DEEN 2007最新カタログ

TEST 1
【ラチェットレンチ編】

TEST 2
【ラチェットメガネレンチ編】

TEST 3
【モンキーレンチ編】

TEST 4
【L型ヘックス編】

TEST 5
【スクリュードライバー編】

TEST 6
【ニッパー編】

At a fraction of the cost of the premium brands, Deen Tools are tested against all comers by Takanokura's *Factory Gear* magazine. Since the magazine is edited by the tool manufacturer, skeptics could suggest that the tests are tailored to favor Deen. Perhaps, but the tool battles really seem to be fair fights. It is fascinating to see the breaking points and types of failures of the different brands.

in selling to amateurs, and I've learned that you can't force companies to do business with you.

As amateurs, we need a comprehensive tool store. In addition to the premium brands from Europe and the United States, the ultimate amateur tool store would sell a professional-grade house brand that would be designed by individuals passionate about the elegance of tools.

With best-in-class quality control, these tools would be exhaustively tested against leading brands and, rather than anecdotal reviews, the tools would be pushed to the point of breaking. The results would be published with graphs and photos to show the point of failure of comparable brands. Naturally, we would expect these tools to be reasonably priced with a straightforward, unencumbered warranty. This is no quixotic exercise, as such a store exists in Japan.

Enchanted by the design of high-quality hand tools but disappointed by dirty, disorganized Japanese tool retailers, Masato Takanokura opened the pristine and hip Factory Gear tool stores and published a tool magazine of the same name. Recently, Takanokura visited my shop along with his chief tool designer, Kazumi Nakajima, and I was terrifically impressed by their deep knowledge of hand tools. For six hours, we examined my ancient tools as they pointed out subtle design features that made the old tools better — and stronger. Takanokura and Nakajima are seriously geeked-out tool guys and they bring this obsessive eye to their house brand of meticulously detailed hand tools, Deen Tools.

With such attention to finish and quality, how can Deen manufacture such beautiful tools for a fraction of the cost of the prestige brands? Forget your preconceptions about tools imported from China, because Deen tools are made in Taiwan. And they are exceptional.

Cheap Chinese imports will be here for a long time, but with the right individuals designing and steering manufacture, we are going to see more extremely high-quality products coming from China.

➕ Check out Factory Gear at f-gear.co.jp and Deen Tools at f-gear.co.jp/deen

All the awl you'll need, a kit to build your own yo-yo, wireless SD memory cards, and the maker before MacGyver.

TOOLBOX

Indiana Jones and the Solar Bag of Doom

Noon Solar
$274–$412 noonsolar.com

Flexible solar cells were all the rage in '07 and likely will become even more ubiquitous in '08. Leading the charge is the awesome line of bags (I lied about the "doom" part) from Noon Solar. The Logan is a very handsome bag that'd look right at home over the shoulder of our favorite archaeologist or any cosplaying steampunk. The materials are first-rate: Bavarian vegetable-tanned cowhide, shibori-dyed hemp/cotton with natural pigments. The 9½"×8¾" solar panel, which takes up one side of the bag, is a wonder. In person, it looks like just another piece of the fabric. It connects to a Li-ion "Power Bank" inside, which connects to your phone, iPod, or other handies (not your laptop, though). You can also plug the bag into AC power for rapid juice-ups. My only criticisms are that the carrying strap is unpadded and the collar-stud closures smack of form over function. That said, this is a bag that'll have geeks and fashionistas alike green with envy.   —*Gareth Branwyn*

ANALOG + DIGITAL

Who says analog can't play with digital?

Analog » PicoPad

$4 everydayinnovations.com

In a world full of photo-taking, MP3-playing, text-messaging digital gizmos, sometimes what you really need is a pen and paper.

The PicoPad is a slim, credit card-sized notebook that combines tacky notes with a surprisingly compact and extremely functional pen.

The secret sauce behind the PicoPad is the Flexigrip (the finger tabs that resemble wings), which allows you to grip and write with the pico-sized pen. The pages are refillable too, so unleash the creative maker in you and scribble notes and project ideas to your heart's content.　　　　　—Mike Lin

Digital » Eye-Fi

$100 eye.fi

I don't know about you, but I am notorious for taking pictures and letting them fester in my camera for months on end before digging out my USB cable, downloading the images to my computer, logging in to Picasa, and then finally sharing my photos with family and friends.

The Eye-Fi wireless SD memory card is nothing short of pure magic. Right out of the box, I was amazed by how easy it was to install and set up. Stick it in your camera, take a picture, and it automatically transfers your photo via wi-fi to your computer, a web-based photo sharing site, or both!

The Eye-Fi is perfect for makers and Instructables enthusiasts to capture their projects in images and set them free on the world!
　　　　　—Mike Lin

Editors Phillip Torrone and Arwen O'Reilly talk about kits from makezine.com/blog.

Solar Power House Kit

$125 electronickits.com/kit/complete/solar/solarhouse.htm

This kit focuses on both heat and light energy from the sun, plus wind, electrochemical, and plant energy as well. A great starter kit for learning about alternative energy.

Alarm Clock Countdown Kit

$56 denkimono.com/timer

Looking for a countdown timer and/or an alarm clock — maybe even one with stopwatch functionality? All in a "memorable" package? The Denkimono alarm clock/timer kit was tons of fun to build, and when friends come over it always gets a reaction. I don't watch TV, but I'm told this belongs in *24*. It's a nice kit because you end up with a practical object, plus it's a great base for lots of projects. Now I'll have this clock for life! —*PT*

Feel the Pulse
$47 makezine.com/go/magnetometer

Take the magnetic pulse of the solar system and compare your results to NASA's. Citizen scientist Dr. Shawn is at it again.

Linear Acceleration
$30 makezine.com/go/stepper

This definitely looks interesting: a linear stepper motor controller kit, open source, for CNC machines!

Wooden Clock Kits

$150 wooden-gear-clocks.com/kit_description.htm

Clock kits abound, but these surreal wooden shapes make Dali's imagination reality. Your clock will be a work of art.

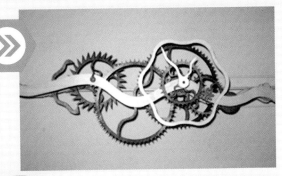

Yo-Yo Kit

$7 and up pennstateind.com/store/yoyo.html

Shoot the moon with your homemade yo-yo, built using this basic kit. More components, like chrome ball bearings, exotic wood blanks, and even a blank cutter, are available online.

Electric Plane Launcher Kit

$15 makezine.com/go/planelauncher

Spinning motors and plastic discs launch paper airplanes at up to 31mph! Build a launcher with this kit and get instant feedback on your paper airplane designs.

Tricks of the Trade By Tim Lillis

Rock steady with guitar effect cheat cards.

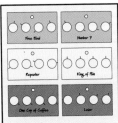

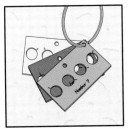

Have a hard time remembering all the guitar effects pedal settings for different songs? Use this trick and you'll be on the fast track to stardom at some bar.

Use thin plastic, and make cards the size of the control knob area of the pedal. Make holes for each knob and the LED. Mark the cards with the song name and the corresponding settings.

If you have many cards, you can arrange them according to your set list and attach them to a key ring for ease of use.

Stomp that pedal with the confidence that only your intended sounds will rock forth from your amp!

Have a trick of the trade? Send it to tricks@makezine.com.

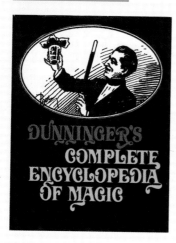

« The Total Trickster

Dunninger's Complete Encyclopedia of Magic by Joseph Dunninger
Spring Books $6–$15 (used)

In the old days, magicians had to make their own magical apparatus. This aspect of magic — as a handicraft — is wonderfully demonstrated in the out-of-print, but not hard-to-find, book titled *Dunninger's Complete Encyclopedia of Magic*.

This book is a compilation of short 1920s magazine articles about stage illusions, party tricks, puppet construction, pocket tricks, tricks employing electricity, and kitchen table science. The pages cover hundreds of illusions, from the very simple to the extremely complex. One trick requires only a deck of cards, a sharp knife, and a few minutes of practice. The illusion on the very next page requires a theater stage, a windlass, stagehands, and an armored knight on horseback!

The author assumes the reader is a capable maker: essential secrets are revealed and diagrammed, but step-by-step instructions are rarely given. The 288 pages are profusely illustrated with vintage black-and-white line drawings. The type is blotchy or small in a few spots, but always legible. The somewhat overly formal writing is delightfully old-fashioned.

Published several times over the last four decades, *Dunninger's* can be found in red paperback or black hardcover (shown).

—Dug North

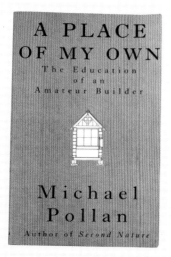

« Tales of the First Build

A Place of My Own by Michael Pollan
Random House $14

Being somewhat more accustomed to the tools of pen and *The Chicago Manual of Style* than to hammer and nail at the start of his project, Michael Pollan was somewhat apprehensive about his sudden compulsion to build himself a treehouse library in the woods up the hill from his home. We can see what the studio did for his work: *The Botany of Desire* and *The Omnivore's Dilemma*, two of his more well-known works, were written after its construction.

He soon realizes that this notion of his is a bit romantic, especially as he doesn't quite know how to hold a level, but like most of us who have made anything, he perseveres, with the chisel, the saw, and the sander. He learns that the joy of building is somewhere between plumb and clumsy thumbs, and the compromise between the ideal and the actuality of craftsmanship may mean your treehouse is out of square, but that's OK.

As Winston Churchill said, "First we shape our buildings, and thereafter our buildings shape us." There is much to be said for the amount of deliberation required for building a structure; would that our own makings take on the same weightiness.

—Andrea Dunlap

« Before MacGyver

Modesty Blaise by Peter O'Donnell

Titan Books, prices vary (used)

MacGyver was resourceful on television, while "Q" provided high-tech gadgets for James Bond to destroy onscreen. But before all of them there was Willie Garvin, the ingenious, inventive, and highly resourceful sidekick and partner of Modesty Blaise.

The fictional duo are successful international criminals who retire to England after they become rich. Despite their luxurious lifestyles, retirement soon palls. They snap at the opportunity to get back in action by working for the Special Intelligence Section of the British Foreign Office. We're introduced to Garvin's skills in the first novel, *Modesty Blaise* (O'Donnell wrote 10 more between 1965 and 1985). There he demonstrates some tricky devices designed to give Blaise a sneaky edge over the bad guys, like lipsticks that also give off a blast of tear gas, to gain a few vital seconds of advantage. His inventiveness is not limited to the bench — he is equally adept at improvising in the field.

As criminals Garvin and Blaise had stayed alive by being smarter and better prepared than their competitors. This talent remains, and readers are treated to escapades and escapes made possible by the ingenious use of whatever is at hand. I won't give you details, since it's more fun to revel in the creativeness of the moment.

—Kes Donahue

Some of the many adventures of Modesty Blaise.

« Makers of Necessity

Home-Made by Vladimir Arkhipov

Fuel Publishing $35

"In the depths of those stagnant times, when there were shortages of everything ..." begins a typical description in this incredible collection. Shortages of everything, that is, save ingenuity. Shovels made of street signs, television aerials made of forks, a colander patched in four different places, and a bubble wand for children made out of a spoon — each page has a description of how an object came to be. Many were made to entertain cranky babies, mollify grumpy husbands, or help elderly aunts navigate their uncomfortable outhouses in the wintertime.

Vladmir Arkhipov began assembling his collection of eccentric and beloved objects 13 years ago — "things that were never meant to be for sale." It's really the portrait of an era, the era of perestroika, when "everything had just disappeared" from the shops. There was no money, nor was there anything to buy. But always, life continued to be lived, and tools were needed: hair clips, kettles, playing cards, toilet seats, and a contraption to keep your boots dry.

—Caterina Fake

As chosen by John Lovick of *Magic* magazine

❮❮ Holonzki Wall Lamp by Ingo Maurer

ingo-maurer.com

This is really cool. I first saw it in the home of David Copperfield's executive producer, Chris Kenner. Here's how it works: there's an empty socket with a pull chain. You pull the chain, and a 3D holographic image of a light bulb appears and it illuminates — the hologram light bulb generates light just like a real light bulb. Well, not really, but that's the illusion that's created. There's sometimes a very fine line between science and magic.

SkyRoll Garment Bags skyroll.com

Any good magician knows that when you step onstage you gotta look your best. The hassles of travel have never been worse, and anything that can help you avoid having to check your bags is a godsend. This unusual carry-on garment bag can hold a couple of suits, some shirts, several ties, a pair of shoes, a shaving kit, and more.

❮❮ Creative Whack Pack creativewhack.com

Magicians of necessity must look at things (objects as well as people) in unusual ways. This illustrated deck of 64 creative-thinking strategies is based on the book *A Whack on the Side of the Head: How to Be More Creative*, by Roger von Oech. The strategies are designed to whack you out of habitual thought patterns and enable you to look at life in a fresh way. With this pack, you can practice your sleight of hand and stimulate your creativity at the same time.

❮❮ Peanut Butter in Plastic Squeeze Tubes peanutbutter.com/squeezeproducts.asp

Why did it take 100 years to put peanut butter in a squeeze tube? Let's not be bitter about it, just be glad they finally did.

❮❮ "The Ex" Voodoo Knife Holder

thinkgeek.com/homeoffice/gear/86dd

Teller (of Penn & Teller fame), one of magic's creative geniuses and a man who delights in all things macabre, has one of these in his kitchen. Do you need to know any more than that?

The Expert at the Card Table by S.W. Erdnase erdnase.com

Dai Vernon (the Stanislavski of close-up magic) described this book, first published in 1902, as the "bible" of card handling, both for magicians and for cheaters. Bill Kalush and the Conjuring Arts Research Center have produced this handy new pocket-sized edition of the book that — purely coincidentally — looks like a small New Testament. You can buy them individually or in 12-packs. Let us now open our hymnals to "the diagonal palm-shift."

John Lovick is the author of two critically acclaimed books on the performance of sleight of hand, and an associate editor at *Magic* magazine, the world's premier periodical for magicians. Handsome Jack, his secret alter ego, is a regular performer at the world-famous Magic Castle in Hollywood.

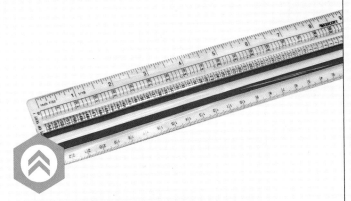

One Rule to Rule Them All

$2 makezine.com/go/ruler

Sometimes the most useful tools are also the most low-tech. Growing up, I always remember my dad (a dental school professor) having one of these and using it to save his eyesight when digging through reference books with tiny fonts. As an editor, I found myself squinting to figure out whether that quotation mark is a "straight quote" or a "curly quote" and straining to determine whether there's an extra space in the text or if it's just my eyes playing tricks on me. I was so excited to rediscover this magnifying ruler. With its bold blue lines surrounding the magnified strip, my squinting days are over. We love it so much that we ordered one for each of our editors. Truly the best 2 bucks I've spent in a long time!

—Goli Mohammadi

For Eyes

Prices Vary glassyeyes.com

Terribly nearsighted from childhood, I've always dreaded the trip to the optometrist's shop. It's clear that the markup on eyeglasses has been out of control; to be happy, you have to buy into a fantasy that there's an optician carefully hand-crafting your lenses. Well, you don't have to pay for that fantasy any longer.

Ordering glasses online has been around for a while, but I'd never heard of it until I was pointed to the Glassy Eyes weblog, which has links to everything you need to know about ordering glasses online. Since I'd just gotten my eyes checked and had a prescription in hand, I called my ophthalmologist and got my pupil distance.

I got the works — bendable titanium frames, highest high-index lens material, anti-reflective coating — for a total of $71. They arrived yesterday, and I'm wearing them as I write this. They're great, and the price is a far cry from the $350 I would have paid at a local optometrist. Had I opted for a basic frame and regular lens material, my total would have been a paltry $17! That means I'll be getting spares — maybe a little something in a leopard print or rhinestones. Rawr.

—Terrie Miller

Awl Good

$12 awlforall.com

The "Awl for All" may not be the prettiest awl around, but after having used one for years, I can safely assert that it is by far the best awl ever made. What makes this superior to all other awls is that, where a normal awl just punctures thick fabrics, leather, and vinyl, this awl simultaneously punctures and stitches these materials. Ever since it was bestowed upon me by another true believer, I've used it to reupholster chairs, perform emergency tent repair, patch clothing, and add a nifty little nylon hoop to my climbing harness. And because a fine needle comes conveniently stored in the screw-off handle, I am fairly certain that should the need ever arise, I can use this amazing awl to stitch closed any gaping flesh wound with ease.

—Randy Sarafan

Andrea Dunlap is a documentary filmmaker for seedlingproject.org.

Caterina Fake is the co-founder of Flickr and a recent devotee of the I Ching.

Dug North is the voice behind automataonline.com.

Gareth Branwyn is a contributing editor at MAKE.

Kes Donahue is a rare books and special collections librarian at UCLA.

Mike Lin is a mechanical engineer at Potenco (potenco.com).

Randy Sarafan is an artist who likes making fun things.

Have you used something worth keeping in your toolbox? Let us know at toolbox@makezine.com.

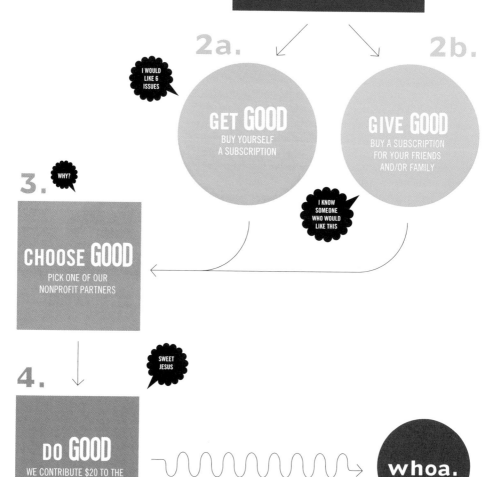

1.

LEARN ABOUT GOOD

GOOD IS FOR PEOPLE WHO GIVE A DAMN.
IT'S AN ENTERTAINING MAGAZINE
(PLUS WEBSITE, VIDEOS, AND EVENTS)
ABOUT THINGS THAT MATTER.

2a.

2b.

I WOULD LIKE 6 ISSUES

GET GOOD
BUY YOURSELF
A SUBSCRIPTION

GIVE GOOD
BUY A SUBSCRIPTION
FOR YOUR FRIENDS
AND/OR FAMILY

3. WHY?

CHOOSE GOOD
PICK ONE OF OUR
NONPROFIT PARTNERS

I KNOW SOMEONE WHO WOULD LIKE THIS

4. SWEET JESUS

DO GOOD
WE CONTRIBUTE $20 TO THE
NONPROFIT YOU CHOOSE

whoa.

FIND OUT MORE AT **GOODMAGAZINE.COM**

Shoot. Edit. Print.

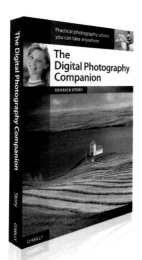

Practical Artistry
Learn how to apply the techniques and principles of classic photography so you can create great images with today's digital equipment.

Digital Photography Companion
Use these creative tips to take top-notch digital photos that reflect your artistic spirit.

Creative Digital Darkroom
Make your photographs shine with this clear, concise, insightful, and inspiring guide.

From capture to print, master the art of digital photography. O'Reilly digital photography books mentor you each step of the way as you reach your potential as an artist.

Buy 2 books, get 1 FREE!
Use offer code opc10 when you order directly from
O'Reilly at http://www.oreilly.com

O'REILLY®

Join the conversation digitalmedia.oreilly.com

1. Publication Title: Make Magazine; 2. Publication Number: 1556-2336; 3. Filing Date: 10/01/07; 4. Issue Frequency: Quarterly; 5. Number of Issues Published Annually: 4; 6. Annual Subscription Price: $34.95; 7. Complete Mailing Address of Known Office of Publication: O'Reilly Media/MAKE, 1005 Gravenstein Hwy North, Sebastopol CA 95472; 8. Complete Mailing Address of Headquarters: same; 9. Full Names and Complete Mailing Addresses of Publisher, Editor, and Managing Editor: Publisher: Dale Dougherty, Editor: Mark Frauenfelder, Managing Editor: Shawn Connally, all at O'Reilly Media/MAKE, 1005 Gravenstein Hwy North, Sebastopol CA 95472; 10. Owner: O'Reilly Media, Inc., 1005 Gravenstein Hwy North, Sebastopol CA 95472; 11. Known Bondholders, Mortgagees, and Other Security Holders Owning or Holding 1 Percent or More of Total Amount of Bonds, Mortgages, or Other Securities: Tim O'Reilly, O'Reilly Media, 1005 Gravenstein Hwy North, Sebastopol CA 95472; 12. Tax Status: [x] Has Not Changed During Preceding 12 Months; 13. Publication Title: Make Magazine; 14. Issue Date for Circulation Data Below: August 2007 (Vol 11); 15. Extent and Nature of Circulation, Avg. No. Copies Each Issue During Preceding 12 Months/No. Copies of Single Issue Published Nearest to Filing Date; a. Total Number of Copies (Net Press Run): 111,003/132,964; b. Paid Circulation (By Mail and Outside the Mail) (1) Mailed Outside-County Paid Subscriptions 44,833/46,255, (2) Mailed in-county Paid Subscriptions 0/0, (3) Paid Distribution Outside the Mails 26,708/33,078, (4) Paid Distribution by other Classes of mail through the USPS 0/0. c. Total Paid Distribution (sum of 15 b, (1), (2), (3), and (4)) 71,540/79,343 d. Free or Nominal Rate Distribution (1) Outside-County Copies 205/233, (2) In-County Copies: 0/0, (3) Mailed at other Classes through the USPS: 0/0, (4) Distribution outside the Mail: 0/0; e. Total Free or Nominal Rate Distribution (Sum of 15d (1), (2), (3), and (4)): 205/233; f. Total Distribution (Sum of 15c and 15e): 71,745/79,576; g. Copies Not Distributed: 39,258/53,388; h. Total (sum of 15f and g): 111,003/132,964; j. Percent Paid (15c divided by 15f): 99.71%/99.71%; 16 Publication of Statement of Ownership: [x] Publication Required. Will be printed in the March issue of this publication. 17. Signature and Title of Editor, Publisher, Business Manager, or Owner [signed] Heather Harmon, Business Manager, 10/01/07. I certify that all information furnished on this form is true and complete. I understand that anyone who furnishes false or misleading information on this form or who omits material or information requested on the form may be subject to criminal sanctions (including fines and imprisonment) and/or civil sanctions (including civil penalties).

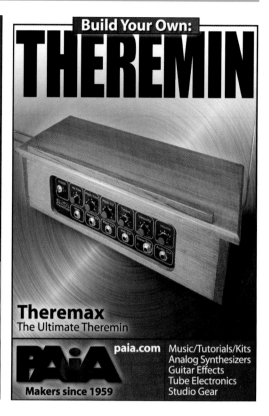

My Own Relay Computer

By Harry Porter, Ph.D.

When I was a small boy, my dad brought home relays salvaged from a decommissioned telephone exchange. With abundant enthusiasm, I set out to build a computer from a dozen dusty, nonfunctioning telephone relays. I worked on it for a while, but eventually gave up and moved on to other things.

However, I became mesmerized with the idea that machines might someday be made to think, and the possibility of mechanizing consciousness itself. I spent years studying computation in the abstract, but I never lost my fascination with simple machines. This unfinished project remained in the back of my mind, long after my mom tossed out those grimy old relays.

Then one day I realized that I had really, truly grown up. I could now do things I could only dream about as a child. I now had the time, the money, the knowledge, the patience, and the determination to complete this long-abandoned project.

My relay computer contains eight general-purpose 8-bit registers, a 16-bit program counter, and an 8-bit ALU capable of performing addition, logical operations, and shifting. The CPU can execute all common instructions including conditional branching and even procedure call and return. Other than main memory, this is an electromechanical computer, not an electronic computer.

Hand-assembled machine code programs are toggled in bit by bit, by flipping switches on the front panel. The only output is from glowing LEDs that reveal the internal state of the machine. Designing it forced me to think through the question of what truly constitutes the core of any computer. My design makes clear the big picture of how computers work, which so often gets lost in the complexity of contemporary processor designs and society's relentless quest toward efficiency, optimization, miniaturization, and specialization.

Although the machine contains only 415 relays and runs at a mere 6Hz, the sound of the clicking relays makes this the most physical, alive computer I've ever encountered. The experience of finally completing a project once dreamt of as a kid has been enormously gratifying. I can finally check "build a computer out of relays" off my to-do list!

Harry Porter teaches computer science at Portland State University. He's married with a sixth child on the way, which he looks forward to programming. makezine.com/go/relay

Photograph by Harry Porter